Glacier National Park

T0303612

America's National Parks promotes the close investigation of the complex and often-contentious history of the nation's many national parks, sites, and monuments. Their creation and management raises a number of critical questions from such fields as archaeology, geology and history, biology, political science, and sociology, as well as geography, literature, and aesthetics. Books in this series aim to spark public conversation about these landscapes' enduring value by probing such diverse topics as ecological restoration, environmental justice, tourism and recreation, tribal relations, the production and consumption of nature, and the implications of wildland fire and wilderness protection. Even as these engaging texts cross interdisciplinary boundaries, they will also dig deeply into the local meanings embedded in individual parks, monuments, or landmarks and locate these special places within the larger context of American environmental culture.

Glacier National Park

A Culmination of Giants

George Bristol
Foreword by Dayton Duncan

UNIVERSITY OF NEVADA PRESS   Reno & Las Vegas

The author and publisher extend special recognition and thanks to the Glacier National Park Conservancy for its support and financial assistance toward the development and research of this book.

The Glacier National Park Conservancy preserves the park for generations to come through philanthropic outreach, park stores, and friends from across the world. To learn more or to connect, go to www.glacier.org.

University of Nevada Press | Reno, Nevada 89557 USA
www.unpress.nevada.edu
Copyright © 2017 by University of Nevada Press
All rights reserved
Cover photographs: (*left*) © ricktravel / adobestock;
(*right*) courtesy of Harpers Ferry Center, West Virginia
Cover design by Erin Kirk New

LIBRARY OF CONGRESS CATALOGING-IN-PUBLICATION DATA

Names: Bristol, George Lambert, author. | Duncan, Dayton, co-author.
Title: Glacier National Park : a culmination of giants /
George Bristol, Dayton Duncan.
Description: Reno : University of Nevada Press, 2017. | Series: America's
national parks | Includes bibliographical references and index.
Identifiers: LCCN 2017005501 (print) | LCCN 2017007380 (e- book) |
ISBN 978-1-943859-48-1 (paperback : alkaline paper) |
ISBN 978-0-87417-658-2 (e-book)
Subjects: LCSH: Glacier National Park (Mont.)— History.
Classification: LCC F737.G5 B73 2017 (print) | LCC F737.G5 (e- book) |
DDC 978.6/52—dc23
LC record available at https://lccn.loc.gov/2017005501

The paper used in this book meets the requirements of American National Standard for Information Sciences — Permanence of Paper for Printed Library Materials, ANSI/NISO Z39.48-1992(R2002).

This book has been reproduced as a digital reprint.

Manufactured in the United States of America

To Nina Harrison,
who gave me food, shelter, and grand conversation
throughout a great deal of my Glacier National Park journey.
Nina passed away in October 2016.
She will brighten heaven with tales of her mountain home
and a smile that will shine all the way to Ireland.

Contents

Illustrations

Foreword

A century and a half ago, in 1868, a young man unsure of the direction of his life—he called himself "an unknown nobody"—wandered into the Sierra Nevada in California and found himself transfixed. John Muir, born in Scotland and raised in Wisconsin, had never seen anything quite like these western ramparts and the beautiful Yosemite Valley they surrounded, so he returned the next summer for a deeper immersion.

"We are now in the mountains and they are within us," he wrote that second summer, "kindling enthusiasm, making every nerve quiver, filling every pore and cell of us. Our flesh-and-bone tabernacle seems transparent as glass to the beauty about us, as if truly an inseparable part of it . . . a part of all Nature, neither old nor young, sick nor well, but immortal."

Muir would call the moment his "unconditional surrender to Nature," and in that surrender, he found his life's calling. He became Yosemite's most eloquent champion, instrumental in getting it set aside as a national park. Then his devotion to Yosemite broadened to embrace other wild landscapes—places that seemed destined for destruction in the last half of the nineteenth century in the midst of the nation's headlong rush to "conquer" the continent. He emerged as a leader of the budding conservation movement, awakening his adopted country to the understanding that "going to the mountains is going home; that wildness is a necessity; and that mountain parks and reservations are useful not only as fountains of timber and irrigating rivers, but as fountains of life."

Muir's writings brought public attention to Alaska's Glacier Bay, Arizona's Grand Canyon and Petrified Forest, California's Sequoia and Kings Canyon, Washington's Mount Rainier, and other majestic landscapes that would soon find protection as national parks. He helped found the Sierra Club. And he would use his fame and persuasive powers in the realm of politics, including a remarkable three-day camping trip in Yosemite with President

Theodore Roosevelt in which the two men—so different in many respects, but so united in their love of the outdoors—bonded over their nightly camp-fires and pointed the United States on a new course for conservation for the twentieth century.

Given the breadth of Muir's impact, it's easy to forget that it all started when a young "unknown nobody" from the flatlands entered the Sierra, fell in love with the mountains, and, in that transcendent moment, decided to do everything in his power to encourage others to do the same. The place had connected him with something much bigger than himself; then he, in fact, *became* bigger.

In that, John Muir's story, remarkable and profoundly consequential as it is, in actuality is merely one story among many others in the long history of our national parks. Look into the background of virtually any national park—how it came to be set aside or how it continues to be protected—and what you invariably discover is one person's (or a small group of people's) affection for a particular place, an affection so deep, so transformative that they devote themselves to making sure that other people, people they will never meet and in generations they will never know, will have the opportunity to fall in love with it just as they did. It's always personal. It's always inspiring. And, I might add, it always requires hard work, persistence, and complete dedication.

So it is with my friend George Bristol. Nearly a century after young John Muir entered Yosemite and found his destiny, Bristol boarded a train in Texas in 1961 at age 21 and ended up in northwestern Montana to take a summer job at Glacier National Park. Imagine a kid from Austin stepping off that train and experiencing his first mountains (and what magnificent mountains they are!), his first view of snow in midsummer, his first scent of pines, his first alpine waterfalls, his first look at a trout leaping in the eddy of a cascading mountain river. "I thought Glacier was the most beautiful place on Earth," he said. "I still do."

Like Muir, Bristol returned to his now-favorite place on Earth the next summer and, as he described it in his earlier book, *On Politics and Parks*, realized that "converging influences were merging into a rushing river that would sweep me along in its flow, carrying me toward a life purpose."

Texas would remain his physical home, but Glacier, he said, became "the home of my heart." Politics and public relations would become Bristol's profession (and his career in presidential campaigns is as colorful as it is distinguished), but Glacier National Park would remain his deeper love, which broadened to encompass the entire national park system, the salvation of Texas's state parks, and conservation in general.

His tireless work as a board member of the National Park Foundation (I was a fellow board member and saw him in action firsthand) was responsible for raising millions of dollars to support the parks. He served as a trusted advisor to the PBS documentary Ken Burns and I made, *The National Parks: America's Best Idea*. Back home, at a time when other states were closing their parks for lack of money, Bristol's leadership with the Texas Coalition for Conservation somehow secured a bipartisan consensus to provide Texas state parks with reliable funding. His beloved Glacier, of course, was not overlooked; Bristol was a driving force in forming a friends group, now called the Glacier National Park Conservancy, the nonprofit organization that underwrites vital park projects that otherwise would not exist.

Bristol's exposure to Glacier's beauty also spurred his passion for photography and poetry, and his recurring visits to the park over the course of half a century fired his interest in its history.

This book, *Glacier National Park: A Culmination of Giants*, is the result of that passionate interest. He tells the park's story—from the geologic forces that created those astonishing mountains to the Blackfeet Indians who considered them sacred, from the railroad magnate who saw both profit and beauty in them to the conservationist who called them the "Crown of the Continent," from the visionary leader who both created the National Park Service and built one of the nation's most spectacular roads through the heart of Glacier to the young men of the CCC who found both dignity and a much-needed paycheck laboring in the park during the Depression.

Bristol calls them—and other important figures in the history of Glacier National Park—"giants." He holds them up as more than characters in a history book, disembodied figures from the past. They still speak to us today, he believes, calling on us to follow in their footsteps, to take up their cause and build a better tomorrow—to become bigger than ourselves.

As he weaves Glacier's narrative into the larger story of the national park idea, Bristol makes sure that John Muir gets proper attention as one of those "giants" and notes that Muir paid a visit to the Crown of the Continent in 1901, nine years before it was preserved as a national park. It was, Muir wrote, "the best care-killing scenery on the continent," and his recommendation was straightforward: "wander here a whole summer, if you can."

Sixty years later, a young George Bristol arrived at the same place and, as if the Mountain Prophet's voice was still echoing through the valleys, heeded the advice, starting his own journey in pursuit of his own life's purpose that built on Muir's. Muir, I think, would have approved. Time spent at Glacier, he wrote, "will not be taken from the sum of your life. Instead of shortening it, it will definitely lengthen it and make you truly immortal."

—DAYTON DUNCAN
Author and co-producer of
The National Parks: America's Best Idea

Preface

In my earlier book, *On Politics and Parks* (Texas A&M Press, College Station, Texas), I wrote a prologue (excerpted below) that spells out how I first came to Glacier National Park in the summer of 1961. Those few days in June 1961 would forever change my life and establish my love affair with the park.

In the early evening, the train stopped at East Glacier. Out the window and up a rise stood East Glacier Lodge, the original showplace hotel of the Great Northern Railway. Behind the lodge and all around were mountains. As a Texas flatlander, I was awed to my depths. As the train proceeded, we plunged into a canyon defined by a river then unknown to me; it sparkled, disappeared, and then reemerged in a new twisting setting. We rattled through what I would come to know as snow tunnels. What we did not do was stop at Belton, my planned stop. That station hadn't opened for the season. A couple from Libby told me not to worry, saying they would take me back from Whitefish, Montana, the next stop.

At dusk, which must have been nine o'clock or so—the sun sets late in northwestern Montana in the summer—we arrived. The Great Northern groaned, buckled, and hissed to a stop. Waiting figures rose from platform benches. Smiles were exchanged when passengers and greeters spied one another. After gathering my meager belongings, I stepped off the train onto Montana soil and saw my first mountain sunset. Dusk gave off a fragrance then unknown to me—pines. We piled into the car and drove toward a darkening canyon—Bad Rock. There, I discovered the blue-green sweep of the Flathead River. Early summer peaks flashed by—Tea Kettle Mountain—still snow-capped and copper-hued in the fading light. Somewhere, a waterfall revealed its slender leg and then disappeared. A mysterious sign appeared for a Lake Five. A solitary silhouette whipped the air, arcing its line toward an eddy. A trout broke the water's surface—and then dissolved in concentric circles that rippled across the fire-red flow.

At just dark, we arrived. Not knowing where I needed to check in, we stopped at the place with the most activity—the West Glacier Bar. With profound gratitude, I thanked the Montana couple—I would never see them again. With my

small suitcase and duffle bag, I stood in the parking lot, surveying my surroundings in the dim light.

I have often attempted to put into words the feelings I experienced in that
moment and what I felt over the next several days. I did not know it then, but I
was gaining my own sense of place. Texas was and is home, but Glacier National
Park would become the home of my heart. Others might share similar feelings,
but mine were my own, special and lasting. What I also did not know then, or
recognize for the longest time, were the reasons. I'd arrived at that entrance to
a small bar in the middle of nowhere. Converging influences were merging into
a rushing river that would sweep me along in its flow, carrying me toward a life
purpose. The people and politics of my early years had coalesced to guide me
to a park. From here, I would have to run rapids and explore tributaries before
arriving at my port of call.

As one steeped in the dual (and sometimes dueling) world of politics
and parks, I have spent a great deal of my adult life attempting to influence
the former to the benefit of the latter. I came to this advocacy, beginning
in my twenty-first year, when I was fortunate enough to obtain the job at
Glacier National Park that summer of 1961. My two summers working in the
park set the hook but did not convert me to an ardent conservationist. That
would come decades later after schooling, family, and career. But it set out
signposts.

For the better part of thirty years, I returned to Glacier practically every
year, often more than once, simply to drink in its beauty and repair my soul.
I came to explore every area of its mountainous magnificence. I accepted
the park without detailed examination of the science, history, or politics
of how it was shaped by nature, discovered by humans, then considered
worthy enough to find a place among those early western wonders that
would come to give legitimacy to America's most original and best idea: our
national parks.

Yet with each visit, I picked up bits and pieces of its history as well as that
of the national park concept and its uniqueness essential to our democracy. By my forties, I realized that Glacier and its vast array of companion
parks, national monuments, national preserves, historic sites, battlefields,
memorials, recreation areas, seashores, lakeshores, rivers, parkways, and
trails were the binding mosaic of our national heritage and sense of shared
civility. I wanted to become an active participant to help ensure their place
of honor in perpetuity.

In 1994, President Bill Clinton and Secretary of the Interior Bruce Babbitt, with the strong backing of the secretary of the Treasury, Lloyd Bentsen, honored me with an appointment to the National Park Foundation. It was the best job—paid or unpaid—I ever had. It opened all aspects of our parks to me. The science, the politics, and the governance of our more than 410 sites under the jurisdiction of the National Park Service flowed through the conversations at board meetings, along trails, and around evening camp-outs and roaring fireplaces in some of our parks' grand hotels. From those experiences of my nearly seven years on the board, I was inspired to continue to expand on my newly found conservation ethic.

My home state of Texas was lacking on many fronts, none more so than funding for state parks. This scarcity of funding not only affected the brick and mortar of parks but also the programs of interpretation and experimentation so vital to families and young children. Through the formation of the Texas Coalition for Conservation, a nonprofit organization, we set about the task of educating and then swaying our elected officials to recognize not only the physical and civic benefits derived from our Texas natural and historical treasures but also the economic benefits obtained by attractive and attracting state parks. After six long years, we succeeded, but it took all of my (and that of others) prior political experiences to move a legislature created by law and tradition not to allow much to happen.

In the process, which often threw me in contact with "pygmies," I discovered leaders of commanding stature in both political parties. They became part of my autobiographical journey, which I incorporated in *On Politics and Parks*, and my growing awareness of the importance of our national parks, including Glacier.

Thus, when I was approached by Char Miller, the W. M. Keck Professor of Environmental Analysis at Pomona College, to consider writing a book about Glacier through the auspices of the University of Nevada Press, I was of several minds. In *On Politics and Parks*, I had covered a great deal about the park and my time there. In addition, I knew plenty of wonderful books on various aspects of the park and park life existed, and I was still vastly uninformed of its science and history. I nearly said no—and did so several times to myself. Then I decided to take a month and go back to the anchor of my soul to explore in detail what and, equally important, who had molded and later championed the "Backbone of the World" so it might be considered for national park status. I discovered giants!

Acknowledgments

One might conclude that my fifty-five-year experience with and within Glacier National Park would be enough to allow me to write a book about the park without a single pause for conversation, research, or reflection. Nothing could be further from the truth. Even though I spent time in Glacier in all seasons from 1961 to 2016, I did so to drink in its beauty and cleanse my soul, not to absorb and digest details of history and geology. It wasn't that I had no knowledge of glaciers, overthrusts, Native Americans, explorers, railroad barons, or park makers; all stuck in my thoughts in passing, but none were ever expanded or connected.

All of that would change when I was approached and encouraged by Char Miller and Matt Becker of the University of Nevada Press to write this book as part of the National Park Centennial in 2016. To them, and later to Justin Race, current director of the Press, I owe dual gratitude—first, for encouraging me to accept the challenge and then, throughout the process, for sharing their knowledge on how best to proceed through the steps toward publication.

I owe much to the Barlow family, Earl, Diane, and her husband, David Laney. Earl instructed me on the ways of the Blackfeet, and Diane and David lent me use of their cabin near St. Mary, Montana, where I read and pondered for a month. At the same time, I began to work with Ann Fagre, a researcher of the first order. Through her, I met her husband, Dan Fagre, who shared his vast knowledge of the geology and glaciers in the park. Theresa Bundick, PhD, was a tremendous help in gathering all things relating to James J. and Louis Hill from the Minnesota libraries and museums. Deirdre Shaw, Glacier National Park Museum curator, and Anya Helsel at the Glacier National Park Library were helpful at every stage of my research. My daughter, Jennifer Bristol, provided the rough draft typing and editing. Her work was followed by the lifesaver of this effort. Sharon McKone is an editor supreme—organized and knowledgeable about aspects of bookmaking about which I know nothing. To Jeff Mow and the Glacier National Park staff who granted me time, information, and interviews: that same spirit of giving was shared by National Park Director Jon Jarvis.

Finally, to my wife, Gretchen Denny, who not only let me wander off to Glacier when needs arose but acted as my proofreader and suggester-in-chief. And then to my children, Jim, Mark, and Jennifer, Andrea, Adam, and Alex, and grandchildren, Evelyn, Sam, Walter, and Henry, who are the legacies I leave for the continuing caring of this good Earth.

The author and publisher extend special recognition and thanks to the Glacier National Park Conservancy for its support and financial assistance toward the development and research of this book.

The Glacier National Park Conservancy preserves the park for generations to come through philanthropic outreach, park stores, and friends from across the world. To learn more or to connect, go to www.glacier.org.

Introduction

It is far more than a place on a map defined by latitudes and longitudes, with boundaries fixed by rivers, treaties, and a once-great nation's reservation. It is more than its histories of geology and humans, great and unknown, who came and went over its billion years' design. Yet, due to the interactions of natural forces then human players, it climaxed into one prized piece of America's best idea. And within those interactions was a culmination of giants who stood on one another's shoulders and created, then preserved, the landscape to be known as Glacier National Park.

But what was within its evolution that made it most appealing to those who came upon it, heeded its call, and then were given the time and wherewithal, either spiritual, mental, financial, social, or all, to cause a crown to be bestowed on it—a national park? This park, created early in the notion of public ownership, shared for the benefit of all, had to have had a fascination so alluring that it overcame its remoteness in the national perception. Yes, it had a railroad moving passengers and settlers toward it, but it was a railroad owned and governed by a man who was captured by the magnificence of its natural artistry and set about to do more than send his railroad through Marias Pass, hauling freight to and from St. Paul and the Pacific. He wanted his railroad to transport tourists from the East and Midwest who would come to share his enthusiasm for the natural beauty. As his infatuation grew, he recognized that the area coming to be known as Glacier needed a preserving mechanism not only to satisfy his own vision but also that of those he brought to East Glacier and Belton stations to experience its grandeur.

And yes, a conservationist and writer who had a national following through his highly regarded magazine would call Americans to what he would deem the "Crown of the Continent." Once he had captured their imaginations, he would call them to action to help him and the railroad baron achieve congressional approval. And most certainly, the voices of a president and a national icon would give the creation of parks a firm foundation of national purpose and pride.

But what was it about this landscape that made it so appealing to cause these giants to set aside great parts of their lives to advocate for parks in general and this park, Glacier, in particular?

It was a million-plus acres so rich in natural treasures that it trumped the designs of destructive forces that had laid waste great swaths of America during the latter half of the nineteenth century. Those treasures accumulated within its mountains and valleys were of such majesty that they captured the minds and hearts of those with counterbalancing influences.

In May 1910, the one million acres would be given preserved status as the tenth national park. Its size and placement were fashioned by the Canada–United States border on the north, the Middle and North forks of the Flathead River to the west and south, connecting with Marias Pass farther south and east, and, finally, framed by the Blackfeet Indian Reservation on its eastern front.

But again, boundaries and maps do not make an icon. It is what is contained within that called and continues to call. It is the accumulated splendor of Glacier that perpetuates its timeless attraction. Even within, it is not one single landscape that gives meaning to visitors, as is the case with many parks and monuments (not that those single or several vistas are not worthy of park status), but Glacier is truly the "best care-killing scenery on the continent."[1]

Or perhaps even better, as Bill Gilbert says in his article "Glacier National Park: An American Place" that appeared in the September 1993 issue of *Life Magazine*, "The main thing is the whole thing, which is why it seems to me that although Glacier lacks a logo-like defining attraction, it, perhaps better than any other place, defines the general purpose and value of our national park system . . . a monument to the underlying forces of nature, not to the unusual feature of it."[2]

NOTES

1. National Park Service, "Glacier National Park Press Kit: Glacier National Park and Other NPS Quotes," National Park Service, accessed April 22, 2015, http://www.nps.gov/glac/learn/news/upload/press_quotes.pdf.

2. National Park Service, "Glacier National Park Press Kit."

Glacier National Park

CHAPTER ONE

Laying the Foundation
Three Giants—Sedimentation, Crustal Movement, Erosion

What was to become the unique mountainous splendor of Glacier National Park in northwest Montana originally lay beneath a massive shallow sea: the Belt Sea that formed 1.5 billion years ago. The sea stretched from what is now the Arctic down through modern-day Idaho, Montana, Washington, and British Columbia. Some have speculated the sea covered the earth's formative crust to a much larger extent, but we have no way of knowing because great masses of the sea migrated to other continents. For purposes of this book, we will consider that which covered what is now much of northwestern America and nearby Canada. It would remain so for more than 700 million years.[1]

But the sea was not static. There was movement. Perhaps not movement by the helter-skelter standards of today but a constant play of ancient winds, waves, and rivers. They tore, poured, and plucked sand and stone, moving them downstream, drawing them beneath the surface where for all those unimaginable eons, compression and heat turned the sediment into hardened layers of different materials and varied colors. During this layering and hardening, something else was happening. The natural order was creating a foundation for mountains. But not just any foundation and not just any mountains!

Over those 700 million years during the middle Proterozoic era, the sea was fed this mix by rivers that carried silt composed of calcium carbonate and quartz, ingredients necessary to completing that phase of this geographical epic. Accumulated over time, the results were sediments, which, when fired by volcanoes and compressed to extremity, gave up layers of quartzite, argillite, limestone, and dolomite.[2] At the same time, the sea waxed and waned, creating coastal wave imprints. Today, these formations and layers are visible throughout Glacier National Park, particularly the one-third of the park above the tree line.

FIGURE 1.1. Fossil stromatolites on the Going-to-the-Sun Road. Courtesy of George Bristol; George Bristol photo collection; George Bristol, photographer.

Where did the rivers originate? Most likely to the west of the sea. But wasn't the west what is now the Pacific Ocean, and don't rivers run to the ocean? They do if they happen to be going that way. But they weren't. Something besides the Pacific must have been out there 700 million years ago. It is believed a substantial landmass was located there with its own east-facing mountains supplying its run-off rivers with mud, silt, and rocks to feed the Belt Sea with those essential foundation materials. To add to the formula, lava flowed to the sea floor about 750 million years ago. This igneous addition can be seen as pillow lava formations in the Granite Park area and as the Purcell Sill in the northeast area of the park.[3]

Somewhere in those hundreds of millions of years, the effects of continental drift (later called the tectonic plate theory) began to cause enormous sections of landmass to break and move away. What happened to our mass, and where is it now? By using modern radioactive isotope technology, we know that grains found in the Belt rocks originated from granite dating to 1.7 billion years ago. No other granite formations of that age can be found anywhere else in North America. But similar rocks have been found in Siberia, Antarctica, and Australia.[4] So perhaps one of those breakaway landmasses played a bit part in the formation of Glacier National Park. It's

FIGURE 1.2. Little Dog Mountain in the Appekunny formation. Courtesy of George Bristol; George Bristol photo collection; George Bristol, photographer.

enough to say that a great deal of pushing and shoving of incredible magnitude was occurring over millions of years that added to the foundation of the equation.

Whatever continent pushed, shoved, and eventually broke away from the North American landmass, it left behind a significant piece of itself in what is now called the Belt Basin, accumulating and compressing to depths of 15,000 to 20,000 feet.[5]

During the course of those eons, the foundation continued to sink, forming the hardening sediment, compacting it into layered formations. Today, the twelve formations are: Prichard, Altyn, Waterton, Appekunny, Grinnell, Empire, Helena, Snowslip, Shepard, Mount Shields, Bonner, and McNamara.[6] When almost a billion years is compressed, matter can become dense to the nth degree.

Eventually, river sediment and some magma flow filled the sea, and there it lay, doing absolutely nothing significant except continuing to compact. And perhaps, if one is so inclined to believe, to figure out how its next moves could accommodate the rise of humankind, who, I might add, were not even on the scene anywhere on Earth and wouldn't be for 600 million years. So maybe it just lay there compressing. During this time, another geological phenomenon was being created: stromatolites—species of blue-green algae formed in the shallow water of the Belt Sea. Starting 1.5 billion years ago, sunlight induced a reaction that allowed the algae to consume carbon dioxide, releasing oxygen in the process. This transformation would, over millions of years, enrich the oxygen-poor atmosphere.[7] As the earth's organisms began to breathe in the oxygen, the life forms developed until mammals appeared, followed by humans. Again, one can speculate why the natural order took this route instead of another to reach an accommodation for homo sapiens to thrive.

Then about 170 million years ago, the earth's tectonic plates collided with such force that the ancient lands buckled, forming about 70 to 90 million years ago what are now the Rocky Mountain ranges. After the initial collisions, matter settled down for another 35 million years, give or take, while the mountains continued to rise, albeit at a slower pace.[8]

At some point, a stirring occurred, a slight shifting as a new plate collision ensued, and out of the great underneath, those ancient, super-hardened layers from the long-gone sea broke the surface, thrusting a huge plate up and over the younger formations. This wedge (later to be named the "Lewis Overthrust" in honor of Meriwether Lewis) would expose those long-dormant Proterozoic layers that were nearly one billion years older than the newly formed crust.

This was not in the natural order. Billion-plus-year-old layers and rocks stood on the shoulders of much younger ones. This was not an abrupt, cataclysmic event. The wedge heaved itself up and over the younger layers, continuing to compress, seeking its final resting place. Creeping in a northeasterly direction at less than a snail's pace, it arrived at its present location some 50 miles from the original eruption site. Over millions of years, it marched, coming to a halt in what is northwestern Montana. Contained in a section of that colossus was the area to be known as Glacier National Park. Even to this day, throughout the park one can witness on the faces of Glacier's mountainsides the first artistry of the earth's evolution.[9]

The landscaping and artistry would change again and again before its designation as a national park in 1910. The overthrust had heaved itself to heights of 15,000 feet in some places. For millions of years, even as the wedge continued to shove toward its current location, other forces of wind and water would tear away at its peaks.

Then to hasten this leveling of mountains, something new began to occur. Ice! Over the past 2.5 million years, a series of ice ages of varying degrees of intensity and duration occurred as the climate cooled. What caused this is open to speculation. Perhaps the formation of the mountain ranges themselves changed the weather patterns, which cooled temperatures enough to facilitate the creation of the key ingredient of glaciers: snow.[10] And not just snow at Christmastime but continuous snow that blanketed and built upon itself for cycles of thousands of years.

As it fell, the second ingredient came into play. The temperature level was cold enough to keep the snow from melting. At some point, after all that accumulation and compression, the ice became so weighty that it reformed its bottom layer to a gel-like substance flexible enough to move glaciers down and through mountains by gravitational force.

The beauty of Glacier National Park's geological handiwork is that it isn't hidden from view, particularly on the east and southeast sides of the park. In some spots, more than a dozen layers of alternating bands of distinctive colors are arrayed within easy viewing from the Going-to-the-Sun Road and on the road to the Many Glacier area.

What is more significant is that this artistry is also visible confirmation of the wedge's final resting place: the billion-year-old sediment standing on the shoulders of the geological newcomers.

To put it all together in one setting, travel Highway 2 near Marias Pass until you locate Little Dog Mountain. In the autumn of 2014, my daughter, Jennifer, and I did just that. There, facing the park from the road is a mountain with a distinctive horizontal break that runs midway across the mountain. Clearly, the wedge that rests on younger layers—the Appekunny formation—is composed of ancient fossils considered to be among the oldest on Earth. Upon discovery and analysis of stromatolites, the origin of animal life was reset by a billion years.[11] All in all, it was an amazing new way to view a mountain we had passed many times over the years, noticing only its distinctive beauty, never knowing its special place among the geological wonders of the park, indeed the world.

But for all the snow and ice, it appears those early ice ages did little to shape the mountains that comprise today's magnificence. The Michelangelo of ice sculpting did not arrive until 3 million years ago. The Great Ice Age came and went several times, covering what is now North America. Again, the causes are varied. For whatever reason or combination of reasons—mountains changing weather patterns, earth wobble, volcanic activity, or solar variations—Earth's climate cooled, heated, and cooled again. This process would continue over 3 million years until 18,000 years ago when the Wisconsin Glaciation covered a third of America.[12] The Wisconsin period would evolve into that moment when the giants of the earth would lock together for a period of time, lasting until 10,000 years ago. At its height of creativity, occurring toward the end of that age, the master artist of ice would leave much of its work on permanent display. But to whom? Before that can be answered, we need to contemplate another important why.

As the mountains and ice were settling into their significant partnership during the Wisconsin Glaciation period, nature, perhaps with human help, was making another change. For reasons not yet fully understood, the woolly mammoth (*M. primigenius*) and other megafaunal species, including a much larger species of bison, began to die to the point of extinction.[13]

A warming trend (the Holocene epoch) could have been only part of the reason because prior warming periods had transpired over the past million years without causing similar megafaunal decline. Whatever else may have hastened the process, it appears that very early hunters of northern Eurasia and America played some role. How large a role will probably remain a mystery. But one major species or subspecies remained and was to be hunted to near extinction at a later time by humans.

The Steppe bison (*Bison priscus*) roamed North America more than a million years ago. Somewhere toward the end of that cycle, it evolved into the giant Ice Age bison (*Bison latifrons*) that lived until approximately 30,000 years ago. It was then replaced by two subspecies, *Bison occidentalis* and *Bison antiquus*. These two species, along with mammoths, mastodons, and horses, were hunted by arriving humans. By 10,000 to 11,000 years ago, most of the *Bison occidentalis* species in North America had vanished.

But one hardy survivor remained: *B. antiquus* stayed around until it evolved into the smaller American bison approximately 5,000 years ago. With the aid of kinder weather, hunting, and plains management practices by what were small numbers of Native Americans and the absence of the white man, the latter-day bison grew to a population of 60 million, ranging from Canada to Mexico to the east coast.[14]

With the disruption of the Euro-Americans, that number shrank to 300 by the end of the nineteenth century. Again, what had taken the natural

FIGURE 1.3. Layered foundations behind the Many Glacier Hotel. Courtesy of George Bristol; George Bristol photo collection; George Bristol, photographer.

order millions of years to cultivate and refine was practically decimated in less than 300 years.[15]

At some point, the "original people" eventually (10,000 or so years ago) arrived at the southernmost area of those mountains of ice, hanging gardens, lakes, U-shaped valleys, rivers, and moraines. Later, they would connect with other travelers and, at an unrecorded moment, deem those mountainous wonders "Mistakis"—the "Backbone of the World."[16]

For the next 8,000 to 9,000 years, as the waves of original people were spilling into the bountiful plains and valleys east and west of the mountains, the glaciers of Montana would continue to shape and sculpt. That is still true today. Even in their diminished states, the remaining glaciers add bits and pieces to the landscape.

Unfortunately, their retreating actions may be akin to cleanup duty before the "Going out of Business" sign is posted. In a little over 200 years, after the earth spent several billion years trying to get it right, humans have set a frightening new timeline for the disappearance of the water and cooling tower of Glacier National Park, and that is being duplicated around the world.

At the creation of the park in 1910, 150 active, vibrant glaciers, many awe-inspiring in their size, were located in the park. During my time in the park in 1961 and 1962, that number had been cut to 80. Today, only 25 remain, and some of those are on life support.[17] The consequences will be catastrophic. The greater irony is that on many levels and areas of the park, the great sculptures will survive. The question will be who will remain to wonder at their majesty? Perhaps they will simply stand there in silence, awaiting nature to recalibrate, which could take a very long time.

As Christopher White put it in his brilliant book, *The Melting World*, "When climate and ice have been in equilibrium, civilization has flourished."[18] One may not want to witness the reverse side of his observation.

NOTES

1. David Rockwell, *Glacier National Park: A Natural History Guide* (New York, NY: Houghton Mifflin, 1995), 7–9.

2. Rockwell, *Glacier National Park*, 11–13.

3. Rockwell, *Glacier National Park*, 22–23.

4. Rockwell, *Glacier National Park*, 9.

5. Rockwell, *Glacier National Park*, 9.

6. Rockwell, *Glacier National Park*, 9.

7. Rockwell, *Glacier National Park*, 13–15.

8. Rockwell, *Glacier National Park*, 26–27.

9. Christopher P. White, *The Melting World: A Journey Across America's Vanishing Glaciers* (New York, NY: St. Martin's Press, 2013), 45.

10. White, *The Melting World*, 47.

11. White, *The Melting World*, 46.

12. Rockwell, *Glacier National Park*, 35.

13. *National Geographic*, "Why Did the Woolly Mammoth Die Out?" *National Geographic*, March 26, 2011, accessed August 29, 2016, http://www.nationalgeographic.com.au/history/why-did-the-woolly-mammoth-die-out.aspx.

14. Roman Uchytel, "Bison Antiquus (Ancient Bison)," Extinct Animals: Images: Prehistoric Fauna Reconstructions, 2012, accessed November 29, 2014, http://prehistoric-fauna.com/Bison-antiquus.

15. U.S. Fish and Wildlife Service, "Timeline of the American Bison," U.S. Fish and Wildlife Service, accessed August 25, 2016, https://www.fws.gov/bisonrange/timeline.htm.

16. C. W. Guthrie, *Glacier National Park: The First 100 Years* (Helena, MT: Farcountry Press, 2008), 9.

17. Justin Franz, "A Race Against Time," *Flathead Beacon*, September 2, 2015, accessed September 8, 2015, http://flatheadbeacon.com/2015/09/02/a-race-against-time/.

18. White, *The Melting World*, 2.

CHAPTER TWO

Footprints
The Original People

The exactness of the when, where, how, and who is forever lost in the mist and mystery of times unrecorded. Yet we know with some certainty that early humans may have migrated from Asia through perhaps different routes in different times. Several possibilities literally opened up as the ice sheets encrusting most of North America drifted apart into pathways. The melting withdrawal of the Cordilleran Ice Sheet created two likely avenues: along the Pacific Ocean coastline and down through Canada from Alaska, extending in a southeasterly direction toward what are now the Great Lakes. It is the movement of these tribes or bands of humans (later to be known as Native Americans) on which I will concentrate due to their impact thousands of years later on what would become Glacier National Park. As the reader will come to appreciate, this will not in any way diminish the history of other tribes that settled west of the Rocky Mountains in Montana and Canada.

Even though scientific holes can be found in all the possibilities of who arrived, how they arrived, and when, it is interesting to explore for no other reason than to observe fact pressed up against foggy windows of mysteries. To do so, we have to step back to the origins of the comings. I stress comings because these arrivals were not an immediate or continuous movement south but were spread over centuries and from different directions. Although new science, coupled with new findings, has recently changed the dates of the earlier arrivals (and may continue to do so), most credible science puts the origins of the coming at 32,000 years ago.[1] During that time, humans from Eurasia and East Asia began to drift in small bands into an area called Beringia. Beringia was a landmass bridge connecting Asia/Siberia with present-day North America. There they stayed for thousands of years, locked in by ocean and ice. While there, they inbred and mutated, creating a new human, no longer Asian, whose strain became the modern

Native American.[2] While I have used the Beringia Land Bridge theory in my discussions in this book, it is important to note that, as previously mentioned, several competing theories of migration exist, and a universal scholarly consensus has not been reached regarding which route brought the earliest humans to the continent. This is to be expected when dealing with histories that are shrouded in mystery and buried in geological layers yet to be explored.

About 16,000 years ago, the ice retreated, creating routes to the south. But here again, a rush of uncontrollable hoards never materialized. At best, a few thousand—5,000 by some accounts—struck out. Eventually, their offspring of thousands of years would wander as far as South America, doubling back toward Texas then into eastern America. Some cut across the northern tier of the Americas, while others moved south as the Cordilleran and Laurentide Ice Sheets deglaciated in Canada. Somewhere between 12,500 to 13,000 years ago, groups came upon the lakes and forests of what are now the Great Lakes. Others may have been settling west of the mountains in Montana, Idaho, Washington, and Canada, suggesting migration from the Pacific coast.[3]

In the grand scheme, exactitude does not have to be the determining drive of all phases of history. It would be good to know, and God bless those who continue to seek out that long-hidden cave for a clue among scatterings of coprolites (human waste) to link the comings and goings of those small bands of wandering explorers who migrated by various routes—sea or land—to a place that had been preparing for their arrival for some billion-plus years.

At this juncture, it is appropriate to speculate on the nature of these original people. For the purpose of their history, I will concentrate on the bands that would later be known as the Blackfoot Confederacy ("Blackfeet" is the Americanized name of the South Piegan [Aamsskáápi Pikunni], who reside in what is now Montana. They, along with the present-day Canadian tribes of the North Piegan [Aapátohsi Pikunni], the Blood [Kainai], and Siksika, also known as the "Blackfoot" [the two Piegan, or Pikunni, tribes use different spellings], form the tribes that call themselves the Niitsitapi [the "Original People"]).[4] I focus on the Blackfeet not in the interest of time but because it is the Montana branch of these tribes that has the most direct bearing on the lands which would become Glacier National Park.

These four distinct tribes—the two Pikunni tribes (several spellings exist for the Pikunni; for clarification purposes, I have chosen the one noted most recently in Sally Thompson's book, *People Before the Park: The Kootenai and Blackfeet Before Glacier National Park*), the Blood, and the Siksika, or Blackfoot—could be found in the area before they migrated south and west toward the "Backbone of the World."[5]

To explain the significance of the Backbone of the World and all other natural (and supernatural) surroundings, the tribes found their creator long before the white man's introduction of religion. His name was Napi, the Old Man. Napi, to the Blackfeet (and, interestingly enough, to other tribes as well), was the maker of the earth, man, woman, and all the wild things. What is most interesting is the sequencing of his work. According to Napi legend, in the beginning, the world was covered by water. Napi, who appears to have preexisted the water, decided to explore what lay beneath and sent Muskrat to find the answers. Muskrat returned with a small ball of mud. Napi blew on the ball of mud and continued to blow until it became the whole earth.

Then he made mountains, rivers, valleys, plains, animals, and, finally, a wife for himself. Napi and his wife would jointly go on to make humans and implant in them standards for living and methods for surviving. Among the Blackfeet, that included how to hunt, kill, and use the bison.[6]

At some point, Napi must have exclaimed in some fashion that it was good. Then he climbed into a mountain and disappeared. If this story among the original people of North America and Canada parallels that of the factual shaping of the land that would become Glacier National Park and its surrounding geography and geology, then we have ample food for thought. And if areas of the tale seem to be biblical, then perhaps there is room for science and religion to coexist in some complementing fashion.

Through the science of mountains, ice, and animals, coupled with the branching at various points of tribes going separate ways and fortified with guidance of Napi's plan, the Blackfeet (along with other Algonquian-speaking tribes, including the Cheyenne, Cree, Ojibwas, Arapahoe, and Gros Ventre) settled in the forested areas around the Great Lakes prior to migrating west onto the Great Plains. Of these, the Blackfeet appear to be the earliest tribe to move west to the Saskatchewan River then toward Alberta and, finally, Montana.

Whatever the reasons, the migration did not take place overnight but over centuries, and, in the coming, the tribe split into the four distinct groups that exist today.

As they came, they were not alone. To the north lived the Sarci (modern-day Tsuu T'ina Nation), who resided in Alberta. To the west were the Kootenai (known in Canada as the Ktunaxa) and Salish, and to the south were the Apsaalooké (Crow) and Shoshones.[7] All would become antagonists to the Blackfeet (and vice versa). Over several hundred years, these conflicts would set the pattern for arms and horse races that would eventually give rise to the Blackfeet domination, allowing them to become one of the most powerful empires of all the tribes of America.

But to become an empire, they first had to walk and fight on foot. That they came, hunted, and wandered afoot there is no question. But it was slow going throughout this prehistoric period. Eventually, through stops and starts, tribal separations to the north, west, and south, and periods of protracted settlements, they came onto the lands butting up against the foothills of the Rocky Mountains north of the Missouri River and south of the Saskatchewan River in present-day Canada.[8] At some moment, a member of the Blackfeet tribe would have mounted a hill or ridge and looked toward those ice- and glacier-covered mountains they called the Backbone of the World or "Mistakis."

To help them make their journey, the Blackfeet relied on a companion: the dog (descendent of the wolf) that was probably first domesticated in the forestlands near the Great Lakes. Dogs were, so to speak, the workhorses of the tribes. Because the tribes were nomadic, moving about with the bison herds and seasons, dogs were trained to haul hide tents and other belongings on long poles. While efficient and supportive, not much ground could be covered in a day—some four to five miles—with long periods of settlement when the herds were plentiful, seasons fair, and geological impediments and hostile tribe encounters minimal.[9]

During these protracted movements west, the bands would come to be known as the Niitsitapi (Blackfoot Confederacy). The four bands, or tribes, were allied through language, family ties, tradition, and strength in numbers. Yet to compensate for the inconvenience of travel time and distance, they formed governing laws and practices for each tribe.[10]

Perhaps as early as 1,000 years ago, the Niitsitapi, along with the Kootenai, began to filter onto the lands to the north, east, and west of what would become known as Glacier National Park. Those furthest to the north were the Siksika, who inhabited the plains of the North Saskatchewan River in Canada. To the south along the Red Deer River and the South Saskatchewan, the Blood held sway. Farther south on both sides of the present-day Canada–Montana border, the Pikunni reigned over an area extending from the Bow River to the north to the Missouri River to the south and all the lands abutting what is now Glacier National Park. In time, the Pikunni would divide into the two separate tribes: the north and south Piegans. The northern tribe favored the plains around Old Man River in present-day Alberta. The South Piegans (Blackfeet) favored the hills and valleys on the slopes of Glacier and the adjacent plains. This southern tribe would become the one most associated with Glacier Park. They often wintered in places now familiar to visitors: the shores of St. Mary's lakes, lower and upper Two Medicine Lakes, and south along the Marias River.[11]

From these strategic locations, the four tribes ruled all the plains and passes east of the Continental Divide. They guarded the passes, not to protect the mountains but to drive off invading western tribes to prevent them from encroaching on the essential bison herds. Even afoot, they were fierce in their protection against all comers. And when they came upon and tamed the horse, they ruled with a swift and deadly iron hand.

The Shoshone appeared to have obtained the horse first and, for a while, held the advantage. The Blackfeet soon acquired guns and horses by raid or trade, and the scales of warfare and domination shifted. With swift mounts and firepower, they would come to rule the Great Plains, forcing the Shoshones, Apsaalooké (Crow), and Kootenais to seek safety in the mountains and lands to the west of the Continental Divide. All this was accomplished in less than a century. It was the end of their migration of thousands of years. It is where they would remain as a people through empire, degradation, and reservation. It would contain within its western reaches a large part of eastern Glacier National Park.

But even as the crown of empire was placed squarely on the head of the Great Plains tribe of the Blackfeet, forces were already afoot that would diminish them to wards of the federal government, at the mercy of its dictate, appetites, and whims along with the corruption of some Indian agents, traders, bureaucrats, and barons.

The empire would last for only one hundred years before it collapsed. After crippling outbreaks of smallpox epidemics in 1781 and 1837, the once-proud tribes were reduced to reluctant ranchers and poor farmers. Their territories were no longer free range and open but were dictated by boundaries prescribed in the 1851 Fort Laramie Treaty that was finally accepted by the Blackfeet in 1855.[12] It must be noted that up until that moment and to a great degree thereafter, the tribes of the plains had no concept of boundaries or landowners save those governed by the mountains, rivers, and other tribes' range of influence.

Running through this history of empire and demise is the parallel near-extermination of the bison. As mentioned previously, it is estimated that early in the history of the Plains Indians, nearly 60 million bison roamed from Canada to Mexico. Given that the population of the various tribes was comparatively small in number and the fact that they hunted and killed only what they needed, it can be imagined that they might have coexisted forever.

But the coming of Euro-Americans bringing with them items to trade, including guns and whiskey, abruptly and irreversibly changed the equation. The Blackfeet became hunters not just for tribal needs but for hides to trade, numbering in the tens of thousands annually. Add to that the ravages of disease, whiskey, fire, drought, and signs of diminishing herds, and soon cracks began to appear in their empire.

Whatever chance of reestablishing a balance was permanently shattered with the arrival of railroads. The railroads made transportation of buffalo hides easy and cheap. Both Indian and white hunters, wasting much of the kill, ran the carnage totals to 4 to 5 million in three years from 1880 to 1883. The final shipment of hides came in 1884.[13] Ironically, the Blackfeet were among the last to suffer the consequences because their herds ranged the farthest west. But confined by reservations and weakened with hunger, malnutrition, and smallpox, they continued to hunt and trade until it appeared that the prophecy "the time is close when the tail of the last buffalo will be seen disappearing from the prairie"[14] would become a bleak truth.

Yet for all the drama of empire and its horrific collapse hastened by overhunting, whiskey, guns, disease, and starvation, nothing had as much impact on the tribes of the Great Plains as the relentless march of the Anglo explorers, traders, and pioneers. Following the Lewis and Clark Expedition of 1804 to 1806, the die was cast. With the Corps of Discovery maps, reports, and, most importantly, establishment of legitimate presence before the territory could be claimed by Britain and other European powers, the gates of western migration were opening. By the 1850s, the trickle was becoming a flood. By foot, horse, wagon, boat, and, finally, railroad, men, women, and children were moving west across the new lands of the expanding United States of America.

But most were avoiding the northern Great Plains. The fierce reputation of the Blackfeet against both Indian and white encroachment was legendary and was, for the most part, cause for avoidance by taking southern routes west to the Pacific Coast. To thwart and contain the Blackfeet and other plains and mountain tribes, the Great White Father had to make treaties and boundaries not only for the protection of the American pioneers but also among the warring tribes. And there had to be peaceful passage guaranteed for the coming of the railroads.

While early agreements and treaties of one kind or another were enacted, it was not until 1855 that the Blackfeet accepted a definition of their lands.[15]

Even though doubts existed among the chiefs and leaders toward white settlers and among each other, fifty-nine leaders representing eight different tribes signed the Blackfeet Treaty of 1855 or, as it was to become known among the tribes, "Lame Bull's Treaty."[16] Among the conditions set forth were promises for $20,000 annually for the benefit of the tribes in exchange for honoring agreed-upon hunting ranges that were described in 1851. Among the land retained in the Montana Blackfeet Reservation was that area of mountains, valleys, and ice that would fifty-five years later become Glacier National Park.[17]

Whether knowingly or not, the once self-sustaining fierce warriors of the northern plains were drawn into the business of trading land for cash, food, goods, services, and peace. But in the years following, much of the cash was wasted; the food was inappropriate, spoiled, or not forthcoming; and peace was elusive with other tribes and white men alike.

It was as if all the rings that had aligned over thousands of years to lead the Blackfeet nation to become the unquestioned empire of the northwestern plains were shattered in an instant. During that short span of time, the population of the tribes (numbering approximately 12,000) that had held sway over a landmass in Montana and Canada larger than the size of all of New England was greatly reduced by starvation, the smallpox plague of 1869 to 1870, continuing warfare with equally desperate tribes, and clashes with white settlers and soldiers. The conflict culminated when a military expedition ambushed and massacred a Blackfeet encampment on the Marias River. The problem (among many) was that it was the wrong camp! The 1870 attack on friendly (but smallpox-riddled) Blackfeet led by Chief Heavy Runner saw the murder of 173 tribesmen and the capture of 140 women and children. The results, once publicized, led to a national outrage and policy change. Thereafter, the practice of employing army officers as Indian Agents was dropped, but matters did not improve much.[18]

For the Blackfeet, the change was for forever. Already weakened by disease, starvation (culminating in the "starvation winter of 1883 to 1884" that killed upwards of one-fourth the tribe), and whiskey provided by uncaring and unscrupulous traders, the disheartened Blackfeet would never again do battle with the white man's army. They were so stricken and spiritually defeated that they would not participate with their other plains brothers in the 1876 Battle of the Greasy Grass, known by most whites as the Battle of the Little Bighorn.

By 1880, U.S. Marshal William F. Wheeler wrote, "Ever since January of 1870, the Blackfeet tribes have been peaceable, and it has been safe to travel in their country. Very few white men have been murdered by them, and they were generally whiskey traders and characters dangerous in any community and caused their own calamity."[19]

As the maladies of resignation and defeat settled over the reservation of the Montana Blackfeet, voices arose anew from settlers, timber operators, miners, and the fast-approaching Great Northern Railway to open up the newly prescribed reservation lands for more concessions. By the 1880s, the Great Northern had obtained right of way for tracks across the reservation. The clamor continued because of mounting belief that rich mineral prospects were located in the mountainous areas to the west.

By that time, the tribe was broken in spirit and had nothing left to leverage—neither bison nor warriors—except their land. By 1895, they knew it and reluctantly agreed to negotiate for a sale of their holdings to the west. The first meeting with the Blackfeet took place on September 20, 1895.[20] The tribe was represented by Chief White Calf and a negotiating team of some thirty-five tribal leaders. The U.S. government's Bureau of Indian Affairs was represented by William Pollock, Walter Clements, and George Bird Grinnell. Grinnell had for the last ten years or so spent time with the Blackfeet and championed their cause. By pointing out their plight,

Grinnell was held in high esteem, and the tribe asked that he be part of the U.S. representatives.[21]

Although they stated the land was of little use to them, the tribal leaders wanted to negotiate as good a deal as possible. The negotiations settled into a give-and-take over land boundaries and price. At some point, the Blackfeet changed their tack, stating that the mountains were the most valuable part of all their lands and that they wanted no less than $3,000,000. It should be noted here that Charles E. Conrad, founder of Kalispell, Montana, and an extremely successful businessman, is often ignored or omitted among the names representing the Blackfeet tribe. It is often the ploy of businessmen and businesswomen such as Conrad to place a high offer—$3,000,000—on the negotiating table with the goal of getting a lower offer raised. This is speculation on my part, but I can well imagine Conrad urging the tribal leaders to do just that. That offer was rejected. Grinnell countered with $1,000,000 and stated that, in his opinion, the land wasn't rich in minerals and, therefore, wasn't worth what the tribe had asked. He would later be proven right.[22]

Finally, after further negotiations between the representatives and among the tribal leaders, the Blackfeet offered to sell 800,000 acres for $1,500,000.[23]

In accepting the deal, Chief White Calf agreed with regret and a warning: "Chief Mountain is my head. Now my head is cut off. The mountains have been my last refuge. We have been driven here and now are settled . . . I shake hands with you because we have come to an agreement, but if you come for any more land, we will send you away."[24]

On September 26, 1895, the commissioners and tribal leaders met to sign the final draft. It was read to them by George Bird Grinnell. Out of a total male population of 381, some 306 Blackfeet warriors signed the agreement of 1895. Among the eleven articles, the Blackfeet further reserved rights for hunting, fishing, and timber so long as the land remained "public lands" of the United States.[25]

Therein lay the continuing and continuous rub. But it did not arise with the swift beginning and end of mining and oil exploration boom and bust. By 1910, all mineral and oil activities died for lack of financially rewarding discoveries in the "Ceded Strip."[26]

The rub lay in the language of the treaty of 1895 that would be just as impactful as the acreage sold and agreed-upon price. It also lay in the seed

FIGURE 2.1. White Calf, Blackfeet Indian chief, 1888. Courtesy of the Montana Historical Society Research Center Photograph Archives, Helena, Montana; *Sport Among the Rockies*, 1888.

FIGURE 2.2. Chief Mountain, Glacier National Park, Montana, 1925. Courtesy of the Glacier National Park Archives; T. J. Hileman, photographer.

planted among those mountains, rivers, valleys, and forests that this was a landscape worthy of consideration for something newly arrived in the American lexicon: a national park.

It would be easy to end on a high national-purpose note, but I cannot ignore the consequences that lay within the language. In my opinion, one was far more egregious than whatever monies may or may not have been left on the table for the purchase of the Ceded Strip. This opinion took form during my conversations with Mr. Earl Barlow, an American Blackfeet who is a bear of a man with a towering intellect. He is the former director of Indian Education for the Bureau of Indian Affairs under President Jimmy Carter. He is an educator and keen observer of tribal history. If he had an opinion on the agreed-upon price for the westernmost area of his tribe's reservation in 1895, it was in passing compared to his outrage over the results of allotment and the swindle it perpetrated.

In Article V of the treaty, a provision was written that prohibited land allotments on the reservation for the length of the agreement. The tribal leaders were adamantly opposed to any form of allotment that had been enacted in 1887.[27]

The Dawes Act of 1887 adopted by Congress authorized the president of the United States to survey tribal lands and divide it into allotments for individuals. Those who accepted and agreed to live separately from the tribe would be made citizens. Its stated purpose was to assimilate Native Americans into white American society by affording them the civilizing experience of private property ownership. But defining "civilized" is in the eyes of the beholder, in this case the author, Senator Henry Dawes of Massachusetts, who declared, "To be civilized was to wear civilized clothes, cultivate the ground, live in houses, ride in Studebaker wagons, send children to school, drink whiskey, [and] own property."[28]

In the name of reform, Dawes sought to give the protection of America's laws to Native Americans by allotting plots of land of 40 to 160 acres to individuals and heads of households. Even if the original goal of Dawes and others was noble in intent, the act was written for ignoble conclusions. Anyone with an ounce of legislative knowledge could have seen through to the underlying motives. It was, in my opinion, a bribe connected to a theft wrapped in a swindle. It would destroy family and tribes, stripping them of their remaining dignity and traditions. It was racism and ethnic cleansing cloaked in the sanctimonious aura of divine guidance for heathens. Furthermore, it was a land grab without the necessity of treaties or negotiation.

Senator Henry Teller of Colorado spotted this hypocrisy before passage. In 1881, he said, "The real aim (of allotment) was to get at the Indian Lands . . . and open them up to settlement. The provisions for the apparent benefits of the Indians are but the pretext to get at his lands and occupy them. . . . If this were done in the name of Greed, it would be bad enough; but to do it in the name of humanity . . . is infinitely worse."[29]

The amount of land in native hands, according to one calculation, was slashed and grabbed from 138 million acres in 1889 to 48 million acres by 1934.[30] Even if one still clings to the reformers' stated intent, the math of allotment destroys their position. At 160 acres multiplied by those eligible to receive it, vast amounts of acreage would be left over to declare as "surplus" to be sold to non–Native Americans.[31]

In 1934, Congress ended the allotment process of the Dawes Act. In 1936, a study commissioned by the secretary of the interior concluded fraud and misappropriation by government agents were rampant and the

General Allotment Act had been used to illegally deprive Indians of their land rights.[32]

Using these findings, coupled with the legislative intent of the 1934 Indian Reorganization Act as well as the 1993 Alaska Native Claims Settlement Act, a lawsuit was filed to correct and terminate the improper management by the Bureau of Indian Affairs of revenues meant for tribes from oil, mineral, timber, and grazing leases. *Cobell v. Kempthrone* (secretary of the interior under George W. Bush) was settled in 2009 for $3.4 billion in the Indians' favor.[33]

I use the example of the abuses and corruption fostered by the allotment program to point out two occurrences related to Glacier's history. First, the tribal leaders who negotiated the Ceded Strip sale had every reason to be suspicious of the implementation and results of allotment propagated by the Dawes Act and thus demanded that land allotments on the reservation be prohibited. Because it was written into the agreement without much fanfare, we can only surmise that Grinnell and the other commissioners agreed with the tribe's concerns.

They should have been suspicious because the ink was barely dry before the abuses and legalized swindling began. But its consequences were more than the highway robbery of land. It was an attempt to convert a people who needed little help in matters moral, ethical, or religious.

Walter McClintock in *The Old North Trail* wrote,

> The Blackfeet are firm believers in the supernatural and in the control of human affairs by Good and Evil powers of the invisible world. The Great Spirit, or Great Mystery of Good Power, is everywhere and everything—mountains, plains, winds, waters, trees, birds, and animals.... All animals received their endowment of power from the sun, differing in degree, but the same kind as that received by man and all things animal and inanimate. Some birds and animals, such as grizzly bear, buffalo, beaver, wolf, eagle, and raven are worshiped because they possess a larger amount of the Good Perfect than others and so, when a Blackfeet is in trouble or peril, he naturally prays to them for assistance.[34]

The Good Perfect. And this is the race of original Americans the white man and "black robes" were determined to Christianize and civilize! The incivility lay with the congressional perpetrators and exploiters that followed.

The other flaw within the language of the treaty was the failure to recognize the impact the legal definition of public lands as it applied to the agreed-upon rights to hunt, fish, and cut timber for enumerated purposes for as long as it remained public lands of the United States.

And that was the case until fifteen years later when Glacier National Park was created in 1910. The land was judged no longer to be public land. Obviously, this led to deeper suspicion and hostility among the Blackfeet, and the legal fights to correct the issues raged until well into the 1990s.[35] For a thorough reading of the legal struggles, I recommend Christopher Ashby's 1985 thesis, *The Blackfeet Agreement of 1895 and Glacier National Park: A Case History*. It is enough to say here that even though Ashby and I arrived at the conclusion that neither Grinnell nor others on either side of the negotiations were in collusion or at fault, waiting-in-the-wings individuals, traditions, and greed were ready to terminate or interpret the treaty language to suit others' purposes.

The results of these actions after the fact would continue to create ill will among the tribes and individuals in conflicts that last to this day. Whatever the final determinations through the courts or negotiations, if there can be such a finality, the tribes possess a constant in which they can take pride. It is something all of us should honor and strive to emulate.

The original people left only footprints over thousands of years—and few of those on the landscape that would come to be known as Glacier National Park. That is not to say they did not camp, hunt, and fish among the valleys and mountains or that they did not find and use passes and trails or find sacred grounds where they held religious ceremonies and, yes, even do battle with the competing tribes to the west. But because all things—mammals, fish, trees, sky, earth, and rocks—had meaning, life, and place, they tread lightly on the land over the centuries. Most giants are applauded for doing something. But there is an equally strong case to be made that *not* doing something—destroying the land—is just as meritorious. The problem is that these giants are difficult to discover, so when they are discovered, they are due recognition and honor. And even if left undiscovered, they are giants nonetheless.

NOTES

1. Scott Armstrong Elias, "First Americans Lived on Bering Land Bridge for Thousands of Years," *Scientific American*, March 4, 2014, accessed September 7, 2016, http://www.scientific american.com/article/first-americans-lived-on-bering-land-bridge-for-thousands-of-years/.

2. Elias, "First Americans Lived on Bering Land Bridge for Thousands of Years."

3. Glenn Hodges, "First Americans," *National Geographic*, January 2015, 127.

4. Sally Thompson, Kootenai Culture Committee, and Pikunni Traditional Association, *People Before the Park: The Kootenai and Blackfeet Before Glacier National Park* (Helena, MT: Montana Historical Society Press, 2015), 11.

5. C. W. Guthrie, *Glacier National Park: The First 100 Years* (Helena, MT: Farcountry Press, 2008), 9.

6. John C. Ewers, *The Blackfeet: Raiders on the Northwestern Plains* (Norman, OK: University of Oklahoma Press, 1958), 3–4.

7. Guthrie, *Glacier National Park: The First 100 Years*, 8.

8. Guthrie, *Glacier National Park: The First 100 Years*, 8.

9. Mari King, "NITS-STI-TA-PII: The Real People: Imataa Manistsi: Blackfoot Dog Travois," Pitt Rivers Virtual Collections, 2010, accessed September 7, 2016, http://web.prm.ox.ac.uk/blackfootshirts/attachments/028_Imataa Manistsi- Blackfoot Dog Travois.pdf.

10. St. Rosemary Educational Institution, "The Blackfoot Indians: History, Culture, Society," SchoolWorkHelper, 2016, accessed September 5, 2016, http://schoolworkhelper.net/the-blackfoot-indians-history-culture-society/.

11. Guthrie, *Glacier National Park: The First 100 Years*, 9.

12. William E. Farr, "'When We Were First Paid': The Blackfoot Treaty, the Western Tribes, and the Creation of the Common Hunting Ground, 1855," *Great Plains Quarterly*, April 1, 2001, accessed September 5, 2016, http://digitalcommons.unl.edu/cgi/viewcontent.cgi?article=3226&context=greatplainsquarterly.

13. Shepard Krech, III, "Buffalo Tales: The Near-Extermination of the American Bison," Native Americans and the Land, accessed September 7, 2016, http://nationalhumanitiescenter.org/tserve/nattrans/ntecoindian/essays/buffaloc.htm.

14. Reports of the Commissioner of Indian Affairs, 1879, 90; Young to Commissioner of Indian Affairs, March 1, 1878, Indian Office Records, quoted in Ewers, *The Blackfeet*, 280.

15. Ewers, *The Blackfeet*, 217.

16. Thompson, Kootenai Culture Committee, and Pikunni Traditional Association, *People Before the Park*, 12–13, 25.

17. Thompson, Kootenai Culture Committee, and Pikunni Traditional Association, *People Before the Park*, 25.

18. Ewers, *The Blackfeet*, 249–52.

19. Ewers, *The Blackfeet*, 252–53.

20. Christopher S. Ashby, *The Blackfeet Agreement of 1895 and Glacier National Park: A Case History*, Master's thesis, University of Montana, 1985 (Ann Arbor, MI: ProQuest LLC, 2012), 22.

21. Dave Walter, "Past Times: The Ceded Strip: The Blackfeet, Glacier National Park, and the Badger-Two Medicine," *Montana Magazine*, September/October 1998, 57.

22. Ashby, *The Blackfeet Agreement of 1895 and Glacier National Park*, 25.

23. Ashby, *The Blackfeet Agreement of 1895 and Glacier National Park*, 26.

24. Walter, "Past Times," 58.

25. Walter, "Past Times," 59.

26. Ashby, *The Blackfeet Agreement of 1895 and Glacier National Park*, 32.

27. Alysa Landry, "Native History: Dawes Act Signed into Law to 'Civilize' Indians," Indian Country Today Media Network, February 8, 2014, accessed August 24, 2015, http://indiancountrytodaymedianetwork.com/2014/02/08/native-history-dawes-act-signed-law-civilize-indians-153467.

28. Landry, "Native History."

29. Frank Pommersheim, *Broken Landscape: Indians, Indian Tribes, and the Constitution* (Oxford, UK: Oxford University Press, 2009), 128.

30. Steven Newcomb, "The 1887 Dawes Act: The U.S. Theft of 90 Million Acres of Indian Land," Indian Country, February 8, 2012, accessed September 5, 2016, http://indiancountry todaymedianetwork.com/2012/02/08/1887-dawes-act-us-theft-90-million-acres-indian-land.

31. Ward Churchill, *Struggle for Land: Native North American Resistance to Genocide, Ecocide and Colonization* (San Francisco, CA: City Lights Books, 2002), 48.

32. Lewis Meriam, "Meriam Report: The Problem of Indian Administration," National Indian Law Library, 1936, accessed September 7, 2016, http://www.narf.org/nill/resources/meriam .html.

33. Patrick Reis, "Obama Admin Strikes $3.4B Deal in Indian Trust Lawsuit," *New York Times*, December 8, 2009, accessed September 7, 2016, http://www.nytimes.com/gwire/2009 /12/08/08greenwire-obama-admin-strikes-34b-deal-in-indian-trust-l-92369.html.

35. Walter McClintock, *The Old North Trail: Or, Life, Legends and Religion of the Blackfeet Indians* (London, UK: MacMillan and Company, Limited, 1910), 167, accessed September 7, 2016, https://books.google.com/books/about/The_Old_North_Trail.html?id=ro_YAAAAMAA J&printsec=frontcover&source=kp_read_button#v=onepage&q&f=false.

35. Walter, "Past Times," 61.

CHAPTER THREE

The Coming of Napikwan
Explorers, Settlers, and a One-Eyed Baron with Vision

Like the bands that came before, the appearance of the white man began with shadows moving through forests then out onto the plains of Canada. Originally, the impetus was a quest to discover a passage to the Pacific Ocean and Asia and to establish French domination of the New World. One of the earliest explorers was Jacques Cartier, who traveled up the Saint Lawrence River in 1535.[1] Although impeded by rapids, he was convinced he had found the passage, claimed the land for France, and named it Canada (probably from the Iroquois name "Kanata"). All told, he would make three voyages to the newfound land. He set up rudimentary trade with the Iroquois yet never found the passage to Asia or discovered the rich minerals of gold and silver that were reported to lie to the west. But in his trading, he found beavers in abundance that soon became the pelt of choice for French and European hats. So popular were the beaver pelts that they were trapped out by the 1600s, leading to expeditions farther west by the French and then the British.[2]

The competition for trade and territory would lead to a two-hundred-year conflict for domination of the Canadian lands and those soon to become part of the newly formed United States of America. While French traders pushed west in the 1600s, the British sailed into the Hudson Bay to the north and west and founded the Hudson's Bay Company in 1670.[3] For the next hundred years, the competition continued, moving to open conflict in 1754. The French and Indian War raged until 1763, ending with the defeat and expulsion of the French and leaving all their North American possessions to the British.[4] Among those newly gained possessions was an area far to the west embracing a large section of present-day Glacier National Park.

It was this junction of the histories that brought all the forces of future dominance of the Great Plains toward conclusion in the creation of a national park. By then, the Blackfeet were gaining horses and guns. The

British were fortifying trading posts to the north in Canada under the jurisdiction of the Hudson's Bay Company. French and Scottish traders formed
the North West Fur Trading Company in 1775, setting up posts from Mon-
tréal to the Pacific.[5] And in 1803 to 1806, President Thomas Jefferson sent the
Corps of Discovery under the leadership of Meriwether Lewis and William
Clark to explore the territory acquired from the French in the Louisiana
Purchase.[6]

In the interim prior to the purchase, the French Canadian and Scottish
trappers openly competed with the British for trade and influence among
the tribes of the Canadian Plains. The vanguard of these were more than
likely the first whites to encounter the Blackfeet. Sacagawea, the wife of one
such trader/explorer, Jean Baptiste Charbonneau, would guide Lewis and
Clark over the Rocky Mountains toward the Pacific.

Although it is reported that a young servant of the Hudson's Bay Company, Henry Kelsey, was the first British white man to come upon the great
herd of bison on the plains in 1690, no contact with the fearful Blackfeet was
made until much later. As a general rule, early traders and expeditions both
British and French tended to avoid the areas dominated by the Blackfeet to
the west and south. Because of this, from 1763 until the Louisiana Purchase
in 1803, the lands of the Missouri River basin were left largely unexplored,
uncharted, and uncontested.[7]

Yet there was contact. In 1772, a Hudson's Bay party attempted to encourage trade with the North Piegan. A trading post was established on the Saskatchewan River. By 1792, another Hudson's Bay Company trader, Peter
Fidler, in the company of a member of one of the South Piegan tribes (the
tribe now located in Montana), arrived at the mountain where he bestowed
the first recognized place name, "King's Mountain," which would later be
changed to "Chief Mountain."[8] This geological wonder stands alone at the
northeast corner of Glacier and is a singular study of the Lewis Overthrust.
It was also one of the places held sacred by several tribes.

With the purchase of this vast, uncharted territory and its subsequent
exploration and mapping by the Corps of Discovery in 1803 to 1806, the
floodgates of exploration, trapping, and trade would open for a new wave
of white men—the Americans. Unfortunately, an incident involving Lewis,
his men, and a small band of Blackfeet would poison the relationship of the
tribe and Americans for years. In the shadow of Glacier's range, Lewis and a
group that had split off from Clark to explore the headwaters of the Marias

River hoped to establish the American–Canadian boundary at the 49th parallel or higher.[9] However, the mountains of the land that would become known as Glacier were left unexplored. The men of Camp Disappointment, the northernmost encampment, were forced to turn back due to weather, lack of food, and the need to complete the journey home. On the second day of the expedition, they came upon eight members of the Blackfeet. After initial friendly overtures, the tribesmen tried to steal guns and horses because they were furious that the white men said they would trade with all tribes—Blackfeet and their enemies alike. Two tribesmen were killed. The encounter would lead to open hostilities with the Americans while at the same time driving the Blackfeet firmly into trading with the Canadians for the next thirty years.[10]

Be that as it may, the report of the Corps of Discovery sparked immediate interest in the Missouri River region. Manuel Lisa, an entrepreneur of St. Louis, established the Missouri Company and set out to monopolize the upper Missouri fur trade, particularly beaver.[11] The British responded, sending expeditions from their trading companies to open up new opportunities in the fur-rich area east and west of the Rocky Mountains. But more was at stake than fur. The boundaries of the Louisiana Purchase were ill defined. The northern boundary between the United States and England's Canada was in open dispute. One of Jefferson's primary charges was to establish the point farthest north for the lands encompassed by the northern branches of the Missouri River.[12]

The issue was not settled until 1818 in a treaty, which formally recognized a border at the 49th parallel from Lake Superior to the eastern edge of the Rockies. But that treaty left the land west of the Rockies to the Pacific in limbo. This northwestern territory included a part of present-day Glacier west of the Continental Divide. The British wanted the boundary fixed at the 46th parallel, and the Americans argued for the 54th parallel. This long-running friction gave rise to the political slogan "Fifty-four Forty or Fight." In 1848, President James K. Polk accepted the British compromise to establish the boundary at the 49th parallel. At that moment, the United States had in its jurisdiction the western lands, mountains, and rivers that would become Glacier National Park.[13]

But there was one matter left unresolved. The land east of the Continental Divide containing that section of Glacier belonged to the Blackfeet, and they weren't ready to give it up. They would finally do so half a century later in 1895.[14] It must be remembered that at that point in midcentury, the Blackfeet were still in ascendancy with little contact with the Americans. They still reigned supreme, with bison in abundance and dominance over the other plains and mountain tribes. They were an empire.

That said, nothing remains static. While governments negotiated, British and American traders and explorers were encouraged to expand their range of influence to establish evidence of jurisdiction in order to make their respective cases for possession both east and west of the Rockies. For decades following the return of Lewis and Clark, trading companies such as the Missouri Fur Company and John Jacob Astor's American Fur Company set about building forts and trading posts across the plains of Canada, the upper Missouri, and farther south with eyes at all times on the Pacific Coast.[15]

What they did not do in the early part of this march (1800–1809) was infringe on the lands of the Blackfeet, who were hostile to the Americans as well as others due to prior grievances and conflicts. The exceptions to this were the Hudson's Bay Company and the Nor' Westerners, who were predominantly French and had established good and fair trading relationships with these tribes in decades past. The Americans, in particular, experienced the brunt of these hostilities until well into the 1820s. Forts and posts were attacked; some burned. The western march was one of two steps forward, one step back, with relocation of routes to the north and south to avoid the Gros Ventre, Apsaalooké (Crow), and, assuredly, members of the tribes of the Blackfoot Confederacy. But all the time, whether it was the British to the north in Canada or the Americans to the south, movement toward the mountains that were known by some, but explored by few, increased.

In the early 1790s, Hudson's Bay agents, skirting the mountains to the north to avoid the Blackfeet, ran into members of the Kootenai (Ktunaxa) tribe, who had lived west of the Rockies for at least a thousand years. This meeting was the first time these generally peaceful people had seen a white man. For the most part, the Kootenai would remain friendly to traders, trappers, and settlers from that moment forward.[16]

Although I have chosen to concentrate on the Blackfeet tribe due to its proximity to and possession by treaty of the lands that would become Glacier, the Kootenai played a role throughout the centuries, occupying the western slopes of the Rockies. For at least 3,000 years, they traveled through the passes to the east to hunt bison. However, they did not rely solely on the herds for livelihood. Their subsistence was more varied, including fish, berries, herbs, deer, elk, and other big game. Because they, like the Blackfeet, were without horses until the 1700s, they hunted and gathered by foot as well as their own unique invention, the sturgeon-nosed canoe. This unique canoe allowed them to move about the lakes, rivers, and streams with ease, carrying with them fresh kill and other foodstuffs.[17]

Although little is known of their origins or language, which is like no other within the region, by all accounts, it is a certainty that the Kootenai had the longest relationship with the areas to the north and west of the lands and mountains that would become known as Glacier National Park. It is also certain that they encountered the Blackfeet as they moved east onto the plains. The encounters escalated into open conflict for land and bison, with the Kootenai being forced off the plains and back to the west of the mountains. By then, the tribe had divided into the lower and upper Kootenai. It was the upper tribe that was most affected by these clashes with the Blackfeet. Because they still relied on the bison for part of their subsistence, the Kootenai continued to cross to the plains to hunt, becoming the Blackfeet's sworn enemy. That would last until the mid-1800s, when the western expansion of the Americans brought a need to resolve the conflicts among the tribes for the protection of the ever-growing number of settlers and soon-to-be expansion of the railroad.

In 1855, Washington Territorial Governor Isaac Stevens persuaded the Kootenai, Salish, and Kalispell tribes to form a confederation and accept a reservation (now known as the Confederated Salish and Kootenai Tribes) near Flathead Lake.[18] The remainder of the tribal territory, including Glacier's west side, was open to settlement. Later in 1855, Stevens met with the Blackfeet, and after negotiations, the new Blackfeet territory would include much of north-central Montana and all of Glacier's eastern boundaries. It was hoped that these negotiations and the treaty would also foster a common hunting ground for all tribes that was to be located south of Blackfeet lands. It never came to be. Several leaders would not accept being excluded from their ancestral hunting grounds, and the Blackfeet and their western enemies fought for land and bison for fifteen years thereafter.[19] But it was not tribal conflict that would end an empire. It was the unstoppable march of white Americans that brought that chapter to a close.

Within the short span of forty years, the collapse of the Blackfeet empire and its ruin would be complete. By 1895, with the acceptance of the Ceded Strip Treaty, the once-proud warriors of the plains were left with no alternative. They had traded away their empire's wealth of beaver and bison pelts and hides for guns, whiskey, and creature comforts. All that was left to be bartered was land—800,000 acres for $1.5 million. It would not be enough (if there is such a thing as enough) to resurrect a new empire. Within the next ten to fifteen years, the Blackfeet of Montana would be reduced to bit actors invented by the public relations geniuses of the Great Northern Railway.

At some point in 1886 or 1887, some members of the Montana Blackfeet were surely confronted with a new phenomenon both frightening and fascinating. Perhaps at first, it was distant sounds unheard before: a clanging bell, rattling steel, and hundreds of voices shouting orders and directions. Then the sounds took on form: a one-eyed Cyclops, belching steam and smoke. Before it came men laying steel tracks, allowing the monster to move forward and dissecting the Blackfeet reservations, as the Great Northern Railway topped the horizon.

But if it was the men, materials, and monstrous locomotives that moved one another across the plains of Montana, it was the one-eyed giant in his private railroad car in the rear who drove the entire project toward completion with an all-encompassing vision, grit, and goal.

James J. Hill of the Great Northern Railway was about the business of creating a line from St. Paul, Minnesota, to Seattle, Washington. And it was to be built on careful planning, routing, and sound financing. The railroad and the man would take the name "The Empire Builder." Who was this man other railroad magnets declared foolish, calling his project "Hill's Folly"?

Self-made is a too-often-overused and -misapplied phrase, but self-driven and self-confident are the epitomical reckoning of James Jerome Hill. He was born in Canada in 1838. Although blinded in one eye as a boy by an arrow that backfired from a broken bow and destroyed his optic nerve, he would become a prodigious reader and student. He studied reading, writing, math, and the classics under the tutelage of an English Quaker. He had a particular bent for men who took risks, dared venture, and built empires. After his father's death, he took on clerking jobs, learning the practical aspects of business and commerce. As with his academic studies, he took in all this knowledge and retained it. He would continue to read and retain knowledge all his life. But unlike many other geniuses, he could connect all the dots.

In the late 1850s, after a series of missteps, he arrived in St. Paul, Minnesota. St. Paul was teeming with trade, with ox carts bustling along its streets and riverboats hauling goods up and down the Mississippi and to trading posts on the plains in Canada. Within a day of his arrival, Hill was hired as a clerk for J. W. Bass and Company. With a solid grounding for figures and a seemingly entrepreneurial instinct for business, he soon knew every aspect of the Mississippi packet trade and, in a short time, was running Bass and Company.[20]

Although incredibly strong in body and mind, his blind eye would disqualify him from service in the Civil War. If he regretted this, it did not deter him from honing his skills. By the end of the war, he was a forwarding agent for the Northwestern Packet Company that had arrangements with the Chicago, Milwaukee, and St. Paul Railroad and the Illinois Central. A year later, he would become agent for the St. Paul and Pacific Railroad, and the die was cast. Railroading would appeal to his passions for entrepreneurship, finance, competition, detail, and empire. But he needed a railroad. To get there, he would buy warehouses, steamboats, coal shipping companies, and then coal lands in Iowa. It was the trading and ownership of coal that led Hill to his abiding destiny: railroads.

During the same period, he would also attain another of his primary groundings: marriage and family (the others being Christianity, public schools, and the railroads). He and Mary Theresa Mehegan were married in 1867 and would have ten children. Although Hill, often with his family in tow, would travel the world, he, unlike other wealthy parents who migrated to New York City, always returned to St. Paul and the family mansion on Summit Avenue. For a variety of reasons, it was here that Hill could clear his head, surrounded by loved ones and the ability to look west toward the expanses of empire to be accomplished by his transcontinental railroad.[21]

The opportunity for ownership came with the nationwide financial crash of 1873. In addition to the Northern Pacific, other railroad companies went under, declaring bankruptcy. One was the St. Paul and Pacific. With his partners in the Red River Transportation Company and support from key banks and individuals, Hill pursued the crippled railroad for five years. In March 1878, he consummated the deal. James J. Hill had a railroad company, although bankrupt and seemingly mortally wounded. But it was not without assets, and now it had a chief who knew every account and expenditure by heart.[22]

One of those assets was Minnesota's land grants (devised by the federal and state governments to encourage new settlement and commerce), which would add enormous wealth to a company bought for 20 percent of its value. The challenge was that track had to be laid to Alexandria, Minnesota, then on to the Canadian Pacific connections at Winnipeg, Canada. Simultaneously, he had to stave off the Northern Pacific from competing for business in Manitoba. On the latter, he outmaneuvered them, and on the former, he overwhelmed the competition through attention to every expenditure and personal supervision of construction, driving his crews through the heat and cold.[23]

In January 1879, Hill's railroad was up and running in Winnipeg. With the St. Paul and Pacific purchase, he became the recipient of more than 2.6 million acres of state land grants worth more than $7 million that he packaged and sold to the flood of Scandinavians who were eager for homesteads. All in all, his company would reap more than $13 million, placing it on sound financial footing, which would allow him to do more than look west—he could actually go there. That James Hill would look west is no surprise. Since boyhood, he had been intrigued with the West as far as Asia. He left home in Canada in 1856 with the intent of reaching Philadelphia to sign on with a ship heading to Asia. Failing that, he decided to find his way cross-country to one of the Pacific ports with the same hope of gaining passage to the Orient. With information he had gathered about fur trappers who left that spring for the Rocky Mountains, he hoped to catch them in St. Paul and sign on with them. He arrived a week late, settling in St. Paul for the rest of his life but with his dream intact.[24]

But Hill was not one to let dreams trump detailed planning and solid financial foundation. He took his time, consolidating his gains in the Red River Valley and Manitoba. By clever and continuous promotion of the richness of the lands, immigrants flowed onto the surrounding prairie. Farms and towns sprang up. By 1881, 40,000 new arrivals were plowing crops and setting up businesses. By 1883, Hill claimed that his St. Paul, Minneapolis & Manitoba Railroad hauled one-fifth of U.S. spring wheat. His shares of ownership of the St. Paul, Minneapolis & Manitoba Railroad were then worth $5,000,000 (equal to $119,000,000 in 2015).[25]

Yet here again, he would not let the dreams overshadow the necessity for planning, and it was a plan like no other railroad to date. He would build his transcontinental railroad to the Pacific without additional government subsidies or land grants, as was the practice of other railroad barons. He would accomplish it by creating (as he had done in the Red River Valley and Manitoba) markets as he went. His primary tool would be the Homestead Act of 1862 that created the availability of tracts of land. He would seek out and recruit immigrants who were farmers, ranchers, and sheep men to the northwest plains. To jump-start their endeavors, he would help with seed stock and supplies to take their products to market.[26]

In particular, he encouraged wheat farmers to settle more than one million acres. To ensure they had the best seed and utilized the best practices, he created an agronomy department within the railroad. To encourage ranching, he imported the best cattle breeds and then gave away 7,000 head of purebred breeding stock. He built or supported the building of stockyards and grain elevators. When integrated, this system would create a self-financing bank for Hill's grand vision, and the tracks rolled west across the plains of the Dakota Territory. By 1884, he had laid 1,300 miles of track to the edge of what is now Montana, with the Rocky Mountains and the Pacific beckoning in the distant west.[27]

But then he came upon another potential impediment—Indian reservations. To enter those lands, Hill needed congressional permission. After a furious confrontation with Jay Gould of the Union Pacific, who Hill was certain had enlisted his lackeys in Congress to kill his bill, he redoubled his own efforts and had his allies pass his bill.[28] No man crossed or double-crossed Hill. That certainly applied to Gould, who seemingly bounced from rags to riches to rags, and Gould was ragged at the time. Unfortunately, all the congressional wrangling was done without consultation or negotiation with the tribes.

While the bill was being passed, Hill had used the past several years to consolidate his gains and expand markets on his steady but slow march west. He was ready to accelerate the pace. But the need for haste did not dictate waste or the jettisoning of Hill's careful routing plans. Unlike his prime competitor, the Northern Pacific, which was built on grades too steep, dangerous curves, and unsound financing, Hill insisted on keeping with a well-laid route with no grade exceeding 31.1 feet to the mile. The engineers and workmen of the Great Northern Railway (GNR) (formed and named by Hill in 1889 to consolidate his holdings) maintained that requirement over miles of Montana plains, partly because it made sense but also because their one-eyed leader was often there, watching all aspects of the project with his good eye on the smallest detail.[29] It is said that when his managers brought out their data books for discussion on inspection tours, Hill recited the figures before his managers could find them.

It is also true that Hill built his railroad on the backs of his low-wage workers. It was part of his formula. It worked because supplies of able-bodied laborers were readily available but also because, like all his other attributions for detail, Hill knew most of the men by name. When occasion dictated, he joined them in shoveling snow and rock. So while there was grumbling and talk of unionizing (which would come later after the completion of the line to the coast), the workers in the summer of 1887 laid the longest stretch of track ever built in one season: 643 miles between North Dakota and Helena, Montana.[30] If James J. Hill could take a shovel in hand, the workers would follow suit.

But Helena and points south were not James Hill's primary goal. He had already decided he wanted to go by the shortest route possible to Seattle and the West Coast. To do so, he would have to find a pass through the Rockies.

Today, the Burlington Northern/Santa Fe and Amtrak glide around the southern boundary of Glacier National Park paralleled by U.S. Highway 2, allowing freight, tourists, and locals to flow from the east and west sides of the Rockies with ease in a short period of time.

But as late as the 1880s, this wide, relatively flat valley was undiscovered, protected by myth, fog, and the Blackfeet's determination not to aid the white man's further invasion. By the time of Hill's railroad appearance, gathering evidence suggested that such a pass, suitable for his line to traverse, was out there—somewhere.

Lewis and Clark nearly got there but turned back after their first encounter with the Blackfeet warriors. Though minor as far as clashes go, it added to the growing legend of the warriors of the plains. Thereafter for decades, traders and settlers skirted north and south of the tribes, leaving active exploration for the pass until eighty years later.[31]

Again, James Hill's passion for detail led him to explore every map and journal that might shed some light on the mysterious pass's whereabouts. By 1889, his railroad had reached Havre, Montana. To proceed over the most direct route with the lowest possible grades, he had to find that pass.

In John F. Stevens, he found his man to scour the mountains and locate the elusive pass. The thirty-six-year-old Stevens was already a near-legend.

He'd laid routes for numerous railroad companies around and across mountains and challenging terrains. His exploits had earned him the reputation as the best mountain location engineer in the country.[32] What may not have been appreciated at the time was that he was a man of unwavering courage and perseverance. He would need both, plus his prior experience, to find, recognize, map, and conquer the long-hidden pass.

His first thought was to enlist the help of the Blackfeet at the reservation agency at Badger Creek. The once-proud people of the plains had been reduced to docility by smallpox, whiskey, starvation, and nearly depleted bison herds. Yet they would not accommodate Stevens no matter their condition. They knew the railroad would flood their remaining lands with trainloads of settlers, traders, and exploiters.[33]

Finally, with a Salish guide, Coonsah, Stevens traveled toward the mountains in the gathering winter of December 1889. So bitter was the cold and so deep the snow that Coonsah gave up somewhere east of the pass. By chance, relying on reports and maps from others who had attempted passage and from those of the Blackfeet, Stevens walked into the mystery.[34]

Although 40 degrees below zero, he kept moving—first to confirm his findings and second to keep from freezing to death. Stevens crossed the Continental Divide, turned back, and set out for Badger Creek. He knew he had found the pass. By pure luck, he came across the all-but-frozen Coonsah. Reviving him, they went on to Badger Creek together.[35] The short and easy grade to the west was in hand.

Stevens's report could not have pleased Hill more. The mountain pass, later to be called Marias Pass (Lewis named the Marias River in honor of Clark's cousin, Maria Wood, in 1805; since the pass contains the headwaters of the river, it became known as Marias Pass[36]) was acceptably wide with a summit of only 5,200 feet and grading of less than 100 feet per mile. Coupled with minimum excavation and no tunneling, cost estimates were approximately $160,000 per mile.[37] Contracts to build to the pass and through it were met and completed in record time by crews numbering in the thousands. To the north as they laid track, they built snow sheds to protect the coming trains from avalanches and bridges of awesome span. The partnership of mountains and glaciers continued to ready the landscape, grinding and gorging, even as the glaciers were beginning to retreat. Their magnificent sculpting accomplishments now lay ready for eyes that would recognize a land suitable for national park status. But conquering the pass was but another leg of Hill's master vision. He was going to the coast and would retain Stevens to take his railroad there.

The GNR tracks from east of the pass ran south and west then northerly along the Middle Fork of the Flathead River to the Belton Station on the west. They then ran on to Columbia Falls, moving toward the rail line being laid from Spokane heading east. From Spokane, Stevens was mapping the route across Washington through the Cascades and then to Everett, Washington, where the tracks would connect with Hill's Seattle to Montana Railroad to the coast. In the process, Stevens would engineer a two-and-a-half-mile

FIGURE 3.1. John Stevens at the unveiling of the statue at Marias Pass, 1925. Courtesy of the Glacier National Park Archives; T. J. Hileman, photographer.

FIGURE 3.2. John F. Stevens, the famous engineer who explored the Marias Pass area looking for railway routes, date unknown. Courtesy of the Glacier National Park Archives.

tunnel that was bored so straight that a person standing on one end could see the light at the other end. For this, the pass would be named for John F. Stevens.[38] The legend was now complete.

Years later, following the worst avalanche disaster in history at Wellington, Washington, in 1910, a replacement tunnel was built that not only eliminated the original two-mile tunnel but also the eight miles of switchbacks James Hill despised. It was completed in 1929 and is still the longest railroad tunnel in the United States.[39]

Stevens would go on to bring order out of chaos and disgrace on the construction of the Panama Canal. Then, following the collapse of Imperial Russia in 1917, President Woodrow Wilson appointed Stevens as chair of a group of railroad experts to bring order out of that chaos. His legacy would be the Trans-Siberian Railway as well as the Chinese Eastern Railway.[40]

With the driving of the last spike in January 1893 in the Cascade Mountains, James J. Hill had completed the vision of a young man who had looked west across the span of Canada and then from the hills of St. Paul, Minnesota.

But it was more than a line on a map from St. Paul to Seattle and the Puget Sound. To quote C. W. Guthrie from her book, *All Aboard for Glacier*,

> James J. Hill was like the locomotive he sent west: a one-eyed, self-propelled engine of unstoppable force. He made the country from the Great Lakes to the Puget Sound and Oregon his empire. He is credited with desolating Minnesota, populating the Dakotas, making Montana a state, and stealing the Puget Sound. Loved and despised, respected and feared, he would become the greatest railroad baron of them all.[41]

I would add that with his all-encompassing vision, he would ensure that his railroad was self-financing because he took the time to build it right, creating markets of wheat, coal, timber, copper, and towns while recruiting immigrants and workers as he went. At the same time, Hill made sure new opportunities to compete with and break the Northern Pacific were never overlooked.

Because the Northern Pacific to the south, which more or less paralleled Hill's Great Northern, was so ill constructed and financed, it should have been an easy target for takeover. That finally came about in 1901 after a fierce Wall Street battle with E. H. Harriman and through Hill's partnership with J. P. Morgan. The Hill–Harriman battle would involve other lines and intrigue and eventually prompt a Justice Department lawsuit that wound up in the U.S. Supreme Court in 1903, involving restraint of trade under the Sherman Act. On March 14, 1904, the Court ruled in favor of the government and against the railroads and the barons who had woven the lines together from coast to coast in a maneuver to restrict competition. While monumental and innovative in its thrust, the decision did little to break up Great Northern's system or other rail giants' conglomerations. James J. Hill said, "I've still got the railroads, haven't I?"

Not only did Hill still have them, he had—even as he battled Harriman, other competitors, and the courts—continued to refine and grow opportunities on his existing lines while adding others in Washington and Oregon and finally purchasing steamships to trade with Asian countries, fulfilling his boyhood dreams of going to the Orient.[42]

One of the opportunities that did not escape his attention was the allure of the beautiful scenery and serenity of the lands, lakes, streams, hanging gardens, and mountains to the north of the Marias Pass route. They were natural magnets to potential visitors from the East and beyond who were becoming enamored with the West. Even before the last rails were laid in January 1893, Hill's Great Northern Railway's tickets and passenger agent, F. I. Whitney, was designing, publishing, and distributing advertisement brochures about the wonders of the country, specifically Lake McDonald.[43]

That potential eventually would lead to the establishment of Glacier National Park in 1910, aided by able preachers and publicists for the new wave of conservation gospel sweeping the country. Sadly, this same period would witness the final curtain on the Blackfeet empire of the plains. All the while, the mountains, in partnership with ice, continued to perfect themselves, as if anticipating new guests soon to arrive.

NOTES

1. Guthrie, *Glacier National Park: The First 100 Years* (Helena, MT: Farcountry Press, 2008), 17.

2. Guthrie, *Glacier National Park: The First 100 Years*, 17.

3. Arthur J. Ray, "Hudson's Bay Company," *The Canadian Encyclopedia*, April 2, 2009, accessed August 24, 2016, http://www.thecanadianencyclopedia.ca/en/article/hudsons-bay -company/.

4. Guthrie, *Glacier National Park: The First 100 Years*, 17.

5. Guthrie, *Glacier National Park: The First 100 Years*, 17–18.

6. Guthrie, *Glacier National Park: The First 100 Years*, 18.

7. C. W. Buchholtz, *Man in Glacier* (West Glacier, MT: Glacier Natural History Association, 1976), 15.

8. Buchholtz, *Man in Glacier*, 15.

9. Guthrie, *Glacier National Park: The First 100 Years*, 23.

10. Buchholtz, *Man in Glacier*, 16.

11. Guthrie, *Glacier National Park: The First 100 Years*, 18–19.

12. Guthrie, *Glacier National Park: The First 100 Years*, 23.

13. Guthrie, *Glacier National Park: The First 100 Years*, 23.

14. Guthrie, *Glacier National Park: The First 100 Years*, 24.

15. Guthrie, *Glacier National Park: The First 100 Years*, 19.

16. Buchholtz, *Man in Glacier*, 16.

17. Wayne Louie, "Sturgeon-Nose Creations: History," Sturgeon-Nose Creations, accessed August 30, 2016, http://www.sturgeon-nose-creations.com/history.

18. Buchholtz, *Man in Glacier*, 23.

19. Buchholtz, *Man in Glacier*, 24.

20. C. W. Guthrie, *All Aboard! for Glacier: The Great Northern Railway and Glacier National Park* (Helena, MT: Farcountry Press, 2004), 11.

21. Larry Haeg, *Harriman vs. Hill: Wall Street's Great Railroad War* (Minneapolis, MN: University of Minnesota Press, 2013), 29.

22. Haeg, *Harriman vs. Hill*, 30–31.

23. Guthrie, *All Aboard! for Glacier*, 16.

24. Guthrie, *All Aboard! for Glacier*, 11.

25. Haeg, *Harriman vs. Hill*, 31.

26. Guthrie, *All Aboard! for Glacier*, 19.

27. Guthrie, *All Aboard! for Glacier*, 19.

28. Guthrie, *All Aboard! for Glacier*, 20.

29. Guthrie, *All Aboard! for Glacier*, 23.

30. Guthrie, *All Aboard! for Glacier*, 23.

31. Guthrie, *All Aboard! for Glacier*, 24.

32. Guthrie, *All Aboard! for Glacier*, 30.

33. Guthrie, *All Aboard! for Glacier*, 30.

34. Guthrie, *All Aboard! for Glacier*, 30–31.

35. Guthrie, *All Aboard! for Glacier*, 31.

36. National Park Service, "Glacier National Park: Through the Years in Glacier National Park: An Administrative History (Appendix A: Historic Place Names)," National Park Service, January 15, 2004, accessed February 21, 2017, https://www.nps.gov/parkhistory/online_books/glac/appa.htm.

37. Guthrie, *All Aboard! for Glacier*, 31.

38. Ralph W. Hidy and Muriel E. Hidy, "John Frank Stevens: Great Northern Engineer," *Minnesota History Magazine*, Winter 1969, 356, accessed August 30, 2016, http://collections.mnhs.org/MNHistoryMagazine/articles/41/v41i08p345-361.pdf.

39. Christopher Muller, "Railroad Engineering Records: Bridges & Tunnels," Railserve.com, accessed August 30, 2016, http://www.railserve.com/stats_records/railroad_tunnels_bridges.html.

40. Guthrie, *All Aboard! for Glacier*, 31.

41. Guthrie, *All Aboard! for Glacier*, 9.

42. Haeg, *Harriman vs. Hill*, 283.

43. Buchholtz, *Man in Glacier*, 45.

CHAPTER FOUR

Except for the Founding Fathers

It is impossible to pinpoint who the first advocates for conservation in America were or when they began their efforts, but it is not all that important. What is important and easily identifiable are those who moved from individuals with shared interests in the natural world into a force for a comprehensive national conservation ethic. The gathering strength of that initial movement would begin before the Civil War, recede but not entirely disappear during the war, and then reform in force thereafter, extending well into the twentieth century to the present.

Along the way, from before the birth of the nation up to and including the Civil War, small beacons of conservation lights would glimmer, but most were singular and without form, publicity, or national consequence. In 1767, Virginian Thomas Jefferson, who would soon catapult onto the national scene, personally purchased what is now Virginia's Natural Bridge. He paid King George 20 shillings and swore that he "viewed it as a public trust and would under no consideration permit the bridge to be injured, defaced, or masked from public view."[1]

Even though he returned to the area while president and built a small cabin nearby, he never pursued public status for the Natural Bridge and certainly not through a national park concept. In fact, the Jefferson property would remain in private hands until 2014 when it was deeded over to the state of Virginia with the intent of being designated a state park.[2]

Yet Jefferson, followed by others such as Ralph Waldo Emerson and Henry David Thoreau, began to recognize the bounty of the Creator's handiwork in America and deemed its existence and preservation relevant to the well-being of the individual and the nation as a whole. Thus, God and physical and mental health were being added to the equation of the purpose for conservation and preservation. Thoreau would take it a step further by beginning to define, without saying so, the "essential democracy" theme espoused by Teddy Roosevelt nearly a century later. In *Maine Woods*, Thoreau wrote,

> Why should not we, who have renounced the king's authority, have our own pre-
> serves, where no village need be destroyed, in which the bear and panther, and
> some even of the human race, may still exist, and not be civilized off the face of
> the earth, our forests, not to hold the king's game mainly, but hold and preserve
> the king himself also, the lord of creation, not for idle sport or food, but for in-
> spirations and our own true re-creation?[3]

Thus, we had one of the first inklings of a concept whereby the people had every right to the privilege of kings and the wealthy, but such rights would be obtained by the governed for their shared benefit through shared public ownership.

"We can never have enough nature . . . in wilderness is a preservation of the world."[4] This cornerstone of the new transcendentalist movement forti-fied the thought that God created nature, that God was found in nature, and man would be perfected by going into nature as a tonic against the tide of crowding humanity and the growing blight on the land. But again, Thoreau was a small, respected voice literally crying out from the wilderness. Yet his thoughts and those of Emerson and others would eventually gain credence after concern over vanishing resources took life after the Civil War.

Still, neither God nor man had that voice or voices which could cap-ture the national imagination for the creation of great public parks for the benefit of man, nature, and the nation. Yet seeds continued to be planted. Among them was the outgrowth of President Thomas Jefferson's formation and backing of the Corps of Discovery—the Lewis and Clark Expedition of 1803 to 1806.

While true that the primary purpose of the Corps exploration was a pas-sage to the Pacific and the mapping of the acquired territory of the recent Louisiana Purchase to establish the most advantageous northern boundary between the newly added lands purchased from France and British Canada, Lewis and Clark's reports of the rich abundance of game, fish, and lands propelled traders, explorers, and settlers westward toward the Rocky Moun-tains and beyond. It also fueled the imagination of artists and writers to seek out those places and people described in Lewis and Clark's findings. While not specifically planned as a trek toward a conservation ethic, their discoveries set in motion those who in going west would find landscapes so awesome in natural beauty—truly God's great American handiwork—that their reports, writings, and artistry would kindle thoughts in the East that there were gifts of nature worth witnessing and then saving.

The noted artist George Catlin was among them. Catlin was at first motivated by a desire to go out among the Indian tribes to observe, sketch, and paint them. While doing so on a trip in 1832, Catlin recognized what few, if any, had noted: the flowing herds of bison (buffalo), which on the surface seemed to be an inexhaustible river of beasts, were, in fact, being slaughtered to probable extinction. Struck by this observation, Catlin, with great insight, foresaw the demise of the bison and the Indians who relied on them for food, clothing, and shelter. From this, he had a vision of and for the future:

> What a splendid contemplation when one imagines them ... by some great protecting policy of government, preserved ... in a magnificent park.
>
> A nation's Park, containing man and beast, in all the wild and freshness of their nature's beauty.
>
> I would ask no other monument to my memory, nor any other enrollment of my name amongst the famous dead, than the reputation of having been the founder of such an institution.[5]

With insight given to few, Catlin saw past the immediate and prescribed an alternative: bison and tribes should be preserved in a "national park."[6] But his was a call of concerned observation at a time when few recognized anything was amiss. Yet at least he inserted into the growing dialogue the seed to set aside and protect some of the wonders of the new nation as well as offer sanctuary to their original guardians. Forty years later in 1872, that idea would take root when Yellowstone National Park was established.

Unfortunately, those early importunings of the gospel of preservation ran up against the overpowering national urge to settle, exploit, and tame those very wildernesses and the humans who had lived with nature for thousands of years in a partnership of balance. Trees, streams, and land were there for the taking, and, in the case of Native Americans and the bison, perhaps extinction. In 1884, the last buffalo hides were shipped, and the proud tribes of the plains, decimated by wars, disease, ethnic cleansing, whiskey, and the rapidly dwindling herds of their life-sustaining bison (it is estimated that by 1884, only 325 wild bison existed), were forced to move onto reservations where conditions were little to no better. Ironically, most of this was justified under the banner of "Manifest Destiny," whereby it was America's fate under divine providence to conquer the West (and other countries) without regard to God's natural gifts for his other children who had occupied those lands in harmonious stewardship for centuries.

Fortunately, the other wing of divinity would prevail, but first we would have to fight a great war to perfect a more perfect union. Yet even in the carnage of the Civil War, voices of natural well-being and purpose arose out of the wreckage. One would set the precedent for public ownership of natural wonders. The other would articulate the national purpose for such "parks."

In 1864, United States Senator John Conness of California rose on the Senate floor and introduced an unprecedented bill: the setting aside for public purpose and further enjoyment for all a tract of land. That moved the second actor in this original act of public ownership to exclaim it was "the greatest glory of nature ... the union of the deepest sublimity with the deepest beauty."[7] Frederick Law Olmsted, according to Dayton Duncan and Ken Burns in their magnificent television and written history of the national parks, *America's Best Idea*, had left New York City, having completed his design of Central Park, to work in California and visit the site called Yosemite.[8] His reasoning for doing so was simple enough. No work was available for landscape architects, not even for America's most renowned architect who had designed America's first grand urban park. Even though Yosemite was little visited, by 1864, Olmsted knew of its existence and hastened there as soon as possible.

His arrival could not have been more timely. The measure transferring the lands from the federal government to the state of California was now the law of the land. It is interesting to note that in order to gain approval, Conness had to assure his congressional colleagues that while the land and the Mariposa Big Tree Grove were wonders of the world and should by preservation flow to the benefit of all, they were "worthless" and required no expenditure of federal funds.[9] That argument would be used time and time again in the establishment of future national parks, including Glacier National Park.

A commission was established to give the state guidance on how best to proceed and to protect the bestowed treasure, which was given over with the stipulation that it be held "inalienable for all time" for the "use, resort, and recreation" of the public.[10] While not deemed a national park, it set a precedent: Congress had, for the first time, reserved federal lands for public use and pleasure.

The commission was now confronted with the untried challenge of crafting a plan for this newly preserved land. Who better to recruit to help with this than America's premier landscape architect, Frederick Law Olmsted of New York, the designer, along with Calvert Vaux, of New York City's Central Park? To Olmsted fell the task of writing an unprecedented plan for a park devoted to the benefit of all citizens.

The product of Olmsted's work should have been a lasting blueprint for the need for such parks, their economical and spiritual benefit for those citizens, and the means and direction for governance of our shared treasures. Unfortunately, for reasons of turf protection, petty politics within the commission and the California legislature, and budget concerns, Olmsted's report was buried for nearly one hundred years until discovered in 1962. Nonetheless, his suggestions were so strongly molded and set forth that their influential legitimacy and legacy were passed on, at least to his son, Frederick Law Olmsted Jr., who, more than fifty years later, would incorporate many of them into the drafting of the National Park Service "Organic Act" of 1916, which established the agency.[11]

Although Olmsted was a prophet without honor until after the fact, it is important to set forth some of Olmsted's most salient and timeless observations. I do so because there were later conversations and letters between Olmsted and others that influenced their national park thinking. Furthermore, they are as relevant today as when written in 1865.

Olmsted, who had a keen eye for the artistry of nature, painted a prose picture of Yosemite Valley and its surroundings.

> The central and broader part of this chasm is occupied at the bottom by a series of groves of magnificent trees, meadows of the most varied, luxuriant and exquisite herbage, through which meanders a broad stream of the cleanest water, rippling over a pebbly bottom, and eddying among banks of ferns and rushes, sometimes narrowed into sparkling rapids and sometimes expanding into placid pools which reflect the wondrous heights on either side.[12]

In his descriptions were images enough to draw the readers in and hold them while he made his case for public purpose. He began by establishing the means to protect such scenery. "It is the will of the nation so embodied in the act of Congress that this scenery shall never be private property, but like certain defensive points upon our coast, it shall be held solely for public purpose."[13]

Wisely, he then set forth the economic benefits of tourism. Better the dollar before the ethereal. He compared the financial opportunities of Yosemite to those of the Swiss Alps.[14] If some in California were slow on the uptake, this premise would be the underlying foundation of Louis Hill's vision of his American Alps to lure easterners away from Switzerland and Europe to his own version of Swiss chalet comfort among the mountains of Montana some forty years later.

To the economic argument, he ended on a prophetic note. "That when it shall become more accessible, the Yosemite will prove an attraction of a similar character and a similar source of wealth to the whole community, not only of California but of the United States, there can be no doubt."[15] Because there were and always are doubters, let me point out that Yosemite presently generates more than $300 million annually!

Next, he pointed out parks were good not only for the pocketbook but also for the mental and physical health of those who experienced the wonders of the outdoors.[16] Thus, "the establishment by the government of great public grounds for the free enjoyment of the people *under certain circumstances* [emphasis mine] is . . . justified and enforced as a political duty."[17]

Those "certain circumstances" demonstrated that he was adamant that the natural scenery be preserved and maintained consistent with necessary accommodations of visitors. Furthermore, Olmsted asserted that preservation of flora and fauna was not only important in the present but also in the future when the numbers of visitors would be measured not in the hundreds but in the millions.

This has been borne out by the fact that for the past several years, Glacier National Park's visitation has topped 2 million, up from a few thousand who came in 1910 after its establishment.[18]

Recognizing this potential, Olmsted called for rules and regulations to protect what needed to be preserved as soon as possible. To him, it would be far more efficient and inexpensive to set such rules in place early on when fewer visitors would be less likely to cause damage.

Yet with the possibility of abuses intended or not, Olmsted closed his treatise with a recommendation to make access to the park available and affordable so Yosemite would not remain or become a "rich man's park."[19]

In a few short pages, Frederick Law Olmsted, according to Dayton Duncan, "delivered his own combination of Declaration of Independence and Constitution for the park idea—a lofty statement of principles coupled with the nuts and bolts of how to put them into action."[20]

His problem was he put a price tag on those nuts and bolts: $37,000 for trails, bridges, salaries, and a road.[21] Although the commission adopted his report in August 1865, some members waited until Olmsted left the state and then "deep-sixed" the report for almost one hundred years.[22] Fortunately, as mentioned previously, some copies, supplemented by later letters, must have been circulated, setting the premise for the creation and governance of parks and, in 1916, a National Park Service.

But Olmsted's observations and recommendations would also lay the foundation for the conflict between public use and preservation that was written into the Organic Act of 1916. That healthy give-and-take remains to this day.

If Olmsted, on the framing of a national park statement of principle, did not receive due credit, a prophet of biblical stature was waiting in the wings who would pick up where Olmsted left off, expand on the concept, and, as a result, receive the recognition and accolades that his predecessor never enjoyed. John Muir, born in Dunbar, Scotland, and raised in Wisconsin, could have successfully pursued any number of careers. He was an inventor with a flair for business who knew most of the Bible by heart. But neither profit nor prophet was in his blood—or at least not a prophet of the religion as prescribed by Christianity. His would be the religion of nature, and Yosemite would be his principal temple.

After wandering great parts of America after the Civil War, he arrived in California. Having read a pamphlet about Yosemite, he headed there and toward the discovery of his life's work in 1869.

His arrival in the wilds of Yosemite proved to be transformative. As he would later describe it, "We are now in the mountains and they are in us, kindling enthusiasm, making every nerve quiver, filling every pore and cell of us. Our flesh-and-bone tabernacle seems transparent as glass to the beauty about us, neither old nor young, sick nor well, but immortal. I am a captive. I am bound. Love of pure unblemished nature seems to overmaster and blur out of sight all other objects and considerations."[23]

Within a few short years, the man of the Sierras came to be the true prophet of the "Range of Light," as he once described Yosemite, and the person most often sought out to guide and explain the wonders of his cathedrals of stone, streams, and sunlight. Among them would be the man Muir most admired: Ralph Waldo Emerson. Emerson, who was one of the first to seek God in nature and nature in God, was to have a profound effect on Muir, God's rising star. Of all the influences Emerson would have on Muir, most important was his urging for Muir to broaden his sphere of influence and add disciples to the cause. Reluctantly, Muir understood the necessity of going out and preaching the gospel of nature, so he moved to Oakland and took up the pen. His pen would truly become mightier than the swords of profit.

At last, conservation and parks had an advocate of rare combination. John Muir embodied the talents of preacher, organizer, and publicist. Through articles in magazines of national stature, he would convert disciples who would become not simply followers but generals of various rank in Muir's army: George Bird Grinnell, Robert Underwood Johnson, Louis Hill, Stephen Mather, and Franklin D. Roosevelt, among others. But in the immediacy, there was Teddy!

If John Muir was the quiet voice of shadows and sunlight playing across the face of nature and the need to protect that scenery, Theodore Roosevelt would become the bugler, sounding the charge for conservation and the "essential democracy" of parks.[24]

When joined in harmony around the turn of the twentieth century, Muir and Roosevelt would add their voices, pens, and power to a growing chorus for conservation. They would become an irreversible force of nature. Fortunately for America—then and now—they were, for the most part, naturally admiring allies. They could not have been more different in upbringing, style, and temperament. In my opinion, they saw in each other not only their shared passion for conservation and preservation but also complementing and admired differences.

Teddy Roosevelt was a product of privilege layered on privilege. Although sickly and asthmatic as a child, he would train his mind and body through what he called "the strenuous life."[25] In part, that involved going out into nature, first as a collector of birds and other species, then out West to hunt and work as a cowboy. From those experiences, he would write volumes of well-defined and well-received books on the West, its beauties, and its need to be preserved. As a young New York legislator, he would begin to champion the cause for conservation. He would begin to use the power of his position and knowledge to mount his "bully pulpit." That use of power and the elective office to articulate the good fight would catch Muir's attention.

From Muir, Roosevelt would discover the effective use of poetic phrasing to drive home national purpose. The best examples of those borrowed attributes arose out of the most extraordinary meeting of giants from which flowed a renewing rededication to the cause of Yosemite National Park in particular and national parks in general as a national priority.

In May 1903, by his design and because he was president, Roosevelt arranged a meeting with Muir in Yosemite. But it was not a perfunctory handshake and photo-op. It was to extend over three days, and, for all practical purposes, they would be alone. In those days, they would take each other's measure and discuss their views on Yosemite and future parks. It was observed by one of their guides that it probably took three days "because both men wanted to do the talking."[26]

Nonetheless, both men found greatness in the other, formed a lasting friendship, and set forth on a course for conservation which would not only see the transfer of the Yosemite Valley and Mariposa Grove back to both the federal government and the existing Yosemite National Park but an explosion of parks, forests, and national monuments under the broad umbrella of the Antiquities Act of 1906. That act, for all its seemingly minor status, would be one of the most significant conservation acts in America's march toward conservation and preservation. Within its loosely worded parameters was permitting language that allowed a president of the United States to act unilaterally to protect "historic landmarks and historic and prehistoric structures," adding "and other objects of historic interest." Furthermore, it lifted earlier restrictions on the amount of acreage that could be protected.[27] It was tailor-made for a president of action, and Theodore Roosevelt certainly fit the bill.

Using that act plus others, he would proclaim 18 national monuments, 51 federal bird sanctuaries, and four national game refuges and add 100 million acres of national forest reserves. To top it off, he added, with congressional approval, five national parks (two of these parks were later dropped from the National Park system).[28] But his most defining contribution to conservation was to empower and legitimize the cause. He made it not only the popular thing to do but also the right thing to do. He gave the cause momentum because he was the president who could write, speak, and take action while at the same time allying himself with the other rising and influential

FIGURE 4.1. Theodore Roosevelt and John Muir on Glacier Point, Yosemite Valley, California, 1906. Courtesy of Harpers Ferry Center, West Virginia; Library of Congress photograph, negative number USZ62-8672.

voices who had, by the turn of the century, significant constituencies in their own right. He was, in the eye of a solid majority of Americans, the "Square Deal" warrior wrapped in a hero's status.

Truly, save when the original founding fathers met to proclaim a new nation and then a constitution, Roosevelt, Muir, and their disciples became the most important gathering of leaders within a prescribed period of time to reshape the nation and set it on a new course: the setting aside of great natural and historic wonders by the people for the people. In short, they would fulfill the "essential democracy" aspect of Roosevelt's call to action by saving Muir's beloved scenery, forests, and wild things. Their influences, even though periodically ambushed by pirates and "pygmies," have endured in America and, indeed, expanded to most countries of the world.

The national park concept has become one of our most important legacies and exports. It allowed a nation torn by a great Civil War and the end of the frontier to carve out places that reestablished national pride while at the same time helping bind up our national wounds through shared ownership of those treasures.

NOTES

1. Thomas Jefferson Foundation, Inc., "Natural Bridge," Thomas Jefferson's Monticello, March 1997, accessed August 27, 2016, https://www.monticello.org/site/research-and-collections/natural-bridge.

2. Frankie Jupiter, "Gov. McAuliffe Accepts Deed to Natural Bridge," WDBJ7, May 12, 2014, accessed August 31, 2016, http://m.wdbj7.com/news/local/gov-mcauliffe-to-accept-deed-to-natural-bridge-on-monday/25931884.

3. Henry David Thoreau, "The Henry D. Thoreau Quotation Page: Conservation," The Walden Woods Project, 1906, accessed August 27, 2016, https://www.walden.org/Library/Quotations/Conservation.

4. Dayton Duncan and Ken Burns, *The National Parks: America's Best Idea: An Illustrated History* (New York, NY: Alfred A. Knopf, 2009), 11.

5. Duncan and Burns, *The National Parks*, 11.

6. Duncan and Burns, *The National Parks*, 11.

7. Duncan and Burns, *The National Parks*, 7.

8. Duncan and Burns, *The National Parks*, 7.

9. Duncan and Burns, *The National Parks*, 13.

10. Duncan and Burns, *The National Parks*, 8.

11. Duncan and Burns, *The National Parks*, 162–63.

12. Frederick Law Olmsted, *Yosemite and the Mariposa Grove: A Preliminary Report, 1865* (Yosemite National Park, CA: Yosemite Association, 1995), 3.

13. Olmsted, *Yosemite and the Mariposa Grove*, 9.

14. Olmsted, *Yosemite and the Mariposa Grove*, 10–11.

15. Olmsted, *Yosemite and the Mariposa Grove*, 11.

16. Olmsted, *Yosemite and the Mariposa Grove*, 12.

17. Duncan and Burns, *The National Parks*, 13.

18. National Park Service, "Glacier National Park: Fact Sheet," National Park Service, accessed September 16, 2015, http://www.nps.gov/glac/learn/news/fact-sheet.htm.

19. Olmsted, *Yosemite and the Mariposa Grove*, 24.

20. Duncan and Burns, *The National Parks*, 15.

21. Olmsted, *Yosemite and the Mariposa Grove*, 27.

22. Olmsted, *Yosemite and the Mariposa Grove*, xviii.

23. Duncan and Burns, *The National Parks*, 17.

24. Theodore Roosevelt, *The Works of Theodore Roosevelt* (New York, NY: C. Scribner's Sons, 1923), accessed October 1, 2014, http://www.theodore-roosevelt.com/images/research/txt speeches/51.txt.

25. Theodore Roosevelt, *The Strenuous Life* (New York, NY: Century, 1902), 1, accessed August 31, 2016, http://www.theodore-roosevelt.com/images/research/thestrenuouslife.pdf.

26. Duncan and Burns, *The National Parks*, 97.

27. National Park Service, "American Antiquities Act of 1906 (16 USC 431–433)," National Park Service, June 8, 1906, accessed August 27, 2016, https://www.nps.gov/history/local-law /anti1906.htm.

28. Ken Burns and Dayton Duncan, "Theodore Roosevelt (1858–1919)," *The National Parks: America's Best Idea: A Film by Ken Burns*, 2009, accessed September 2, 2015, http://www.pbs .org/nationalparks/people/historical/roosevelt/.

CHAPTER FIVE

Louis Hill, George Bird Grinnell, and the Fight to Save a Crown

"I sincerely hope that publicity now being given to that portion of Montana will result in drawing attention to the scenery which surpasses anything in Montana or adjacent territories. A great benefit would result to Montana if this section could be set aside as a national park."[1] This letter, written by Lt. John Van Orsdale to the Fort Benton River Press in December 1883, was the first public suggestion that the lands becoming known as Glacier be designated a national park. But he added something else that would become the signature economic argument for Glacier as well as other parks, past and future.

"The country included in such a park is not fit for agriculture or grazing purposes, but by placing it under the protection of the Government, the forest would be protected and consequently some of the sources of water of three great rivers systems: the Missouri, the Columbia and the Saskatchewan."[2] To wit, it was worthless, which was Senator Conness's convincing argument in his explanation of the bill setting aside Yosemite in 1864. It was also prophetic. The three rivers and their ecosystems flowing out of Glacier have now become a matter of grave concern as glaciers retreat and snowpacks diminish.

Among those who were motivated by Van Orsdale's suggestion was George Bird Grinnell. He was a friend of Teddy Roosevelt and an admirer of John Muir. Like Roosevelt and Muir, he would use the pen and politics to advance his causes (and the plight) of Yellowstone, Native Americans, and national park status for Glacier, the Grand Canyon, and Olympic, among others.

Grinnell first came to Glacier in 1885. He would return almost annually on the Great Northern to visit what would become the place of his heart. By 1891, he was already thinking about national park status for these wild and haunting places of mountains, valleys, rushing waters, glimmering lakes, and glaciers. Grinnell became so enthralled with the area that he gave it a name, "Crown of the Continent," in 1901 and began to actively champion its inclusion as a national park.[3] Whenever possible, he called on other supporters such as Dr. Lyman Sperry, Emerson Hough, and L. O. Vaught to join the fight.

But immediate congressional support was not forthcoming. Even after Roosevelt took office in 1901 and began to use his "bully pulpit" to thunder at the abuses of timber barons, miners, cattlemen, and other exploiters, including railroaders, nothing happened. That would hold even after Muir visited Glacier in 1901 and proclaimed that the area was "the best care-killing scenery on the continent."[4]

Nor did matters change after Roosevelt and Muir met for their extraordinary conservation summit in 1903 in Yosemite. It would change when the interest of one man was tweaked and, in particular, after Louis W. Hill, son of James J. Hill, took over the reins of the Great Northern Railway as its president.

Born in 1872, Louis Warren Hill was the third of nine children of James J. and Mary T. Hill. Due to his older brother's lack of interest in western railroading and desire not to live in the domineering shadow of his father, Louis Hill would rise to lead the Great Northern, first as president in 1907 and then board chairman in 1912.

Ironically, it would be a boyhood trip to Yellowstone on his father's chief competitor's line, the Northern Pacific, that planted the seed for Hill's love of nature and western scenery, which eventually blossomed into support for the national park concept. Specifically, as he matured and began to take charge of more aspects of the Great Northern's business, he would come to recognize an opportunity for his railroad to have its own national park: Glacier.

Together, Grinnell, Hill, and their allies would hammer a reluctant Congress into submission through their genius of the pen, public relations, and, in Hill's case, sheer political and financial power.

Both Grinnell and Hill were cut from the same cloth of wealth, privilege, education, and connections. They would use all those attributes to make their way in a world that was changing in the latter half of the nineteenth century and into the twentieth century. Both were successful far beyond their monumental achievements of giving birth, then breath, to Glacier

National Park. But it was their connection to Glacier that would define the underlying purpose of their lives and link them forever to Glacier's creation and history.

By the time Grinnell arrived in the Glacier area, he was already well established as a renowned conservationist and student of Native American life. He also had political clout through wide social and conservation circles and as publisher and editor of *Forest and Stream* magazine, first published in 1873. It would, under Grinnell's genius, become the most influential outdoor magazine in the nation. Through his articles and those of contributing writers such as Teddy Roosevelt, Grinnell turned the magazine into the premier American instrument for the rising conservation movement.

Like Roosevelt and Muir, something in Grinnell's DNA drew the young man of privilege to a vocation, avocation, and admiration of the natural world and the lure of the West. Even before completing his education, he traveled west to participate in the last great bison hunt of the Pawnee in 1872.[5]

In 1874, he accompanied George Custer on the Black Hills Expedition as a naturalist. By great luck and a prior commitment to go to the Montana and Yellowstone regions, he declined Custer's later offer and dodged sure death at Little Big Horn in 1876.[6]

The Ludlow Expedition would take him among the landscapes and people who would forever change his life. He came in contact with various tribes, their way of life, and the rapid demise of the bison and other big game. From that time forward, he would publicize the causes of tribes, wildlife, and parks. He was able to do so because he had his own bully pulpit—the magazine.

Before he had completed his life's work, Grinnell would initiate campaigns to end predatory market hunting and game poaching in Yellowstone that led to the Yellowstone Park Protection Act. He founded the Audubon Society of New York that was the precursor of the National Audubon Society. With Teddy Roosevelt, he founded the Boone and Crockett Club that became the most influential organization for ethical and sustainable hunting and conservation practices. His pen and the influence of the club saved the bison from extinction. He would write nearly thirty books on Indian life, conservation, and sport hunting. He would take up the fight for national park status for the Grand Canyon and Olympic National Parks as well as others.[7]

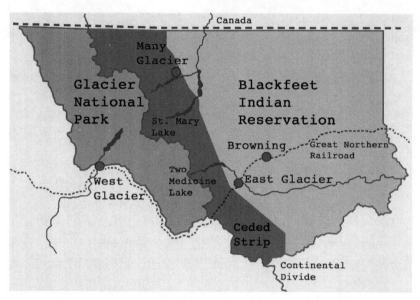

FIGURE 5.1. Glacier National Park and the Ceded Strip. Map created by Mark Bristol and influenced, with permission of the publisher, by the map in *More Montana Campfire Tales* published by Farcountry Press.

But through it all and for twenty-five years, he would return to the landscape of northwest Montana. Under the direction of the area's first professional guide, James Willard Schultz, Grinnell came to intimately know the St. Mary's lakes and Swiftcurrent Valley regions. Schultz would name a glacier and lake in the Swiftcurrent Valley in Grinnell's honor.

While in the area, Grinnell came to know, respect, and defend the Blackfeet. He raged against corrupt Indian agents and illegal grazing. The tribe came to admire him and gave him the name "Fisher Hat."[8]

When it became necessary to resolve the growing problem of the mountain portion of the Blackfeet reservation in 1895, the tribe wanted Grinnell, as discussed in Chapter 2, as one of the government negotiators. At first, he declined, perhaps sensing potential conflict. Eventually, he agreed. While it is well documented that Grinnell finally recommended a lower price than that demanded by the tribe ($3,000,000), he could have run up against the reality of having to propose a more realistic agreement rather than accepting a less satisfactory resolution, such as an uncontrollable gold and copper rush, which would despoil the land to the benefit of no one.

Although Grinnell did not believe profitable veins of minerals existed, the possibility was there. And if a rush was in the offing, neither Grinnell, the tribe, nor the government could have stemmed the stampede.

On September 26, 1895, the "Ceded Strip" Treaty was accomplished. At the tribe's request, George Bird Grinnell read aloud the document. Three hundred six out of 381 tribesmen signed it.[9] Its fairness and Grinnell's role in it have long been debated. For my part, I have concluded that Grinnell may have been conflicted between two worthy callings: he wanted to obtain for the Blackfeet the best deal possible, and he wanted to save the area against exploiters who would have stripped it bare and left it in ruins. Perhaps the answer lay in the future. Until the end of his life, George Bird Grinnell would continue to write about the Blackfeet and Indian life, and he and his wife would dedicate time to spend with them wherever their travels brought them back to his Crown of the Continent or the tribe's "Backbone of the World."

To further blunt the prospects of exploiters, Grinnell, in 1897, hastened to persuade Congress to set aside the area as the Lewis and Clark National Forest Preserve. National Forest status would offer some, but not perfect, protection. But he and others would gain enough time to mount a campaign to convince Congress that Glacier National Park's time had come. He would need all the support he could garner. Waiting just offstage was the difference maker. Even so, it would take another thirteen years to make the dream a reality.

Louis Hill was an unlikely candidate to serve as Grinnell's co-conspirator and partner in the effort to gain national park status for the area they had both come to view as essential, although perhaps through different lenses. Even though both were born into privilege and wealth, it appears on the surface that, unlike Grinnell, Hill's life was prescribed since birth. He would follow in his father's steps. He would be a railroad man. While both graduated from Yale, Grinnell would head west and fashion his own career as a publisher, writer, and conservationist.

Hill, on the other hand, went immediately to work for James J. Hill and the Great Northern. To some, he may have been looked upon as a dandy, while others viewed him as having his career handed to him on a silver platter or, more to the point, on an iron rail. Part of this image may have been fostered by the fact that Louis and his brother James Norman Hill were not good students and only succeeded in school because their parents willed it and intervened with headmasters and professors to get them through what could be best described as an educational ordeal.

But in Louis's case, they would have been wrong on all counts. Beneath the surface and his father's gigantic shadow lay a shrewd business mind with a visionary view of his work and surroundings, fortified by a wide streak of determination.

Shortly after joining the railway, he and his brother were packed off to Duluth to run a small spur line, the Eastern Railway. Louis was the first member of the family to see the potential for the vast deposits of iron ore in Minnesota's Iron Range. When James J. Hill refused to participate in a land purchase, Louis Hill bought it on his own. It pointed out a major difference between father and son: James Hill too often stuck to what he knew best based on past history; Louis could see over new horizons and anticipate new opportunities. Louis Hill's early investments in iron ore lands would make himself, the railway, his family, and his father a great deal of money. Louis wrote,

> During the early period of the acquisition of iron ore properties, I personally acquired the Hill Annex Mine, which to date has shipped about 40,000,000 tons of iron ore. This one mine alone has produced approximately $37,000,000 in freight revenues for the Great Northern Railway and approximately $22,000,000 in royalties to the Great Northern Iron Ore Properties. It was acquired by me personally, prior to being drilled and after my father turned down for the railroad.[10]

Over the years, wherever the railroad went, Louis Hill would invest heavily and successfully in all manner of mining ventures throughout the West. It would make the rich scion of one of America's wealthiest families richer in his own right and, I am convinced, self-confident enough to move out from under his father's shadow, even though, to the best of my knowledge, it was not a rebellious move, rather one of mutual admiration. From every indication, James J. Hill, although often hard pressed to accept change, did so when convinced, as was the case with iron ore properties and trafficking. All told, son and father would acquire more than 55,000 acres. By the mid-twentieth century, Minnesota iron production accounted for two-thirds of all iron mined in the United States.

From that time forward, father and son would grow close, even as James J.'s other beloved and multitalented son, James Norman, grew more distant,

FIGURE 5.2. James J. Hill and Louis W. Hill, 1912. Courtesy of the Minnesota Historical Society; James J. Hill 387, James J. Hill Papers.

finally moving away from the railroad and his domineering father. The path was now clear for Louis Hill to ascend the ladder to leadership of the Great Northern.[11]

As president, Louis Hill was free to pursue his vision for the railroad, including his love of the West and its scenery. This was a part of Hill unrecognized by family or competitors. He threw himself and the railroad behind the creation of his most cherished dream: Glacier National Park.

In addition to his already immense talent for the railroad business, he would reveal his talents for promotion and art. One would play against the other to make Glacier Park an icon that Americans would hasten to witness. "See America First" would be the clarion call.[12]

James J. Hill had little interest in passenger trade unless they were new farmers or settlers who would buy and ship goods up and down the Great Northern lines of the Dakotas, Montana, Idaho, and Washington. Again,

Louis, without abandoning the core business of the railway, saw the potential of the attraction of western scenery and mountains, particularly those
that lay to the north of the Great Northern line that cut through Marias Pass.
He also knew the attraction would be enhanced by tourist amenities that
would surpass those of the Northern Pacific's Yellowstone facilities.

All he needed was a park. To accomplish that, he would need a receptive
Congress to create Glacier National Park. As Hill was turning to George Bird
Grinnell for support, Grinnell was turning to him. Whether their supportive
handshake was real or symbolic, it would tilt the scales in favor of positive
action. The partnership would foster the teamwork necessary for a successful lobbying effort: up-front grassroots building and behind-the-scenes persuasion. Grinnell became Mr. Outside and Hill became Mr. Inside. Even with
this potent partnership, it would take time to persuade, perfect, and pass a
bill in Congress.

All legislation at the national or state level that attempts to confront and
establish new grounds is sure to run up against traditional and entrenched
competing interests. That was the case of the United States Senate at the
turn of the twentieth century. By its history, tradition, rules, and procedures,
the Senate was established and perfected to stop or at least slow any legislation that challenged the old order. Even though seven national parks
were in existence at the time (Grinnell and Hill made their move in 1907),
five had come about in the preceding years under the tireless leadership
of Teddy Roosevelt, yet all seven took time to establish. And all the proponents of these parks, to one degree or another, had to convince a suspicious Congress to gain approval. While the Roosevelts, Pinchots, Muirs, and
others spoke to our better angels and national purpose, it was usually the
argument first adopted by Senator John Conness in championing his 1864
Yosemite bill that the land was "worthless" and no federal monies would
be spent that carried the day. For the most part, Congress bought into that
argument and rarely appropriated funds.

Fortunately for Hill, Grinnell, and other proponents of the park, by 1905,
most of the anticipated mining stampede failed to materialize, taking away
that argument from miners, locals, and even James J. Hill. But other arguments, if allowed to develop, would create substantial hostility at the local
level. The Forest Homestead Act of 1906 opened forest reserves, specifically
agricultural lands not needed for public purposes, to free settlement. All of

what was to become Glacier was in such a reserve, largely at Grinnell's urging in 1897.[13] He had hoisted his park on his own petard.

But Grinnell was not without influential support and the standing to make his case through *Century* magazine, the *New York Tribune*, the Boone and Crockett Club, his editorship of *Forest and Stream*, and, of course, Teddy Roosevelt, the highly popular president of the United States. While Roosevelt did not sign the final Glacier National Park bill, he set the stage, championing the creation of the 5 national parks, 150 national forests, 18 national monuments, and other bird and game preserves.[14]

Grinnell and Hill's targeted audiences were twofold: local backing and the support of Montana's congressional delegation, in particular Senator Thomas Carter. First as congressman and then as a senator, Carter held important committee posts that gave him broad and growing influence. He was also James J. Hill's railroad senator.[15] It would take this connection to override Carter's firm philosophical bent that the federal government (or probably any government) had no right to appropriate lands or impose restrictions on lands that were already settled, paid for, or needed to be settled in the future. To counter that position, Grinnell needed a plausible alternative. The Hills, specifically Louis, would give him the necessary tools of persuasion: money, power, persistence, and public relations. Louis Hill would use all of them, although completely behind the scenes, to secure his vision of true conservation coupled with the ability to offer a first-class tourist experience on his railroad. To generate interest in the latter, he was already spending the Great Northern Railway's advertising dollars on slick and colorful brochures, posters, and the like to lure easterners westward rather than crossing the Atlantic for vacations. The possibility of thousands of tourists attached to their bulging pocketbooks began to turn some heads, at least enough to compel Senator Carter to introduce Senate Bill 2032 late in the 1907 session. It failed to pass and was predestined to do so because Carter appears to have only wanted to appease the Hills and silence Grinnell. He failed to appreciate the depth of Hill's or Grinnell's commitment and willingness to continue to apply the heat. Carter reintroduced a bill early in 1908.[16]

By then, his junior senator, Joseph Dixon, had taken office and was much more inclined to work for passage. But it was still an uphill climb, perhaps insurmountable. Carter was still unenthusiastic, but he also had gained a powerful excuse. Speaker of the House Joe Cannon did not like the concept of national parks at any level. Because he controlled all flow of legislation, he had almost dictatorial power to pass or kill any bill. He refused to allow the park bill to be debated or brought to a vote. The second bill died in March 1909.[17] On the surface, Glacier National Park appeared to be dead.

Teddy Roosevelt was out of office. Taft was an unknown to some but not the Hills. The bill had failed twice, and the lapsed time had allowed some opponents to mount a counter campaign. The Kalispell Chamber of Commerce was particularly agitated by language that seemed to give the Great Northern a monopoly on land travel from east to west.[18] It probably did, but that protest could have been overridden—Cannon's opposition, however, could not.

Grinnell was depressed. Had Glacier's time come and gone? He should not have worried. Louis Hill, with the far-behind-the-scenes support of James J., doubled down. He turned his promotional attention to business leaders and newspapers. Most of his activities were hidden from public view. He did not want to stir up the hornet's nest of anti–big business populism which was spreading across the Plains and mountain states. It was an adroit balancing act. It was enough to keep Senator Carter in line and in the game. Carter would make one last attempt. Hill and Grinnell redoubled their public efforts.

Hill sent salmon to one and all, including President Taft and Speaker Cannon. He entertained Taft at his home in St. Paul. He followed with Flathead apples and Montana potatoes. And then to mellow proponents and opposition alike, he sent whiskey to Montana businessmen and political and newspaper leaders.[19]

Grinnell reinvigorated the conservation community with a nationwide letter writing campaign. In June 1909, Senator Carter kept his promise to the Hills (with the clear understanding that political and financial support would be forthcoming). He introduced Senate Bill 2777 that was sent to the Committee on Public Lands. Besides the tireless and relentless work of Hill and Grinnell, Carter now had the supportive aid of his fellow senator, Joseph Dixon, and Congressman Charles N. Pray.[20] They, unlike Carter, were dedicated to the national park concept and a new Glacier National Park in Montana. Even with full delegation support, pitfalls remained that could torpedo the bill at several junctures.

FIGURE 5.3. Joseph M. Dixon, governor of Montana, U.S. senator from Montana, representative from Montana, and first
assistant secretary of the interior, date unknown. Courtesy
of the University of Montana, Missoula; Maureen and Mike
Mansfield Library/Archives and Special Collections.

The argument of the possibility of minerals and agriculture development
was still in play. This was struck down by Carter's counterargument that
the lands were worthless for commerce. The matter of future railroad construction that seemed to favor the Great Northern was also a concern. The
bill was amended to negate that possibility. Then the persistent argument
of new appropriations to pay for a new park was cited. This was countered
by the argument made by Frederick Olmsted in 1865 that a well-maintained
park would turn the heads of Americans who annually vacationed in the
mountains of Switzerland to the more readily accessible mountains and
lakes of northwestern Montana. A figure of $2,000,000 was thrown out. That,

FIGURE 5.4. Thomas Henry Carter, territorial delegate and U.S. senator and representative from Montana, December 12, 1907. Courtesy of the University of Montana, Missoula; Maureen and Mike Mansfield Library/Archives and Special Collections.

coupled with the Great Northern's "See America First" national campaign, seemed to touch the pocketbooks and patriotism of the senators and representatives.[21]

From that point on, minor squabbles and amendments were debated. A favorable committee vote was cast on February 9, 1910. The bill was headed for the House, to be handled by Congressman Pray—and apparently without the opposition of Speaker Cannon. Why?

Because of his autocratic (some said dictatorial) rule, the speaker was facing a revolution in the House of Representatives—shades of the present. On March 17, 1910, St. Patrick's Day, Nebraska's representative led a coalition

FIGURE 5.5. U.S. Representative Charles Nelson Pray, 1910.
Courtesy of the University of Montana, Missoula; Maureen
and Mike Mansfield Library/Archives and Special Collections.

of 42 progressive Republicans and 149 Democrats in open revolt to strip
the speaker of his chairmanship of the Rules Committee that controlled
the flow of all House legislation as well as his power to assign committees.
On paper, Cannon would have seemed to have the votes, but many of his
staunchest allies were not only Republicans but also Irish, and they were
away from the House celebrating St. Patrick's Day. The battled raged for
more than a day. In the end, Cannon remained speaker, but his iron rule
was ended. He lost the speakership and his seat in 1912 when a Democratic
majority was swept into office under the banner of Democratic presidential
candidate Woodrow Wilson.[22]

Lacking the revolt that took place on St. Patrick's Day, Glacier National Park may not have seen the light of day in 1910 or beyond. Perhaps sensing revolt, Cannon, looking for support in all corners, may have seen a potential vote in Congressman Pray and possible backing by J.J. and Louis Hill. In any case, with continued public relations pressure from Grinnell and Hill, on April 13, 1910, the bill was placed on the calendar. It passed with amendments. After a flurry of final questions and acceptance of differences between the Senate and House versions, on April 29, 1910, Senate Bill 2777 passed both houses of Congress and was sent to President Taft for his signature, which was affixed on May 11, 1910.

America had a new national park. George Bird Grinnell had a twenty-five-year dream fulfilled, and Louis Hill had not only a dream fulfilled but a protected area for developing his vision of a land he was convinced would turn traveling Americans west, all riding on his trains. Furthermore, it was his dream and his project, not an extension of James J. Hill. He would now turn to making the attraction that would make all Americans and perhaps foreigners rush to "See America First"—and Montana in particular.

But something more meaningful happened in and during the legislative deliberations concerning the creation of this park at that time in our history. It would focus the argument on John Muir's pure preservation versus Gifford Pinchot's "the greatest good for the greatest number." It would give rise to a continuing debate, the conflict of which was incorporated in the establishment of the National Park Service Act of 1916, known as the "Organic Act": "which purpose is to conserve the scenery and the natural and historic objects and the wildlife therein and to provide for the enjoyment of the same in such a manner and by such means as will leave them unimpaired for the enjoyment of future generations."[23]

It is that debate in the first part of the twentieth century that propelled the recognition for a National Park Service to establish rules and regulations to govern the growing number of national parks. It is the ambiguity of its dual purpose that has continued the dialogue and debate into the present. In my opinion, it is a healthy balancing act that attracts among its visitors those who will grow to advocate that the natural grandeur of Glacier National Park and others will remain intact. It is a fine line but one that will ensure that both sides of the equation are weighed one against the other.

The debate also fueled discussion that economic value could add to the coffers of local communities and state treasuries far in excess of what might be lost from those revenues generated by whatever small results derived from marginal natural resources or agriculture development. As of this writing, Glacier National Park generates an annual economic benefit to local businesses and communities of $179 million spent by 2.2 million visitors.[24] Of further interest, it was announced in June 2015 that the 100 millionth visitor had passed through the park since its founding.[25]

The congressional debate also brought to the attention of certain members that their region of the United States had no parks. All were being established in the western states. Over the next thirty years, Acadia, Hot Springs, Great Smoky Mountains, Shenandoah, and Isle Royale would be added. Today, 59 national parks are complemented by 118 national monuments spread across the land.[26]

Finally, the debate began the preliminary discussion on what role and how much the federal government would and should play in financing these wonders of America through appropriations. Not that Glacier or others would receive any meaningful funding for a number of years, but the question was raised several times during the Glacier debate and thereafter. It became part of the larger discussions of the need for a national governing body to give a consistency in guiding and governing the growing number of parks.

This aside, May 11, 1910, was a glorious day for George Bird Grinnell. He had his park. In *Forest and Stream*, he would thank Senators Carter and Dixon, Representative Pray, and the Boone and Crockett Club members, taking no credit himself. Carter and Pray publicly thanked Grinnell. However, no one publicly acknowledged Louis Hill. He and his father probably wanted it that way.[27]

In an ironic twist of fate, neither Senator Carter's support for Glacier nor the backing of the Hills was enough to get him reelected in 1910. While I'm sure a number of reasons existed, one may have been that the populist movement was blowing across the West and Montana. Because U.S. senators were elected by state legislators before the passage of the Seventeenth Amendment (popular election of senators) and because Montana's legislature was controlled by the Democrats, Carter saw the probable outcome and retired.

As for Grinnell and Hill, they would both continue to embrace Glacier, but from different perspectives. Grinnell would grow to regret the tide of tourists coming into his park. As early as 1911, he voiced dismay at the developments underway or planned. Yet in his letters over the next fifteen years or so, he always came back to the fact that in order to have a park to protect against exploitation, tourists and accommodations had to exist as well. He simply wished otherwise.

Louis Hill, on the other hand, could not wait to get his hands on those tourists and build those accommodations. Fortunately, he chose to build only to his high standard of excellence.

Interestingly enough, the two founding partners in the drive to create the park apparently did not personally meet until 1912.

> Two days later, as he and [Luther] North rode toward East Flattop, they met three horsemen, Grinnell recorded. The leader spoke and at length asked if this was Mr. Grinnell's party and if I was Mr. G. Just before we turned off to McDermott (now Swiftcurrent Lake), they stopped again and the leader introduced himself as Mr. Louis Hill (president of the Great Northern Railroad). We had a long talk.... Hill seemed a very bright, energetic, and determined fellow. He will do much for the park and I told Jack (Monroe) he is a good man to tie up to.[28]

Whether they met again I do not know.

For fourteen years, Grinnell would continue to return to Glacier over most summers until 1926, when he would, with help, climb to the glacier bearing his name for the last time. After that trip, as he had done before, he wrote his friend L. O. Vaught on his disillusionment but ended as always on his reoccurring justification: "If we had not succeeded in getting these regions set apart as national parks, by this time they would have been ... cut bare of timber, dotted with irrigation reservoirs, the game would have all been killed off, the country would have been burned over."[29]

In spite of his self-effacing manner, Grinnell would gain national recognition, receiving the Theodore Roosevelt Distinguished Service Medal from President Calvin Coolidge in 1925. Coolidge stated among other accolades that Glacier National Park was Grinnell's monument.[30]

Although some of his enthusiasm for Glacier waned, not so his devotion to conservation in general and the lives of the Native Americans. Grinnell continued to write books and articles. He served as president of the National Parks Association and the Boone and Crockett Club. He died on April 11, 1938, at the age of 89. The *New York Herald Tribune* proclaimed him as the "father of American conservation."[31]

Louis Hill, about whom I will speak more in the next chapter, set out on his grand plan to have his railroad take tourists to his hotels, chalets,

FIGURE 5.6. Dr. and Mrs. George Bird Grinnell on Grinnell Glacier, date unknown. Courtesy of the Glacier National Park Archives.

and camps in his park. By 1929, he had finished his task and resigned as chairman of the Great Northern, cutting all ties to the park that Grinnell claimed came about in large part because of Hill's support. To the best of my knowledge, he never returned to Glacier. Unlike Grinnell, he seemed to have completed that chapter of his life, turned the page, and moved on to other things.

Like the landmasses and glaciers that flowed together to form something even more significant than the parts separate, something, perhaps prede-termined, steered George Bird Grinnell and Louis Hill toward their love of nature. That unseen hand steered them westward toward a finite area in the earth's scheme. Both knew within a short period of time—perhaps in the first moment—that they were in the midst of their life's destination and the home of their hearts.

Then, without meeting until after the fact, they joined in a partnership that would assault Congress, including the Montana delegation, which was skeptical at best of this new conservation ethic centered around national parks and forests. Separately, again without meeting, they each knew (and had been prepared to know) what their roles were. Grinnell would take up the pen, and Hill turned to publicity and power.

When they had finished, one received most of the public accolades. The other seemed to have been ignored. It did not seem to have caused any fric-tion between the two, as witnessed in the 1912 meeting high in the Granite Park area. Perhaps like the landmasses and glaciers, they had only to touch for a brief time and then began to move away, never to see each other again.

But in the time before that handshake in the high mountain air of Glacier National Park, they had become a singular force for nature.

NOTES

1. C. W. Buchholtz, *Man in Glacier* (West Glacier, MT: Glacier Natural History Association, 1976), 45.

2. Buchholtz, *Man in Glacier*, 45.

3. National Park Service. "Glacier National Park Press Kit: Glacier National Park and Other NPS Quotes," National Park Service, accessed April 22, 2015, http://www.nps.gov/glac/learn /news/upload/press_quotes.pdf.

4. National Park Service, "Glacier National Park Press Kit."

5. Tony Perrottet, "Chasing a Prairie Tale," *New York Times*, June 23, 2012, accessed August 31, 2016, http://www.nytimes.com/2012/06/24/travel/buffalo-the-pawnee-and-an-old-story -on-a-trip-across-the-plains.html?_r=0.

6. Michael Punke, *Last Stand: George Bird Grinnell, the Battle to Save the Buffalo, and the Birth of the New West* (New York, NY: Smithsonian Books/Collins, 2007), 109.

7. Richard E. McCabe, "George Bird Grinnell: 'The Noblest Roman of Them All,'" Outdoor Writers Association of America, accessed August 7, 2016, http://owaa.org/owaa-legends /george-bird-grinnell-the-noblest-roman-of-them-all/.

8. Dayton Duncan and Ken Burns, *The National Parks: America's Best Idea: An Illustrated History* (New York, NY: Alfred A. Knopf, 2009), 118.

9. Dave Walter, "Past Times: The Ceded Strip: The Blackfeet, Glacier National Park, and the Badger-Two Medicine," *Montana Magazine*, September/October 1998, 59.

10. Biloine W. Young and Eileen R. McCormack, *The Dutiful Son, Louis W. Hill: Life in the Shadow of the Empire Builder, James J. Hill* (St. Paul, MN: Ramsey County Historical Society, 2010), 49–50.

11. Young and McCormack, *The Dutiful Son*, 81–82.

12. Young and McCormack, *The Dutiful Son*, 121.

13. Buchholtz, *Man in Glacier*, 46–47.

14. Ken Burns and Dayton Duncan, "Theodore Roosevelt (1858–1919)," *The National Parks: America's Best Idea: A Film by Ken Burns*, 2009, accessed September 2, 2015, http://www.pbs .org/nationalparks/people/historical/roosevelt/.

15. Andrew C. Harper, "Conceiving Nature: The Creation of Montana's Glacier National Park," *Montana: The Magazine of Western History*, Summer 2010, 13.

16. Harper, "Conceiving Nature," 15.

17. Harper, "Conceiving Nature," 16.

18. Harper, "Conceiving Nature," 18.

19. Harper, "Conceiving Nature," 17.

20. Harper, "Conceiving Nature," 17–18.

21. Harper, "Conceiving Nature," 18.

22. David M. Shribman, "Getting Rid of Uncle Joe," *Pittsburgh Post-Gazette*, March 14, 2010, accessed August 31, 2016, http://www.post-gazette.com/opinion/david-shribman/2010/03/14 /Getting-rid-of-Uncle-Joe/stories/201003140237.

23. Duncan and Burns, *The National Parks*, 163.

24. Denise Germann, "Glacier Creates $179 Million in Economic Benefit," National Park Service, July 21, 2014, accessed July 21, 2014, https://www.nps.gov/glac/learn/news/glacier-creates -179-million-in-economic-benefit.htm.

25. Vince Devlin, "Glacier National Park Welcomes 100 Millionth Visitor: '#WINNER,'" *Missoulian*, June 11, 2015, accessed August 30, 2016, http://missoulian.com/news/local/glacier -national-park-welcomes-millionth-visitor-winner/article_9692204b-8804-544d-8d5d-81893c b54d24.html.

26. National Park Service, "Frequently Asked Questions (U.S. National Park Service)," National Park Service, accessed September 7, 2016, https://www.nps.gov/aboutus/faqs.htm.

27. Gerald A. Diettert, *Grinnell's Glacier: George Bird Grinnell and Glacier National Park* (Missoula, MT: Mountain Press Publishing Company, 1992), 95.

28. Diettert, *Grinnell's Glacier*, 99.

29. Diettert, *Grinnell's Glacier*, 104–5.

30. Diettert, *Grinnell's Glacier*, 106.

31. Diettert, *Grinnell's Glacier*, 109.

CHAPTER SIX

Molding a National Park
1910–1929

"The railroads are greatly interested in the passenger traffic to the parks. Every passenger that goes to the national parks, wherever he may be, represents practically a net earnings," stated Louis W. Hill, Chairman of the Board of the Great Northern Railway, in 1915.[1]

Fortunately for Glacier National Park and national parks in general, Louis Hill had a vision grander than rail revenues. His tough business acumen was cloaked in a sensitivity that included a deep passion for the mountains, outdoors, art, and photography and a skillful sense of promotion. He would wrap all these talents into a force of nature with a Renaissance man's three-dimensional sense of purpose and place. He also had a fourth dimension essential to turning vision into reality: he was president, then chairman, of the Great Northern, which would supply the money and the muscle. He would need a great deal of both.

I am also convinced that Louis Hill had at least the tacit backing of his father. James J. Hill was not only extremely proud of his protégé, entrusting him with his beloved rail empire, but also Louis had made the old man and the family a great deal of money, with more projected for the foreseeable future. James Hill had silently aided in the passage of the Glacier legislation, and he would not stand in the way of Louis completing his vision.

Louis's vision was grounded not only in his deep love for the area (the conservation side of his nature) but also in the fact that the Northern Pacific and the Santa Fe railroads already had proven that the great natural wonders of Yellowstone and the Grand Canyon, respectively, were attracting tourists with attractive hotels and facilities. The Northern Pacific's "Old Faithful Lodge" and the Santa Fe's "El Tovar" were successful magnets for those easterners beginning to look for the Western experience.[2] But neither could compare to Hill's grand scheme.

FIGURE 6.1. Westbound Empire Builder coming into Glacier Park Station, June 10, 1934. Courtesy of the Glacier National Park Archives; George A. Grant, photographer.

Hill was drawn to the concept first propounded by Frederick Law Olmsted's report on the potential of Yosemite. It is only speculation, but not out of the realm of possibility, that Louis Hill had heard of or seen Olmsted's treatise on the benefits and drawing power of such facilities. He certainly became intrigued with the mountain chalets in the Alps of Switzerland. He was determined to build even grander hotels and chalets in the Alps of America. He would follow Olmsted's suggestions not only in the facilities but also in the concept of the human need for care from the spiritual, physical, and mental decay of modern society and industrialization. Hill's hotels and park experiences would be promoted in art, photography, and prose about the blessings of a mountain and lake experience unrivaled by any in Europe, and he could get travelers there in comfort, cheaper, and sooner on his railroad.

He sprang to the task with the same enthusiasm, planning, and attention to detail that were the hallmark legacy of his empire-building father. Parenthetically, he did so without counting on meaningful financial support from

FIGURE 6.2. Major William Logan's camp at Lake McDonald at the mouth of Fish Creek in Glacier National Park, 1910. *Left to right*: William R. Logan, superintendent; Clement S. Ucker, chief clerk; and W. W. Phillips. Courtesy of the U.S. Geological Survey, Denver Library Photographic Collection; U.S. Department of the Interior.

the federal government (or anyone else, for that matter), at least not at the outset. In 1911, only $15,000 was appropriated from Congress for Glacier.[3]

While Hill's own talent, coupled with that of his railroad's public relations geniuses, had already done a great deal of advertising back east over the past several years, he was immensely aided by the constant drumbeat of George Bird Grinnell's weekly *Forest and Stream* magazine, whose audience was national in reach and influential beyond the telling. From 1900 on, starting with a Grinnell article published by *Century* in which he deemed Glacier "The Crown of the Continent," Grinnell's magazine and others he'd influenced seem to come out weekly extolling the wonders of Glacier. They included, among others, Boone and Crockett publications, *National Geographic*, sympathetic newspapers, and individual conservationists extolling the wonders of the area. And always in the background was the thunder and whisper of Roosevelt and Muir.

Fortunately, a growing, receptive audience was listening. America at the turn of the century was growing an expanding middle class that wanted to imitate the traveling upper class. Thus, when the rich began to turn away from Europe and go west, they followed, and "they" numbered in the tens of thousands, unlike the limited number of wealthy.

But most rich and wannabes alike wanted to travel and "rough it" in comfort. Underlying this was a sense of national pride wrapped in a growing patriotism encompassing an embrace of all things American and, at the same time, a gathering sense of loss of the frontier and pristine wilderness that had seemed would always be just over the next horizon. Because Glacier and most of the newer national parks had been created in a relatively short span, 1890 to 1910, they were a fresh idea that peaked Americans' interest, fulfilling and satisfying those dual senses of pride and place.

Louis W. Hill and company were furiously at work to ensure they got what was expected. Between 1910 and 1913, Hill commissioned nine chalet groups as well as his signature hotel—Glacier Park Hotel (now Glacier Park Lodge). Because of a quirk of history, the west side of the park already had a hotel, concessions, and other facilities, so Hill concentrated most of his efforts on the east side of the park.[4]

FIGURE 6.3. Glacier National Park east entrance, 1914. Courtesy of the Library of Congress; Harris & Ewing, photographer; retrieved October 27, 2016, from the Library of Congress.

FIGURE 6.4. Open campfire in the massive lobby of the Glacier Park Hotel, dated between 1910–1920. Courtesy of the Library of Congress; retrieved October 27, 2016, from the Library of Congress.

FIGURE 6.5. Glacier National Park east entrance, 1914. Courtesy of the Library of Congress; retrieved December 1, 2016, from the Library of Congress; Harris & Ewing, photographer.

Construction began on chalets at St. Mary's, Sun Point, Sperry, Granite Park, Cut Bank, Gunsight, Two Medicine, and Swiftcurrent. The exception was Belton, where a station and an accommodating hotel had been built several years before at what is now West Glacier. In addition to the Glacier Park Lodge and chalets on the east side, the Great Northern controlled either directly or indirectly all concessions: boats, horseback rides, and bus service. Every contract carved out a piece of the profit, as well it should have. With the commissioning of the Many Glacier Hotel in 1913 and the Prince of Wales Hotel at Waterton National Park in Canada as well as major expenditures on roads and trails, the railroad's investment is estimated to have exceeded $2.3 million ($31,193,000 in 2015 dollars).[5] In 1930, the railway purchased the existing Lewis Hotel at Lake McDonald (later renamed Lake McDonald Lodge).[6] With that addition (under the ownership of Glacier Park Hotel Company, organized by Hill in 1914 to run the growing tourist business), the company had dominated the market in every arena of the park from Waterton on the north, Many Glacier on the east, Glacier Lodge on the south, and Lake McDonald Lodge on the west, with chalets and tent camps strategically positioned within a day's ride or hike from the grand lodges.

Another aspect to Hill's genius was his eye for beauty and place. He chose sites for his hotels and chalets that would blend into the landscape while at the same time giving tourists views that fostered awe and serenity from the time alpenglow mornings greeted the new day until God-finger sunset rays welcomed the night.

He also built them to last for the ages. The proof is in the present, one hundred years later. In part, the lodges would last because of the Swiss chalet concept that appealed to Louis Hill's aesthetic as well as his practical nature. Their Swiss-style roofs could carry heavy snow loads that have ruined many a lesser-designed facility over the years. Furthermore, they were built of materials (hand-picked by Hill) to last for those hundred years and longer. That is not to say that repairs and renovations have not occurred and are not still needed, often including modernization alterations, but never did these necessary rehabilitations mar the sightlines between structure and mountains.

"The work is so important, I loathe to entrust the development to anybody but myself," noted Louis W. Hill.[7]

That quote was the forerunner to Hill's decision to leave the Great Northern presidency and become its chairman. He needed all the time he could

FIGURE 6.6. Old concession tour buses and autos parked next to the Great Northern Railway Depot at Belton, Montana, early 1920s. Courtesy of the Glacier National Park Archives; T. J. Hileman, photographer.

muster to be in and out of the park and hotels and chalets that were to be part of the landscape when completed. That would require Louis to be on-site with hands and eyes on every detail and change order. According to several accounts, most of the change orders came from Hill himself.

Because I spent two summers (1961–1962) working in the Many Glacier area on the trail crew, I am most familiar with its design and history. For that reason, I will use it as the example of the park's facilities commissioned and built by Hill. Each has its own story and all have the touch of the visionary who wanted to reroute traveling America from east to west to a place that not only would captivate them but would become the magnet to draw them back, along with their families and friends, then children and grandchildren.

Hill knew that Glacier Park Lodge and the Many Glacier Hotel would be a fit, with complementing chalets and tent camps connecting the two flagships. But Hill, like his one-eyed father, saw over horizons and around corners. By instinct and survey, he realized that not all his guests wanted the outback "rough it" experience. Plus, he needed a road to send baggage and supplies as well as construction materials and men to build his hotels. The park had no money for such undertakings, in fact, little for anything else. So the Great Northern financed a new road between the two major facilities at a cost of $90,000.[8]

While the hotel would be a marvel in and of itself, it was Hill's concept and siting which made Many Glacier Hotel, in my opinion, the most perfect lodge among all the great lodges of the national park system.

Approximately 50 miles from East Glacier, Montana, on the road to Babb, Montana, one turned left off the main road into the Swiftcurrent Valley. There, for another twelve miles or so, visitors were drawn around each bend to ever-expanding glimpses of the panoramic views of mountains, valleys, and glaciers until finally arriving at a two-pronged valley, breathtaking in its majesty. With an appreciative eye for the geology that formed the park beginning more than a billion years ago, the newly arrived visitor would recognize they were standing at the pinnacle of the artistry of rock and ice. Then at the end of the valley road, just when the traveler came to think they'd seen all there was to see, a glacier lake (in 1915, Lake McDermott, now Swiftcurrent) of glimmering splendor would appear. Turning left, they crossed a waterfall bridge into the Many Glacier Hotel complex. Because of the way it was nestled among the framing lake, mountains, and glaciers, it came as a hidden surprise. I believe that Louis Hill knew he had to match mountains and water with his hotel to please both tourists and nature. He succeeded in 1915, and that success holds true to this day, slightly more than one hundred years later.

Then, as now, one arrived without the blemish of gaudy billboards or neon lights. It is a place where the rotten layers of stress and the mundane peel away within moments. Again, the setting was such that even as it blended into the landscape, it was also minimalized to the point of no disruption to the towering peaks that surrounded it in every direction: Altyn, Mount Gould, Grinnell, Mount Wilbur, Mount Henkel, Appekunny, and the mountains of Swiftcurrent Pass running west to the Garden Wall. It is this "walled-in" effect that established the panorama that practically lost the hotel in its magnificence, and it is that grand isolation (even with telephone, telegram, and now Wi-Fi) that caused visitors to sense they had found solace. Even those tourists who chose only to sit on the lobby balconies or outside their rooms had their senses drawn away from the hotel toward the mountains, glaciers, and wildlife that included garbage-feeding grizzly bears.

Whatever the level of "roughing it" participation, the amenities would accommodate. The hotel itself was truly a "showcase of the Rockies." The Many Glacier Hotel's lobby was the first experience as visitors entered, rising four stories, supported and dramatized by giant peeled log columns, with two fireplaces and a unique staircase with large west-facing windows looking out on the wonders of the lake moving up into the mountains, framed by an ever-changing sky of brilliant sunscapes at all hours of the day. Along the walls, a mural of eye-catching dimension—180 feet long—told the history of the Blackfeet. Commissioned by Hill, it was painted by Chief Medicine Owl and other elders. It was deemed so outstanding that members of the American Rockies Alpine Club wrote it was "worthwhile to cross the continent to see; it was painted expressly for the hotel and is unique among wall decorations."[9] Unfortunately, wrapped in the guise of cost cutting and renovations, a blatant disregard for all things Blackfeet occurred. The Great Northern, in a failed attempt to sell the Glacier properties in the late 1950s, allowed a manager/contractor, Donald Knutson, to destroy much of the original architectural centerpieces, including the mural and other Indian artifacts.[10] Whether this act was tinged with racism is a matter of speculation, but it severed all ties with the tribes that Louis Hill had so carefully nurtured in true friendship. It should be noted that this took place after Hill's death in 1948. Had he been alive, no one in the organization would have had the nerve or guts to condone this action.

But that was years away. What was there in 1915 was a hotel of such complementing design to welcome all—inside and out—that it accomplished exactly what Louis W. Hill envisioned. For decades, it attracted and retained those easterners and others (into the third and fourth generations) wanting to experience America's gifts to itself in the West. Nearly half of Glacier's 1915 visitors, some 6,732, came through the doors of "Many," causing the Great Northern to immediately authorize expansions with an 80-room annex and swimming pool. This additional expansion brought the room total to 242 by 1918. With the expansion, the Many Glacier Hotel would cost $500,000 (nearly $12,000,000 in 2015 dollars).[11]

To help ensure that sense of satisfaction, barbershops, a tailor, an infirmary, telephone and telegraph services, steam heat, running water, lights, and room rates to suit every need were incorporated. Rooms cost $4.50 without baths and $5.00 plus with baths, which included meals![12]

Through all stages of development of the Many Glacier complex, Louis Hill's hands-on design and management were apparent to contractors,

FIGURE 6.7. Many Glacier Hotel as viewed from the opposite side of Swiftcurrent Lake in Glacier National Park, May 4, 1921. Courtesy of the Library of Congress; C. C. Kiser Photo Co., Fred Kiser, photographer; retrieved October 27, 2016, from the Library of Congress.

employees, and park personnel. No window size, dining room chimney placement, or lobby log selection escaped his ever-probing letters and memos. He knew what he wanted and what would appeal to visitors. He also had the good sense to demand that all that was built would be attractive and attracting for the ages.

He took on the park service when necessary, including the hotel's site selection, stating he would withdraw Great Northern support unless Superintendent James L. Galen got out of his way. He got his way. In my opinion, Hill had every right to stand his ground. First, he knew his eye for placement and that of his architects was keener than Galen's, and he was footing the entire cost of the hotel. In addition, the park had all but ceded near absolute control of the east side of the park to Hill and the railroad while it concentrated what little resources it received from Congress on the west side of Glacier.

Furthermore, Hill had other matters to consider, including better roads and a third hotel in his string of pearls—the Prince of Wales in Waterton

Village, Alberta, Canada. He would first drive there in 1913 over a road that made primitive look good. Standing on a wind-swept bluff overlooking Waterton Lake, framed by majestic peaks on both sides, running all the way into the United States to the south, Hill announced another site to fulfill his vision. In some ways, the view was every bit as awe-inspiring as Many Glacier, with one significant exception. At the Many Glacier Hotel, one looked up at the mountains, glaciers, and waterfalls. At the Prince of Wales, visitors would look down and away, giving them a different perspective of mountains, water, and sky. Same mountains, same water, same sky—different experience!

And because Hill's sense of nature's dramatic presentation was coupled with his and his staff's attention to market, he did not overlook the practicality of this site. The year 1919 ushered prohibition into the United States, and Canada had not bought into that failure of social engineering. It was "wet" and eager to accommodate weary and thirsty travelers. It so happened it was also a personal accommodation to Hill and his friends. He and they liked to tilt a glass (later, drinking would become a problem for Hill). But the Prince of Wales Hotel would have to wait for World War I to run its course. It would not be completed until 1927.[13]

If the Great Northern's east side moved apace under the driven supervision of Hill, the west side was bogged down in lack of funds, conflict of purpose, and, in the first year of 1910, a fire that threatened to consume much of Washington, Idaho, and Montana—including the park.

Although the newly appointed first superintendent, William R. Logan, arrived with a plan to fit his title, superintendent of Road and Trail Construction, he was immediately faced with the task of fighting the fire that swept over Rampage Mountain, Firebrand Pass, DuBois Creek, and Soldier Mountain. Before it was contained with a small hodge-podge crew of rangers, federal troops, and temporary firefighters, more than 100,000 acres of the million acres of the park were destroyed.[14] All plans for roads, trails, and other projects were put on hold until 1911.[15] The enormity and destruction of the 1910 fire would set in motion a forest and park service policy that would create a future climate for disastrous consequences in the decades between 1980 and 2000: the "no burn" policy of managing fire would lead to a tremendous buildup of tinderbox dry timbers, which, once set on fire by lightning or man, would sweep all before it in firestorms that were practically uncontrollable across the West and the western parks, including Glacier.

The 2003 fires (six separate fires) destroyed 135,000 acres, or approximately 13 percent of the park.[16] Save for the heroic work of thousands of firefighters, the Roberts fire alone came close to destroying the entire McDonald Valley and the hotels, homes, and headquarters located therein. The entire area was evacuated. Only strategic backfires and, finally, heavy September rains saved the day and the valley. My daughter and I escaped the Flathead Valley area that was blanketed with dense smoke by taking the Amtrak "Empire Builder" to Seattle.

As a substitute for that year's Glacier experience, we went to the Olympic and Cascades national parks. First Lady Laura Bush, a devoted conservationist and lover of parks, particularly Glacier, and her party had to cancel their 2003 Glacier Park plans as well and went west to Olympic National Park the following summer in 2004. They would return again in 2011.[17]

But future history or flawed policy was not the concern of William Logan and the Interior Department of 1910 to 1911. Once the 1910 fire was contained, they had to return to a far more significant challenge: how to develop a park that would attract visitors to the new recreational "pleasuring grounds" while preserving wilderness and establishing order and authority. It must be noted that in establishing Glacier National Park in 1910, it was done while allowing loopholes and grandfather clauses for in-holders, mining claims, and timber cutting. There were, without question, legitimate claims, but there were also plenty of scoundrels, poachers, and exploiters who had no use for and less recognition of this newfangled government intrusion. Logan's small band of rangers went from fighting fires in 1910 to preventing the "defacing of natural features," "obnoxious persons entering," and any other "activities which might endanger the park."

Regardless of the lack of funds or personnel in the early years of the park, plans were afoot to preserve and develop a park that Logan hoped in 1910 would "develop the park as rapidly as possible . . . keeping in mind the future day . . . when an American traveling public will at last realize that the beauties of their own country are unsurpassed anywhere in the world, and our national parks will come into their own."[18]

The fact was that Logan and his supervisors were rapidly coming down on the "wisest and best use" policy of the conservation equation. This utilitarian philosophy would create the dilemma that confronted and confounded the authors of the 1916 "Organic Act" establishing the National Park Service, extending the debate to this day.

The challenge was to attract scores of visitors who would become constituents of Glacier Park and the park system while preserving wilderness. Through leadership in Washington and in the park, an admirable outcome, with some major flaws, was achieved over time. But it would take patience and compromise to achieve the balance. To all involved—Logan, the Interior Department, Hill, and his railroad—the first order of business was to develop facilities, roads, trails, and a license system for concessionaires to attract visitors in great numbers and then hold their attention and future allegiance to both the park and the national park experience.[19]

Even as the great hotels were being completed in 1913 and 1915, the railroad was building trails, tent camps, and chalets. By 1915, horse concessions operated between the hotels and the more rustic camps and chalets. By 1925, these guided horse rides, with more than 1,000 mounts available, carried more than 10,000 visitors annually to backcountry venues and accommodations over an ever-expanding network of trails.[20] In doing so, it would give visitors the opportunity to go out into the wilderness where around every turn they could witness vistas that had been in the making for more than a billion years. Mountains stretching out in all directions displayed waterfalls, hanging gardens, U-shaped valleys, and glaciers numbering 150 at the creation of the park. What was not noticed at the time was that the glaciers, while still at work carving and creating, were doing so at a slower pace. The end of the last Ice Age had ceased around 1850. The Earth was warming.

Even though all this development would require sawmills, road equipment, horse stables, and crews numbering in the hundreds, the ever-watchful eye of Louis Hill kept track of the progress, insisting on excellence not only in the design and site selection but also in a minimum disruption of the natural order. Hill loved the scenery and wanted it preserved for all time. Hill's primary contribution was his ability to select sites to attract visitors and build hotels and chalets to satisfy their creature needs while drawing them into a sense of a renewing place amid expanses of unending awesomeness.

How he got them there was more than simply loading them on his trains. As mentioned, Hill was a public relations genius who, along with his staff, borrowed a slogan first used in 1906 and made it the trademark advertising scheme for the railroad and Glacier: "See America First."[21] It became not only one of the most successful ad campaigns of American history but Hill's call to patriotism to all the easterners who should see America and glaciers rather than going to Europe or other foreign countries. The slogan became so popular and recognizable (along with Glacier's white Rocky Mountain goat, Rocky) that the first director of the National Park Service, Stephen Mather, later adopted it to herald the wonders of the entire and rapidly expanding national park system.[22]

By 1929, Louis Hill, with the completion of the Prince of Wales Hotel, had, like his father with his vision of a transcontinental railroad, completed his own vision: a national park of the first order, with hotels, chalets, roads, and trails to welcome visitors, along with a developed sense of the scenery at every step of each guest's journey.

In that year, he stepped down as chairman of the board of the Great Northern Railroad.[23] It was probably time. From beginning to end, he had thrown himself into his dream. He had developed a park and facilities to complement each other in timeless excellence. Yet even as Hill strove to make his park the epitome of excellence, he got one thing wrong, even allowing for the best of intentions.

While the artist George Catlin had called for a national park in his 1832 letter, he planted a seed that would have unintended consequences some eighty years later. The park was to be a living diorama featuring man and beast in their natural setting—a kind of Jurassic Park flashed forward: "a magnificent park, where the world could see for ages to come, the native Indian in his classic attire, galloping his wild horses, with sinew bow and shields and lance among the herds of elk and buffalo."[24]

While Catlin was motivated by his heartfelt and perceptive concern that both Indian and bison were headed toward exploitation and elimination, others would come to see the noble natives as an attraction with commercial appeal. None would exploit this possibility more than the Great Northern and its soon-to-be guiding light Louis W. Hill.

It should be pointed out here that nothing I have found has led me to believe that he developed his Native American theme out of a demeaning attitude toward the Blackfeet or other tribes. In truth, it appears that Hill genuinely liked his plains brothers and sisters. But there was a barrier. For all their years of existence with strong ties to the mountains and valleys of what was to become Glacier National Park, the Native Americans were of the Plains, not the mountains. Yes, the eastern slopes provided wintering grounds. And yes, the mountains provided game, fish, and timber, and, most assuredly, certain places, such as Chief Mountain, were deemed sacred, but they were of the plains of Montana and Canada. However, that was a small inconvenience for Hill. Developing publicity and advertisement for American travelers was simple. Their romantic view of the not-too-long-ago "savages" was matched by their ignorance of who they were and where they lived. Who among all recipients of Hill's writers, artists, photographers, and promotions would know, or perhaps even care, if the remnants of the "Empire of the Plains" were, by 1910 or so, transplanted into the mountains of the newly created national park? In a short span of ten years, the perception was not only that the Blackfeet were of the mountains but also were of Glacier National Park's mountains and valleys. They were Glacier Park Indians and had been forever.

With that preconditioning affixed in their imagination, all touring passengers who alighted at the Glacier Park Lodge station at Midvale were met by handpicked warriors with tepees arrayed behind them on the expansive lawn. Pictures were snapped, dances performed, and native artifacts and murals greeted them as they entered the awe-inspiring lobby.

By 1913, with the completion of the Glacier Park Lodge, the transformation of the Montana Blackfeet was completed. A new species, the Glacier Park Indians, had been created. But it was not total exploitation. By all accounts, Hill's affection for the Blackfeet extended to his business relationships with them. For their summer contracts, the railroad paid fair wages. They were paid to set up painted lodges and encampments on the grounds and don feathered bonnets (although most were Sioux—now known as Lakota—not Blackfeet, in design). Hill thought the Sioux (Lakota) swept-back feathers were more Indian and thus more appealing to greet the tourists as they stepped off the train. Others were allowed to be Indian Door Girls, greeting the guests at the lodge. Tribesmen who performed "adoption into the tribes" ceremonies made extra money. Others signed colorful postcards, sold handmade dolls, droves busses, and worked in the hotel.

As mentioned, Hill went so far as to commission an impressive wall mural painted by twenty-five elders to grace the lobby of his newest hotel, the Many Glacier Lodge, in 1915. Hill took the myth making one step further. He invited tribe men, women, and children to several "back East" urban centers. Dressed in full regalia—Sioux bonnets and all—they literally drummed up business for the West. Business aside, Hill invited the delegation to St. Paul and into his home.

FIGURE 6.8. Louis W. Hill and Two Guns White Calf, Glacier National Park, 1925.
Courtesy of the Minnesota Historical Society; Louis W. Hill 2482, Louis W. Hill Papers.

But even though Hill bestowed fair treatment on the hotel Indians, coupled with a true respect for the Blackfeet, particularly chiefs and top warriors, it was make-believe on a grand scale. And the fair treatment was not universal by either the Great Northern or the park service. Those Indians not selected for work or imagery were not allowed in the hotels, certainly not as guests. The promised hunting, fishing, and timber rights vanished. They were even charged admission to the park, although this was park policy, not Hill's.[25]

Pure discrimination aside (and it was there in spite of Hill's personal practices and policies), the promises made in the "Ceded Strip" Treaty (and others) pertaining to enumerated rights and prohibitions to be honored so long as the lands remained public were stripped away with little notification and much mortification on the part of the Blackfeet.

The end result, for all the fair treatment and adoption of Indian art and artifacts, was the perception by most Americans that the Blackfeet were of the mountains and valleys of Montana and, specifically, Glacier. For Hill and his marketing staff, it was, without malicious intent, identity theft. The quest to reestablish the Blackfeet's true relationship with plains and mountains as well as the park service is ongoing. Surely, there is room for meaningful reconsideration and accommodation.

Part of the problem of the failure of reconciliation can to a degree also be attributed to Louis Hill, although it had nothing to do with his relationship with the Blackfeet per se. It had to do with his relationship with the park, his park achievement, as well as the tribe. After he resigned as chairman of the board in 1929, no evidence exists that Louis Hill, who had given some thirty-five years of his life striving to better the lot of all, ever returned to the area.

He simply left them behind. It is not that he did nothing else. He had other businesses and successes. He weighed in on helping the citizens of St. Paul, Minneapolis, and other parts of Minnesota through the Depression and World War II. He turned his attention to his family and children. And there was much to turn to as a family feud erupted over Hill's mother's estate that apparently continues to this day. Unfortunately, his marriage fell apart, and alcohol began to take its toll. He died on April 27, 1948.[26]

Had he chosen to remain active in the affairs of Glacier and the Blackfeet, perhaps he could have, by vent of his power and reputation, made a difference in the future relationship of the park and the tribe. Perhaps he could have helped the tribe reestablish its rightful place in the world of the twentieth century. Perhaps he could have added to his own reputation and history, but, in my opinion, he accomplished all that he intended to accomplish for Glacier National Park. And then he left.

NOTES

1. Biloine W. Young and Eileen R. McCormack, *The Dutiful Son, Louis W. Hill: Life in the Shadow of the Empire Builder, James J. Hill* (St. Paul, MN: Ramsey County Historical Society, 2010), 110.

2. Young and McCormack, *The Dutiful Son*, 111–12.

3. Young and McCormack, *The Dutiful Son*, 113.

4. Ray Djuff and Chris Morrison, *View with a Room: Glacier's Historic Hotels & Chalets* (Helena, MT: Farcountry Press, 2001), 12.

5. Djuff and Morrison, *View with a Room*, 20.

6. Djuff and Morrison, *View with a Room*, 147.

7. Djuff and Morrison, *View with a Room*, 12.

8. Djuff and Morrison, *View with a Room*, 13.

9. Djuff and Morrison, *View with a Room*, 83.

10. Djuff and Morrison, *View with a Room*, 99.

11. Djuff and Morrison, *View with a Room*, 84.

12. Djuff and Morrison, *View with a Room*, 83.

13. Djuff and Morrison, *View with a Room*, 115, 120.

14. C. W. Guthrie, *Glacier National Park: The First 100 Years* (Helena, MT: Farcountry Press, 2008), 47.

15. Donald H. Robinson, "Glacier National Park: Through the Years in Glacier National Park: An Administrative History (Chapter 3)," National Park Service, May 1960, accessed September 1, 2016, https://www.nps.gov/parkhistory/online_books/glac/chap3.htm.

16. Glacier Park Foundation, "The Fires of 2003: An Anthology," The Inside Trail, Winter 2004, accessed September 1, 2016, http://www.glacierparkfoundation.org/InsideTrail/IT _2004Win.pdf.

17. Candace Chase, "Laura Bush Visits Glacier Park," *Daily Inter Lake*, July 16, 2011, accessed September 1, 2016, http://www.dailyinterlake.com/members/laura-bush-visits-glacier-park/ article_9e9a2d0a-af49-11e0-99f4-001cc4c03286.html.

18. C. W. Buchholtz, *Man in Glacier* (West Glacier, MT: Glacier Natural History Association, 1976), 51–53.

19. Buchholtz, *Man in Glacier*, 51.

20. Donald H. Robinson et al., *Through the Years in Glacier National Park* (Whitefish, MT: Sun Point Press, 1960), 70.

21. Young and McCormack, *The Dutiful Son*, 121.

22. Rachel Hartigan Shea, "How Good Old American Marketing Saved the National Parks," *National Geographic*, March 24, 2015, accessed September 1, 2016, http://news.national geographic.com/2015/03/150324-national-park-service-history-yellowstone-california-united -states/.

23. Great Northern Railway, "What Was the Great Northern Railway?" GN History, accessed September 01, 2016, https://www.gnrhs.org/gn_history.htm.

24. George Catlin, "George Catlin: Letters and Notes on the Manners, Customs, and Conditions of the North American Indians, 2 Vols. (1860), 1: 260–64," Franklin & Marshall College, June 5, 1997, accessed November 02, 2016, http://www.fandm.edu/david-schuyler/ams280 /manners-customs-and-conditions-of-the-north-american-indians.

25. William E. Farr, "How the Blackfeet Became the Guardians of Glacier," in *Center for the Rocky Mountain West*, proceedings of History & Memory: Glacier National Park's Centennial Year Symposium, Flathead Valley Community College, Kalispell, MT, April 24, 2010, 4–10, accessed October 4, 2015, http://crmw.org/MP3Files/Kalispell Symposium 4-10.pdf.

26. Young and McCormack, *The Dutiful Son*, 311.

CHAPTER SEVEN

The National Park Service and Park Makers

1915–1933

Even before his first official visit to Glacier in 1915 (before there was a National Park Service), he would meet with leadership of the Blackfeet tribe to hear their complaints about the lack of Indian names for Glacier's mountains, rivers, and lakes. With a sensitivity benefiting the occasion and in good humor, he agreed that changes were necessary. Lake McDermott in the Many Glacier Valley became Swiftcurrent Lake. Others would be changed or added over time.

On his first inspection trip as assistant to the secretary of the interior, he became convinced that the roads (or lack of roads) in Glacier and other parks were terrible and needed to be addressed to meet the rising American love affair with the automobile. He also saw that Glacier required a new headquarters, bought the necessary land out of his own pocket to house it, and gave it to the park.

When necessary (which in the formative years of the park service was often), he would take on the high and mighty to establish firm jurisdiction of the agency so that policy would not be whipsawed by politics, power, or profit. That firmness of purpose would include confronting United States Senator Thomas Walsh of Montana over sheep grazing rights in Glacier during and after World War I.

For the same reason, he would take on Louis Hill and the Great Northern Railroad. After ten years of delay and several renewals, the final extension for the destruction and removal of the sawmill used to build the Many Glacier Hotel was set to expire on August 10, 1925. The permit had been given with the understanding that as soon as the hotel was complete, the sawmill would be removed and the site restored to a natural state. But the sawmill remained, and he set a date when the eyesore must be off the premises.

Great Northern asked for an extension, and he granted it.[1] The day came and went. Instead of reaching in his pocket to pay for the removal, he reached for a match and blew up the mill with dynamite he'd personally packed in. (Author's note: As it turns out, he was at Glacier for his daughter's birthday when the August 10 extension day came and went. With all patience gone, he took matters into his own hands.)

But in August 1924, he would make the decision that forever changed the face and accessibility of Glacier National Park. He approved the road that would not only link the east and west side of the park but would do so in a way that would lay easy on the landscape and the eyes.

Stephen Tyng Mather was old New England establishment by birthright, even though he grew up in California, where he was schooled. Graduating from the University of California at Berkeley in 1887, he moved east and went to work as a reporter for the *New York Sun*, where he honed an essential stock in trade: public relations and media promotion. It would serve him well in both the business and national park phases of his life.[2]

His business was Borax, a common commodity that he took to a new commercial level by advertising it as the "20 Mule Team Borax," first with the Pacific Coast Borax Company and then with the Thorkildsen-Mather Borax Company. Both endeavors were successful and made Mather a millionaire several times over. By 1914, at the age of 47, he was rich for a lifetime and sought other ways to fulfill his restless drive.[3] He also needed another outlet to tame his periodic bouts with serious depression. Already a devoted outdoorsman and hiker, he turned to the western mountains to calm his nerves. During that period (1904 to 1914), he would meet John Muir, join the Sierra Club, and become a lifetime devotee of Muir and his philosophy for national parks.[4]

But Mather had something neither position, genius, nor money could buy. He had presence—what one reporter called "incandescent enthusiasm" and a woman reporter called the looks of all the national idols rolled into one—and, Horace Albright would later write, "a personality that radiated poise, friendliness, and charm."[5] He would have to bring all facets of his multiple attributes to bear on the life-changing experience that was about to present itself.

If the original national parks movement was loaded with first-team talent, its second-generation bench was equally impressive. None was more important than Stephen Mather to the establishment of a coherent system for supervising the growing number of parks whose governance had been wholly lacking, spread over several agencies (Interior, Agriculture, and War departments), and desperately underfunded.

Secretary of Interior Franklin K. Lane was a Woodrow Wilson appointee who knew from the outset that the parks and monuments of America were a hodgepodge of sites without direction or vision. Even within his own department, little to no communication transpired with the parks and even less among park supervisors. It was a mess that Lane, backed by concessionaires, businesses, railroads, and national organizations such as the American Civic Association, was determined to clean up and systemize. But he had no budget and no one in his agency suited to the task.[6]

The story of Mather's recruitment to the Department of the Interior by its secretary is a product of fact and myth. The shorter version is that Secretary Franklin K. Lane and Mather were old friends from their college days and that after a frustrating experience through a number of national parks, Mather wrote a scathing but to-the-point letter to Lane outlining his complaints park by park. Lane was so impressed that he wrote back that if Mather didn't like the way the parks were run, "why don't you come down to Washington and run them yourself."[7]

That the exchange of letters might have occurred was fortified by Horace Albright in his second autobiography on his service in the nation's parks, *The Missing Years*. Might have occurred because the circumstances fit, although no one has ever discovered the letters.

What was myth was that they were old college friends, and the letters were exchanged in that context. The truth seems to be that Stephen Mather wrote Lane out of the blue with his protestations of exploitation and outright thievery among some private businesses of the Giant Sequoia land and that the federal government was complicit by ignoring the problems.[8]

Lane was so intrigued that he asked a mutual acquaintance of his and Mather's to set up a meeting because Lane did not know Mather personally. That meeting occurred in 1913 at the Blackstone Hotel in Chicago.[9]

Lane was hugely impressed with this man of great energy, personality, and wealth. I insert "wealth" because Lane and other cabinet members were always on the lookout for "free" talent, and Mather fit the bill.

As a result of letters, their meeting, or both, a very skeptical Mather, who had no government experience and no desire to sit behind a desk, accepted Lane's invitation to come to Washington.

In mid-December 1914, Mather showed up in Washington with the assurance by Lane that he did not want a desk-bound bureaucrat but a man who could take to the road, selling national parks to the public and Congress with the goal of getting laws passed protecting the parks—the primary one being to establish a functioning and funded national park service. Lane also promised to keep politics out of Mather's way and work. Mather was still not convinced. Off the bench came the man who would convince Mather to give it a try. Horace Albright, who became Mather's alter ego and second in command, would persuade Mather to take on the task.[10]

Albright, who had come to Washington from California a little over a year before as "confidential clerk to the secretary of interior," was at twenty-three already an accomplished quick-study on the law, bureaucracy, legislation, and the politics of parks and the Interior Department. He and Mather complemented each other's styles and skills.

Each convinced the other to stay for a year. By that agreement, the national parks would secure a long-term partnership that would bring direction, purpose, congressional favor, appropriations, and iconic status to the citizens of America. The partnership, coupled with others inside and outside government, would result in almost immediate returns as well as others in the future that are relevant into the present.

In short order, Mather, with Albright's assistance, would lay out an ambitious set of goals for their agreed-upon year of service. To keep Albright in Washington rather than returning to California to practice law and marry his fiancée, Grace Noble, Mather offered him an extra thousand dollars out of his own pocket—a practice Mather would use with personnel and parks time and time again.[11]

First and foremost was the need to establish a national park service, then get it functioning and funded. But to get the credibility and funding necessary, a national public relations effort would have to be devised. To accomplish this, Mather would use his own public relations genius, supplemented by that of his former newspaper colleague, Robert Sterling Yard, an editor at the *New York Herald*. Again, Mather got Yard by personally paying his $6,000 a year salary.[12]

But if increased park visitation were to be realized, better and more accommodations and roads to service the tourists would have to be built. The publicity and increased visitation were essential to persuade a reluctant Congress to appropriate additional funds.

FIGURE 7.1. Yellowstone National Park Superintendent and National Park Service Deputy Director Horace M. Albright (*left*) and National Park Service Director Stephen T. Mather (*right*) standing next to a Packard with license plate "U.S. N.P.S.1", 1924. Courtesy of Harpers Ferry Center, West Virginia; National Park Service photograph.

All had to be packaged and fit into 1914 to 1915 not only to meet Mather's and Albright's personal deadlines but to create a critical mass of public support and growing numbers of people going to parks to foster legislative action. While support was growing in the hinterlands for more parks and a national park service (Rocky Mountain National Park was established in 1915), Congress was another matter. Mather's first budget for more staff and roads was cut. Limitations on per-park spending were adopted. Mather then found he could not personally pay for a road in Yosemite without congressional approval. He got the law changed, and he convinced his wealthy friends and the Sierra Club to buy the road and gift it to Yosemite.[13]

Undeterred, Mather, with Albright in tow, headed out of Washington for a series of conferences and meetings to generate support among elected officials, business leaders, and organizations such as the General Federation of Women's Clubs, whose 2 million members were working for the establishment of more national parks and a national park service.[14]

It is always a shame to find that large segments of the population, any segments, have been denied a place at democracy's table. When it is nearly half or more of the population, it is a travesty. That was made blatantly clear with women and the parks. We've already seen that the Federation, under the leadership of Mary Belle King Sherman, was 2 million members strong in 1916. And the Garden Club of America membership was coming up fast. Both were forces not to be ignored with the Nineteenth Amendment looming, giving women the right to vote.[15]

In a number of states, such clubs were already active by the turn of the twentieth century. They gained influence because most of their states had given them the right to vote even before the turn of the century and prior to the national granting of that right.

One such state was Colorado. Its women's right to vote came in 1893. Virginia Donaghe McClurg pushed for several years in the 1880s and 1890s to save Mesa Verde cliff dwellings. Frustrated with the lack of support, she joined the Colorado Federation of Women to save the ruins. The Colorado Federation championed the site as a national park, built a road to the dwellings, and worked to allow the Ute to remain on the lands. To avoid opposition from those who harbored fears of Indian displacement, McClurg fashioned a lease between the tribe and the club. So favorably were their actions received that probability of a new national park grew.[16]

As that prospect became a reality, McClurg changed her position. She wanted the area to become a state park operated by the women of the Colorado Cliff Dwelling Association. Her stance caused a rift. Lucy Peabody of the Cliff Dwelling Association stepped in and pushed for national park designation. She traveled to Washington to lobby for the bill. McClurg's reactions and future actions became so abrasive to so many that they resigned in protest. In 1906, the bill creating Mesa Verde National Park passed.[17]

Peabody was nationally praised for her accomplishments. McClurg was not mentioned. She spent the rest of her life trying to gain recognition. It should have been granted.

Mary Belle King Sherman, accompanied by Marion Randall Parsons, director of the Sierra Club, attended Mather's 1916 conference. Sherman brought with her a reputation for getting things done. Working with Enos Mills, she caused the Federation to join the drive to create Rocky Mountain National Park. They succeeded in 1915. So even though they were the only two female delegates of the conference, they were given a place on the program and heeded. After all, they were calling for more parks and the establishment of a national park service. Their Florida affiliate went on to establish Royal Palm State Park, which became the forerunner to Everglades National Park some thirty years later.[18] In the interim, the women of the Florida Federation owned and operated the state park—perhaps to the eternal mortification of Virginia McClurg.

In 1916, with a mailing list of 275,000 names at the ready, the Federation gave Mather's team its major publicity tool, and on August 25, 1916, they had their National Park Service, with more parks to follow. Sherman would thereafter be known as the National Park Lady.[19]

Mention must also be given to the Daughters of the American Revolution (DAR) for two reasons. First, on a number of occasions, it, as a national organization or state affiliates, joined with the General Federation of Women's Clubs and others to support the national park proposal. Its Denver chapter was cited by Sherman as being instrumental in the drive for Rocky Mountain National Park.

Equally important, women, through organizations such as the DAR and the United Daughters of the Confederacy, had become the promoters and protectors of historic sites, particularly those of battlegrounds and sacrifice. Because of their commitment to their cause of promoting patriotism and protecting those hallowed grounds, coupled with their links to other women's organizations championing parks, they were a significant factor in Albright's plan to place all military historic sites, memorabilia, and monuments under the umbrella of the National Park Service. By executive order, President Franklin Roosevelt did just that in 1933.[20] The good works of protection and remembrance by the Daughters of the American Revolution and others are carried on to this day.

In Glacier National Park in 1915, Mary Roberts Rinehart, after a 300-mile horseback ride through the park with forty-plus companions, half of them women, would tell of its wonders. Already famous for her crime novels, she was hired by the Great Northern Railway to further publicize the park, appealing to the women of America to come west to the mountains of Montana. When they planned family vacations, Rinehart exhorted them to come: "If you are willing to learn how little you count in the eternal scheme of things, go ride in the Rocky Mountains and save your soul."[21]

Though late to the scene, women as individuals and through organizations, national, state, and local, have often made the difference not only in

FIGURE 7.2. Mary Roberts Rinehart posing with three Blackfeet men at tepee camp, 1914. Man on the right is Two Guns White Calf. Courtesy of the Glacier National Park Archives; Ted Marble, photographer.

park creation but in demanding that our parks remain preserved for all and all generations. "We want more national parks," Mary Belle King Sherman, conservation chairman of the clubs, told the conference, "and we are going to keep right on working to get them!"[22]

Fortunately, Mather turned to all groups, men and women, that could carry the message. More fortunately, with the Nineteenth Amendment approaching in 1919 through the work of the nationwide suffrage movement, more of the males elected were beginning to pay attention to women, specifically their wives!

In the meantime, Stephen Mather welcomed women's support as well as others where he could find it, and when not forthcoming, he created it. Mirroring his heroes John Muir and Teddy Roosevelt, he planned and assembled a trip into the wilderness of the California Sierra Nevada in July 1915. Each member of the party was hand-picked by Mather, Albright, and Yard for his potential influence either in Congress, national publications, newspapers, or business. Mather paid for the outing.

They camped among the Giant Sequoias, climbed Mount Whitney, and traveled over the Tioga Road, for which Mather and others had paid, into Yosemite Valley. So successful was the outing that all came away as ardent park supporters, so much so that Gilbert Grosvenor of the National Geographic Society compelled his organization to donate $20,000 to help purchase the Giant Forest. Most would come away with similar zeal. Emerson Hough of the *Saturday Evening Post* wrote that the Kings Canyon country "is too big for any man or men to own . . . it belongs to humanity, as it is, unchanged and never to know change."[23]

Congressman Frederick Gillett of Massachusetts, an influential member of Congress, ranking Republican on the Appropriations Committee, and soon-to-be (1919) speaker of the House, gave his support then and later to the parks and the National Park Service.[24]

Following the "campout" in the Sierras, Mather and Albright continued on through the western parks on an inspection trip, with a final stop at Glacier National Park. While there, he and Albright would hike to Gunsight Pass in heavy snowfall, staying at Sperry Chalet and Going-to-the-Sun Chalet. From there, they planned to tour by automobile but found roads impassable and less than facilitating to tourists trying to get to and from the Great Northern's hotels. Furthermore, they found the existing park headquarters shoddy and ill located. Mather found a site on private land, but it was not for sale, so he located another nearby, purchased it, and gave it to the park.[25]

The upshot of his first trip to Glacier National Park was that Mather concluded that the parks absolutely had to have better roads and facilities if they were to entice enough visitors to capture the support of Congress. The circle of complementing influences had to remain unbroken if one were to cause reaction in the other.

It was that inspection trip, culminating in Glacier, that would put Mather squarely in the "wisest and best use" camp, but it would be one of his own making, with "best" and "wisest" defined by Mather. He concluded that in order to have sustainable and substantial congressional support, he had to attract the people to their parks. While losing the backing of some preservationists, he correctly developed an entire new constituency—the American people, who were beginning to have more leisure time, money, and automobiles. Yet throughout his tenure as head of the park service, he was forever mindful of the need for scenery, wildlife, and wilderness. His every action was to attain that fine balance between man and nature.

FIGURE 7.3. National Park Service Director Stephen T. Mather on Piatt Path along the top of the Garden Wall overlooking Grinnell Glacier, Glacier National Park, 1920. Courtesy of Harpers Ferry Center, West Virginia; National Park Service photograph, negative number GLAC #915.

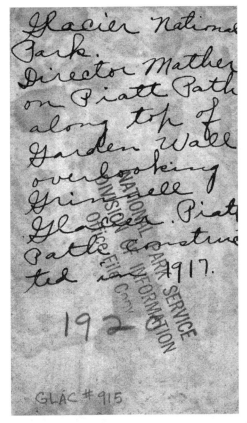

FIGURE 7.4. Handwritten description on the back of the photo of Mather on Piatt Path overlooking Grinnell Glacier, 1920. Courtesy of Harpers Ferry Center, West Virginia; National Park Service photograph, negative number GLAC #915.

Of all the parks Mather helped bring into the system as well as the projects on which he passed, none would dramatize this adherence to both sides of the people and preservation equation more so than his decision to obtain funding for a road through Glacier: the Going-to-the-Sun Road.

But before this happened or could happen, Mather and Albright had to turn their prodigious talents to the primary task at hand. They had to have legislation passed creating a National Park Service. Neither of them was the first advocate for such a unified national service. Since the turn of the century, there were calls for a service or bureau, but they went unheeded for reasons coupled to the mind and philosophy of President Teddy Roosevelt. First, in my opinion, Roosevelt sensed there needed to be a larger critical mass of parks to generate citizen and elected official support strong enough to carry the day and to override the objections of Forest Service Director Gifford Pinchot's opposition. Pinchot saw national parks as a threat to the Forest Service, and his utilitarian conservation philosophy held as much sway with Roosevelt as did that of Muir and other preservation advocates. So Roosevelt chose not to weigh in, allowing Pinchot to kill all early legislative attempts.

But by 1911, Roosevelt and Pinchot were out of office, and President William Howard Taft and his secretary of the interior Walter Fisher were supportive of the idea.[26]

With the constant support of friends organizations such as the American Civic Association, the General Federation of Women's Clubs, the Sierra Club, national publications, newspapers, and influential individuals, private and elected, the idea began to gain acceptance. By late 1915 into early 1916, the time for action and results seemed at hand.

As a positive signal, bills were introduced to create sixteen new parks, including Lassen Volcano in Hawaii, Mount McKinley in Alaska, and Sieur de Monts National Monument in Maine, which would become Acadia National Park. Bills were drawn up, then refined. The vexing question of conflict between use and preservation was debated, with use receiving equal status because even Mather, Albright, and others recognized parks needed people to trump politics and congressional purse strings. Though finalized into law, that debate continues and necessarily must do so to maintain that fine and delicate balancing act.

Other matters such as grazing rights, roads, buildings, accommodations, and automobile entrance fees had to be glossed over or compromised. One of Mather's strengths, particularly for one used to getting his way, was an ability to compromise when necessary, with an eye toward fixing the issues in the future.

All the while, even as the bill wound its way through committee hearings, Mather kept the publicity on the benefits of national parks at maximum pitch. He would need every bit he could generate. Even for all the support from without and within Congress, there was still opposition.

Finally, while Mather was on another publicity trip through Wyoming and California and after a few additional compromises were reached, Congress passed "an act to establish a National Park Service and for other purposes." President Woodrow Wilson signed it on August 25, 1916.[27]

Now the real work would begin—organizing a new service out of the separate, unequal, and underfunded national parks and monuments. If Stephen Mather's genius for public relations carried the act to creation, it would be his business acumen and management experience that would mold the service into a working unit with purpose and vision. It would not be simple or without mistakes, but it would be accomplished in a relatively short period of time, even as he battled a debilitating disease that would create gaps in his tenure. Fortunately for him, the parks, and the nation, he always had his alter ego and equal to fill the void—Horace Albright. And because of the seamless nature of their relationship and the fact that, in that time, long absences from Washington were commonplace, hardly anyone noticed Mather was missing.[28]

The startup of any government agency (or business or nonprofit) is a daunting task, particularly when that agency's assets are scattered across the far reaches of the states and territories of Alaska and Hawaii. By the time of the creation of the National Park Service in 1916, twelve national parks (with others in the pipeline), nineteen national monuments, and two reserves covered approximately 5 million acres.[29] But for all intents and purpose, that was as far as it went.

As mentioned before, the parks had been under the jurisdiction and administration of several agencies (Interior, Agriculture, and War departments), with no coordination, often dueling purposes, and turf wars. No funding was available for a Washington staff and less for parks. It was a governance nightmare, with chaos and roadblocks at every turn.

Neither time nor the purpose of this book allows complete coverage of all that faced Mather and Albright. Seemingly every park had its own vexation that required immediate attention and funding. To get a complete picture of the enormity of the task confronting them, I suggest the reader obtain a copy of Horace Albright's insightful book, *The Birth of the National Park Service: The Founding Years, 1913–33*. It is a masterful tale of two men who went to Washington for a year in 1915 and stayed to mold a visionary wilderness empire for the benefit of citizens, nature, and history. However, a few examples will suffice to demonstrate how they accomplished the tasks that lay before them with help from kindred spirits and unyielding determination.

Blessedly, the "Organic Act" was simple and brief in wording and direction. It created a park service and set forth its basic purpose. It gave the director the power to manage and control the parks. The secretary of the interior was authorized to make rules and regulations for park management along with the authority to grant permits of up to twenty years as well as grazing rights (a provision necessary to gain critical congressional support) and provisions pertaining to previously agreed-upon rights of way through parks, reservations, and public lands.[30]

What it didn't designate were appropriations for staff, roads, and facilities or operating funds, although it spelled out salary limitations for the director and other employees in Washington D.C. In other words, it left Mather and Albright in much the same status with most of the same problems they had confronted in 1915.

In order to gather his thoughts and discuss them with Albright, Mather planned a trip to Glacier. It seems, based on research, that Mather found special solace within the soaring confines of Glacier, even though Yosemite was the place of his heart. Throughout his official association with the parks, he often returned to Glacier. But when he did so, he always had several purposes in mind. Fact finding and problem solving were simply part of the makeup of this driven man with a mission. While he hiked and rode, he planned and questioned.

From Glacier, he sent Albright to Yellowstone to supervise the transition of the Army's long-held (and originally justified) role of protecting and preserving the park. Consolidating management and control of the parks under the umbrella of the National Park Service was one of Mather's unmet goals. By 1916, with a potential war, the Army wanted out from under the responsibility of Yellowstone and other parks.

War or not, the presence of the Army in Yellowstone would go unresolved due to the interference of Congressman John J. Fitzgerald, chairman of the House Appropriations Committee until his retirement in 1917. In 1918, Congress gave complete jurisdiction over the parks to the National Park Service and called for the removal of the Army and the Corps of Engineers.[31]

But even though that battle was won and Fitzgerald was gone, Senator Thomas Walsh of Montana remained a force with which to be reckoned. Two confrontations are of note. One would affect Glacier in its result, and the other would directly affect Glacier in its conclusion.

Stephen Mather's business sensibilities led him to the conclusion that competition among concessionaires was not desirable as it pertained to the parks. It was his view that a regulated monopoly would protect parks and the public.[32] Several practicalities formed his thinking.

First, only a monopoly would be attractive to outside investors with deep pockets; one only has to look at the situation surrounding Louis Hill and the Great Northern investment in Glacier to make the point. Only by a near (but perhaps unspoken) monopoly on the east side of the park were they enticed to build the hotels, camps, chalets, and roads to attract tourists. Surely Mather picked up on this during his early trips to Glacier.

In 1916, he and Albright found quite the opposite in Yellowstone. Multiple concessionaires with services that ran from shoddy to "Ponzi," with disease-ridden food thrown into the mix, had a lock on concessions in the park. Inferiority, a result of reducing costs to beat the competition, was the order of the day. That year, Mather vowed to put a stop to it. He took away the franchise of the Old Faithful Camp Company, whose franchise had been arranged by Senator Walsh. Walsh called for all who wished to operate concessions to be allowed to do so, and he took his criticism of Mather directly to Secretary of the Interior Lane.[33]

It is here that two of Mather's hold-card attributes came into play. He told Secretary Lane in no uncertain terms that concessionaires, Senator Walsh, and others had pressured him to renew the license. In each instance, he, Mather, had refused and concluded, "If now my positions are reversed by you, every concession in the parks will say, very properly: never mind what Mather says or does; the Secretary will do what our senators ask."[34]

Because Mather had Lane's assurances going into the job that political influences would not be tolerated and because he'd only signed on for a short stint, such a reversal on Lane's part would have caused Mather to resign. Lane backed Mather! The fact that Mather's wealth allowed him to stand up against external or internal pressures was also in the background. He didn't need the salary, although events soon proved he needed the parks.

Even with threats and grumbling as part of their everyday life, Mather and Albright proceeded with the implementation of their proscribed plans to perfect a functioning service. Of strategic importance was a nationwide conference to highlight the passage of the act as well as the benefits such a united and well-managed National Park Service would provide. Delegates from every park discipline attended. Leaders in their field spoke on the role of people, women, art, and physical and spiritual well-being that parks afforded the American people.[35]

Both to rally congressional support and hopefully blunt the criticism of senators such as Walsh, Mather invited key House and Senate proponents who spoke glowingly of the parks and their need for adequate and immediate funding. Senator Reed Smoot of Utah summed it up: "I do not want to see any of the natural resources taken from them that would in any way mar their beauty. I think it would be the best money that Congress could spend to place the Parks in a condition that they can be enjoyed by the people of the United States."[36]

It could not have gone better, and yet a shadow hung over the conference. Unknown to all but his wife and doctor, Stephen Mather had had a nervous breakdown in 1903 due to work-related stress. During the 1916 conference, Albright recognized that his friend and mentor was depressed and incoherent in speech. He and other friends quietly called Mather's wife, who took him to a sanitarium in Pennsylvania. He would remain incapacitated for a year and a half. Albright, having been appointed acting director by Secretary Lane, seamlessly stepped in, filling the void so adroitly that few guessed that Mather was missing or sick.[37]

Mather's cure lay not in the hands of doctors or drugs but in the solitude of his room filled with pictures of Yosemite, coupled with Albright's weekly visits where matters of the parks were discussed without the stress of worrisome problems.[38] Through this singular treatment of park impressions in photos and paintings, combined with Albright's comforting conversations about all things park, Mather slowly renewed himself in the manner proscribed by Frederick Law Olmsted some fifty years before.

As Olmsted noted,

> It is a scientific fact that the occasional contemplation of natural scenes of an impressive character, particularly if this contemplation occurs in connection with relief from ordinary cares, change of air, and change of habits, is favorable to the health and vigor of men and especially to the health and vigor of their intellect beyond any other condition which can be offered them, that it not only gives pleasure for the time being but increases the subsequent capacity for happiness and the means for securing happiness.[39]

Perhaps Jane Mather or Mather's doctor read a secret copy of Olmsted's 1865 Yosemite report or instinctively knew that parks and nature were the only cure. Stephen Mather's life had come to be the national parks, and their survival depended on a renewed Mather. Conversely, his survival depended on them.

Since organizing a fully functioning National Park Service, with competent men filling every superintendent post, and persuading Congress to fund the new agency were at the forefront of Mather's agenda, Albright would remain on the job in Mather's absence to see the tasks through to completion.

Money to operate came first. After a round of contentious hearings in the House, including the removal of troops in Yellowstone (Congressman Fitzgerald got his way), an appropriations bill was passed in 1918 giving the parks all that Mather and Albright had requested. That was followed by a supplemental appropriation for the hiring of personnel.[40] Albright now had the money to seek out the best talent for Washington and field staff alike.

Having secured a fine Washington D.C. staff, Albright took to the road, looking for superintendent talent, confronting concessionaires' issues, and continuing to drum up public support. He would also begin the process of scouting for new park sites. The need for capable superintendents and concessionaires was potentially troublesome due to the prior lack of supervision and unified purpose.

In the void, many park superintendents and concessionaires were the creatures of political appointments and meddling. But armed with Mather's guarantee from Secretary Lane not to let politics interfere with the running of the parks, Albright was able to find solid men who not only were good administrators but also shared with Mather and Albright the love for the parks in their charge. In Glacier, they had to replace a political appointee so inept that he had been assigned to patrol a railroad track lest he wander off into the forest![41]

To fortify policies for high standards, basic principles were drafted, supplemented by twenty-three specific points.[42] All were aimed at molding a park service that would not only be allowed to function efficiently but also meet the dual purposes of use and preservation. With this manifesto as the foundation, the National Park Service has become one of the most respected agencies within the government and among the citizens it was created to serve.

But problems continued. The Penfold Sheep Company, which had among its investors Senator Walsh, obtained grazing rights to Glacier through pressure from Walsh. Through counterbalancing pressure, Albright came up with a solution that took the ability to grant those grazing rights out of Penfold's hands, to the chagrin of the embarrassed senator.[43]

Fortunately, shortly thereafter, Mather was able to return to duty full-time. By taking strong stands, the National Park Service was well established in the minds of Congress, concessionaires, and the American people by the end of World War I. The result was that a new Congress elected in 1920 was of a more receptive mind to providing adequate appropriated funding for operations, maintenance, facilities, trails, and roads.[44] Interestingly enough, part of the universality of the parks' popularity was the promotional genius "See America First" campaign first launched by Louis Hill and the Great Northern Railroad to ballyhoo the attractions of Glacier. During the war, when travel to Europe was forbidden, Mather and company, with the support of a number of railroads, turned the promotion into a national campaign. An unintended consequence of its success was that more Americans were prompted to travel to their parks by automobile rather than by rail.[45]

From the outset, Stephen Mather was a proponent of automobile roads in the parks, but he insisted only one scenic road should run through each park and each road be built "without disturbing the solitude and quiet of other sections."[46] Throughout the 1920s, he and his superintendents made ready for the eventuality of congressional appropriations that with each passing year grew more likely. One such project would be the Transmountain Highway through Glacier National Park. It, and other parks' roads, would now be championed by many automotive clubs and good roads associations.

Small appropriations for such roads were forthcoming in 1921, and the Transmountain's first 20 miles were completed to the head of Lake McDonald. A similar road from St. Mary's Village was begun on the east side. But the main challenge lay ahead: building a road up along the west face of the Garden Wall to Logan's Pass. In 1924, Congress appropriated $7.5 million for such roads. It then fell to Mather to approve the location of Glacier's mountain pass road. The debate about what the Transmountain Highway would be and where it would be located was joined. It would pit the park service's foremost road-building engineer George Goodwin's plan for a series of fifteen switchbacks against that of a young landscape architect, Thomas Vint. Vint suggested having only one switchback that was also more expensive. In Vint's report, he exclaimed that Goodwin's plan "would look like miners had been there."[47] Mather would make the final decision.

More was riding on just the road through Glacier. The National Park Service and Mather's reputation depended on getting this spectacular and monumental undertaking right. It could not be simply a finely engineered road; it had to be a road not only to take visitors and their automobiles up and over the pass but also a road that would least disturb the scenic and natural landscapes and that would please the eye as it wandered toward the pass. In other words, this road had to embody the language of the Organic Act: to provide and preserve.

In the end, Vint's concept, after heated discussions, Goodwin's resignation, and an inter-bureau agreement, was selected. Those debates and that agreement became the policy foundation for all future national park roads and highways, and it is still in effect today.[48]

Mather's one-road philosophy of high construction standards, coupled with "lying lightly on the land," would lead to what was to become the Going-to-the-Sun Road, dedicated in July 1933 and completed in 1934. By then, Mather's ill health would catch up with him, and, after a series of strokes, he died on January 22, 1930.[49]

On June 15, 1933, at the official dedication of the Going-to-the-Sun Road, a memorial plaque was unveiled in Mather's honor for not only his role in making the road lay lightly but for his contributions to all national parks. The plaque reads, "He laid the foundation for the National Park Service, defining and establishing the policies under which its areas shall be developed and conserved, unimpaired for future generations. There will never come an end to the good he has done."[50]

As Horace Albright observed on Stephen Mather's first trip to Glacier in 1915, "It seems impossible that every new national park appeared more spectacular than the last—or at least more unusual . . . as I stood gasping at the awesome beauty, Mather joined me. Neither of us spoke for some time. Then I heard him say, 'Horace, what God-given opportunity has come our way to preserve wonders like these before us. We must never forget or abandon our gift.'"[51]

NOTES

1. Horace M. Albright and Robert Cahn, *The Birth of the National Park Service: The Founding Years, 1913–33* (Salt Lake City, UT: Howe Brothers, 1985), 170.

2. American Academy for Park and Recreation Administration, "Stephen Tyng Mather," American Academy for Park and Recreation Administration, accessed August 7, 2016, http://www.aapra.org/pugsley-bios/stephen-tyng-mather.

3. American Academy for Park and Recreation Administration, "Stephen Tyng Mather."

4. American Academy for Park and Recreation Administration, "Stephen Tyng Mather."

5. Dayton Duncan and Ken Burns, *The National Parks: America's Best Idea: An Illustrated History* (New York, NY: Alfred A. Knopf, 2009), 138.

6. Albright and Cahn, *The Birth of the National Park Service*, 7.

7. Horace M. Albright and Marian Albright Schenck, *Creating the National Park Service: The Missing Years* (Norman, OK: University of Oklahoma Press, 1999), 32.

8. American Academy for Park and Recreation Administration, "Stephen Tyng Mather."

9. Albright and Schenck, *Creating the National Park Service*, 32.

10. Albright and Cahn, *The Birth of the National Park Service*, 17.

11. Albright and Cahn, *The Birth of the National Park Service*, 18.

12. Albright and Cahn, *The Birth of the National Park Service*, 24.

13. Philanthropy Roundtable, "1916: Stephen Mather Builds the National Park Service," Philanthropy Roundtable: Nature and Parks, accessed August 7, 2016, http://www.philanthropy roundtable.org/almanac/nature/1916_stephen_mather_builds_the_national_park_service.

14. Duncan and Burns, *The National Parks*, 98–99.

15. Duncan and Burns, *The National Parks*, 102.

16. Polly Welts Kaufman, *National Parks and the Woman's Voice: A History* (Albuquerque, NM: University of New Mexico Press, 1996), 33.

17. Duncan and Burns, *The National Parks*, 102.

18. Kaufman, *National Parks and the Woman's Voice*, 33.

19. Kaufman, *National Parks and the Woman's Voice*, 32.

20. Kaufman, *National Parks and the Woman's Voice*, 44.

21. Mary Roberts Rinehart, *Through Glacier Park* (Helena, MT: TWODOT, 2016), 1.

22. Albright and Cahn, *The Birth of the National Park Service*, 23.

23. Albright and Cahn, *The Birth of the National Park Service*, 26.

24. Albright and Cahn, *The Birth of the National Park Service*, 24–26.

25. Albright and Cahn, *The Birth of the National Park Service*, 29.

26. Albright and Cahn, *The Birth of the National Park Service*, 34–35.

27. National Park Service, "History (U.S. National Park Service)," National Park Service, accessed September 2, 2016, https://www.nps.gov/aboutus/history.htm.

28. Albright and Cahn, *The Birth of the National Park Service*, 51–52.

29. National Park Service, "History (U.S. National Park Service)."

30. Albright and Cahn, *The Birth of the National Park Service*, 44–45.

31. Albright and Cahn, *The Birth of the National Park Service*, 45–46.

32. Albright and Cahn, *The Birth of the National Park Service*, 46.

33. Albright and Cahn, *The Birth of the National Park Service*, 48.

34. Albright and Cahn, *The Birth of the National Park Service*, 48.

35. Albright and Cahn, *The Birth of the National Park Service*, 49–50.

36. Albright and Cahn, *The Birth of the National Park Service*, 50.

37. Albright and Schenck, *Creating the National Park Service*, 202.

38. Laura Lee Richmond, "Stephen Mather of the National Parks Believed That the Outdoors Ward off His Mental Illness," Lauraleerichmond, May 7, 2015, accessed September 2, 2016, https://lauraleerichmond.wordpress.com/2015/05/07/stephen-mather-of-the-national-parks -believed-that-the-outdoors-ward-off-his-mental-illness/.

39. Frederick Law Olmsted, *Yosemite and the Mariposa Grove: A Preliminary Report, 1865* (Yosemite National Park, CA: Yosemite Association, 1995), 12.

40. Albright and Cahn, *The Birth of the National Park Service*, 57.

41. Ken Burns and Dayton Duncan, "Episode Four: 1920–1933: Going Home," *The National Parks: America's Best Idea: A Film by Ken Burns*, 2009, accessed September 2, 2016, http://www.pbs.org/nationalparks/history/ep4/2/.

42. Albright and Cahn, *The Birth of the National Park Service*, 68–72.

43. Albright and Cahn, *The Birth of the National Park Service*, 73.

44. Albright and Cahn, *The Birth of the National Park Service*, 56–57.

45. Duncan and Burns, *The National Parks*, 147.

46. C. W. Guthrie, *Going-to-the-Sun Road: Glacier National Park's Highway to the Sky* (Helena, MT: Farcountry Press, 2006), 19–20.

47. Guthrie, *Going-to-the-Sun Road*, 22.

48. Guthrie, *Going-to-the-Sun Road*, 23.

49. Albright and Cahn, *The Birth of the National Park Service*, 248.

50. Duncan and Burns, *The National Parks*, 241.

51. Albright and Schenck, *Creating the National Park Service*, 101.

CHAPTER EIGHT

A Road, Another Roosevelt, and the CCC

It would traverse then transform with minimum transgression a valley, a wall, and the Continental Divide over miles of impossibility. It would take more than twenty years to complete, ground into the possible by hundreds of men with hammers, shovels, blasting powder, and machines capable of conquering obstacles laid down by nature no matter how many millions or billions of years in the making. It was and is worthy of any superlative applied or award given. As viewed by Michael Jamison of the *Missoulian* newspaper, "It is a marvel traversing an even greater marvel."[1]

On completion, the Going-to-the-Sun Road would stretch over a 50-mile span from West Glacier to St. Mary, Montana. From east to west, it would be built in stages, commencing in 1911 and concluding in 1934. The primary reason for the length of time was the intervention of World War I and the initial sporadic funding and underfunding by Congress. None of this dissuaded Mather, Albright, or their team of engineers and landscape architects.

Although often frustrated, they took what was given and did with it what they could, always hewing to Mather's high standards and one-road vision. Finally, starting in 1921 and culminating in 1924, Congress began to heed Mather's call for adequate dollars to fund the longest and most challenging sections: the head of Lake McDonald to Avalanche Creek (1922–1923), Logan's Creek (1924–1925), Logan's Creek to Logan Pass (1925–1928); on the east side: St. Mary's Lake to Rising Sun (1922–1925), Rising Sun to Logan Pass (1931–1932), then a rework from Rising Sun to St. Mary (1933–1934).

All told, it would cost $2.4 million by the time it was dedicated on June 15, 1933. It would consist of only one switchback on the west side, two tunnels, and eight bridges made of native stone retaining walls at the Triple Arches along the Garden Wall and the Golden Stairs above St. Mary's Lake.

Although the route was longer and more expensive than the alternatives, because it was built to Mather's specifications, it remains after eighty-two years a wonder of engineering and landscaping. It was relevant then and now. Because of its high-quality construction and its "lying lightly on the land" across the historic and wildlife bounties of Glacier National Park, it would set the standard for all national park roads to follow.

It was the first road to be designated a National Historic Landmark, is the only road recognized as a National Civil Engineering Landmark, and is listed in the National Register of Historic Places.[2]

But one crucial point of its initial benefit was not fully appreciated. Few saw the road for what it was: a proof-positive model, along with the Hoover Dam and other projects, of an endeavor that could put hundreds of thousands of needy men to work and help break the back of the ever-deepening Depression.

Although a good man and great humanitarian, Herbert Hoover, and most of those around him, was tied to a political philosophy that relied on volunteerism, local relief, and balanced budgets. He simply could not accept that the federal government could or should help the governed in their time of need. By the time events shook Hoover awake to action, the Great Depression was well into its second year, swirling downward and entrenched across the nation. Although he tried to act, establishing some federal funding relief programs, his earlier paralysis assured they would be ineffective, except at the margins.

Crippled by polio, Franklin Delano Roosevelt had no such compunction against trying something new and bolder. He would immediately on taking office as president of the United States begin to help a paralyzed nation walk again.

"Today, for the first time in my life, I have seen Glacier Park. Perhaps I can best express my thrill and delight by saying that I wish every American, old and young, could have been with me today. The great mountains, the glaciers, the lakes, and trees make me long to stay here for the rest of the summer."[3] But FDR's radio address delivered from Two Medicine Chalet in Glacier National Park in August 1934 was more than praise for the beauty of the park. It was the complete embodiment of the national park history, experience, and purpose. Because it was so meaningful on so many levels, I have included his speech (and the travel plans for the park visit) at the end of the book. Both are worth readers' attention.

Among his pronouncements were a commitment to and pride in the work of the young men of the Civilian Conservation Corps (CCC), who were

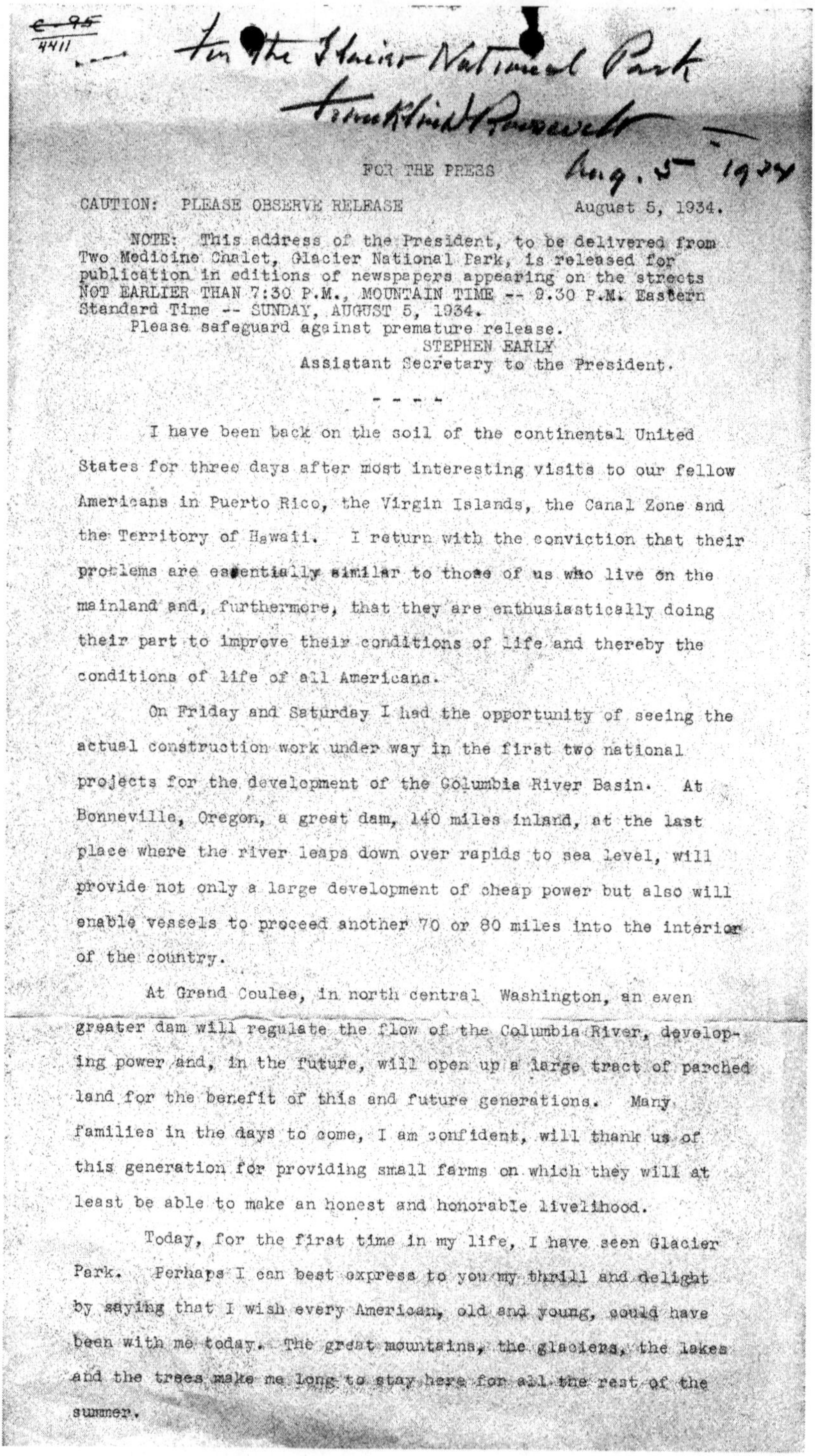

C-95
4411

for the Glacier National Park
Franklin D Roosevelt

FOR THE PRESS   *Aug. 5 - 1934*

CAUTION: PLEASE OBSERVE RELEASE   August 5, 1934.

NOTE: This address of the President, to be delivered from
Two Medicine Chalet, Glacier National Park, is released for
publication in editions of newspapers appearing on the streets
NOT EARLIER THAN 7:30 P.M., MOUNTAIN TIME -- 9.30 P.M. Eastern
Standard Time -- SUNDAY, AUGUST 5, 1934.
        Please safeguard against premature release.
                                STEPHEN EARLY
                        Assistant Secretary to the President.

                        - - -

I have been back on the soil of the continental United
States for three days after most interesting visits to our fellow
Americans in Puerto Rico, the Virgin Islands, the Canal Zone and
the Territory of Hawaii. I return with the conviction that their
problems are essentially similar to those of us who live on the
mainland and, furthermore, that they are enthusiastically doing
their part to improve their conditions of life and thereby the
conditions of life of all Americans.

On Friday and Saturday I had the opportunity of seeing the
actual construction work under way in the first two national
projects for the development of the Columbia River Basin. At
Bonneville, Oregon, a great dam, 140 miles inland, at the last
place where the river leaps down over rapids to sea level, will
provide not only a large development of cheap power but also will
enable vessels to proceed another 70 or 80 miles into the interior
of the country.

At Grand Coulee, in north central Washington, an even
greater dam will regulate the flow of the Columbia River, developing power and, in the future, will open up a large tract of parched
land for the benefit of this and future generations. Many
families in the days to come, I am confident, will thank us of
this generation for providing small farms on which they will at
least be able to make an honest and honorable livelihood.

Today, for the first time in my life, I have seen Glacier
Park. Perhaps I can best express to you my thrill and delight
by saying that I wish every American, old and young, could have
been with me today. The great mountains, the glaciers, the lakes
and the trees make me long to stay here for all the rest of the
summer.

FIGURE 8.1. First page of Roosevelt's speech during the presidential visit to Glacier National Park, August 5, 1934. Courtesy of the Glacier National Park Archives.

at work in Glacier and across the nation. Because of their accomplishments in a little over a year's time, Roosevelt had every reason to be pleased. After all, of all his New Deal programs ushered in during his first hundred days in office, the concept of such a national corps was Franklin Roosevelt's own idea from the start of March 1933.[4]

That is not to say that no one other than Roosevelt thought of the need for programs for the unemployed to save the nation's lands and forests. A number of limited forest service schemes cooperating with state and local officials sheltered, clothed, and fed unemployed men in return for their work in reforestation. But it was Roosevelt—first with a limited program as governor of New York during the initial years of the Depression and then as a new president—who, with the force of Congress behind him, quickly molded a concept into an immediate call to action on a national scale. As viewed by Arthur Schlesinger, "He felt the scars and exhaustion of the earth almost as a personal injury."[5] And he meant to use his presidency to right the wrongs—for the lands and for the youth of America.

Franklin Roosevelt came by his love of nature and desire to repair the broken parts of it from his boyhood at his home in Hyde Park, New York, in the Hudson River Valley.[6] Throughout his life until his death in 1945, he took great delight in his home's natural world. But as a young adult, he also witnessed and then addressed the need for renewal of his family's lands, which were exhausted by overuse, poor stewardship, and neglect. When he took over the estate in 1910, he set about implementing major reforestation projects. It was that experience that forever transformed FDR into an ardent conservationist on two levels: if reforestation worked in Hyde Park, it could also serve as a blueprint for saving America's forests and natural resources. It also demonstrated that good, honest work in the outdoors would benefit body and soul as well as the pocket book.

Even as he honed his personal conservationist knowledge in Hyde Park, he also had an opportunity to expand on it, having been elected to the New York State Senate in 1910. He sought the chairmanship of the Senate's Fish and Game Committee and introduced several conservation and reforestation bills.[7]

But Roosevelt also had another influence. He had the benevolent ghost of his fifth cousin, Teddy Roosevelt, smiling down on him. Franklin Delano Roosevelt not only greatly admired the "father of American conservation and national parks," he also considered Teddy his role model for life and politics. Although a Democrat, he would seek every office held by Teddy:

assistant secretary of the navy, vice presidential candidate, governor of New York, and president.

But he contracted polio at the age of thirty-nine just as he was coming into his own. While devastating politically and personally, it gave FDR an extra dimension that is a hallmark of many great men and women: time to think and reflect without interference of a demanding career, family, or other obligations. During that time, through his discovery of the hopefully healing powers of the waters of Warm Springs, Georgia, he also witnessed the helplessness of others, an experience that greatly affected his philosophy of support for the less fortunate. Seeing their struggles, particularly that of the young with their attitudes of hope, gave Roosevelt another dimension that would serve him well—an aura of optimistic purpose for himself and his country. It would buoy him and the nation in times of crushing depression and devastating war.[8]

In 1928, he returned to public life as governor of New York. He immediately set about the task of conservation where he'd left off. Among the acts passed was a reforestation program coupled with employment for men on relief programs. While small and experimental in scope, it was the genesis of Roosevelt's plan to combine saving natural resources and men at the same time. Nationally, it would draw favorable attention to FDR from conservation leaders who were politically influential in many states.

As his term as governor (1929–1933) entered its last year, the Great Depression got worse. The Republican Party was mired in the old, tired policies of market adjustment and riding out the storm. The Democrats looked to FDR. As governor, he not only was acting to stem the tide, he was doing so with the smiling buoyancy that would become his trademark: The Happy Warrior.

Roosevelt was ready to right the foundering ship of state, but the tasks were enormous on every front. A quarter of the workforce was unemployed. Farm prices had fallen by 60 percent. Production was down by half. Banks were closed in thirty-two states. In response to the nation's deepening crisis, Roosevelt's first hundred days would target immediate relief. Among those measures proposed during that time was his Civilian Conservation Corps. In truth, the bill simply gave to the president the broad authority to get programs up and running. Even though some labor and Republicans opposed the measure, it had broad bipartisan support that it would retain throughout its short life from 1933 to 1942.

Working with teams from the War, Agriculture, Labor, and Interior departments, a plan was quickly fashioned and set in motion. Among its many innovations, the plan would directly involve the federal government in state and local park projects. Coupled with work in our national parks, an initial team of more than 250,000 men was mobilized by the summer of 1933. This mobilization was the largest in the nation's history, excluding that of World War I, and would ultimately produce a national pool of 3 million young men trained in numerous disciplines with a variety of work skills. As an unintended consequence, this pool of men who had learned to build bridges and roads were a civilian force in waiting, readied for World War II.

Each recruit enrolled for an initial six months, with the possibility of re-enrolling for three additional six months of employment. Each man received $30 per month, of which $25 was sent home to destitute families. More skilled men were paid $45 per month. Once accepted by the Labor Department, each man would be assigned to a quasi-military district where they would be trained, fed, equipped, and housed. From these district camps, they would be assigned to the departments of Agriculture (forests and soils erosion) and Interior (national and state parks). At the district camps and within the specific work camps of approximately two hundred enrollees, they would continue to be under the command of at least two Army officers, who were mainly called up from reserve units. For national and state park projects, the National Park Service acted as the "technical agency" charged with hiring skilled architects and engineers and other professionals.[9]

In Montana, the Missoula District of the Ninth Corps encompassed eight states, which included Glacier. Of the 65,000 enrollees positioned by the end of 1933, approximately 1,278 would disembark at Belton (now West Glacier).[10] All were under the age of twenty-five, and most had never seen a mountain, glacier, waterfall, or forest.

It would be a new experience for them, the Army, and the National Park Service staff of Glacier. Fortunately for the Glacier experience, Superintendent Eivind T. Scoyen was not only ready with projects to be addressed, but he was enthusiastic about the CCC concept. As well he should have been. Many worthy plans had gathered dust due to lack of funding over the decades. With this influx of ready labor (the largest ever before or since), park leaders and staff were organized to put men and plans to work.

It also came at a time when the Great Northern Railway was beginning to become disenchanted with the Glacier enterprise, in large measure due to the absence of Louis Hill's leadership and the crippling loss of business due to the Great Depression.

To add to the park's woes, the automobile tourists were in full bloom. What had been a one-in-every-two arrivals by automobile in the early 1920s had risen to nine-auto-travelers-to-one-rail arrival in 1930. The opening of what is now Highway 2 between East Glacier in 1930 and the Going-to-the-Sun Road in 1933 only added to the problem.

These tourists were staying in newly opened auto-cabin campgrounds (motels) and campsites that accommodated cars and personal camping gear. To compound the problem, they also used the packhorse tours less and less between chalets. They simply drove. Chalets and the Prince of Wales Hotel closed in 1933.[11] Thank God and FDR, prohibition had ended.

Whatever chance there may have been to reorganize, the Great Northern business plan was torpedoed by World War II. Three chalets were never reopened after the war: Going-to-the Sun, St. Mary's, and Cut Bank. Belton, Sperry, and Granite Park chalets were sold.[12] The Saddle Horse Company also shut its doors.[13]

In 1948, with the passing of Louis Hill, the death nail was driven for the Great Northern hotel-chalet presence in Glacier Park. The railroad began to look for a buyer. It changed the name of the operations company to Glacier Park, Incorporated (GPI) to attract a buyer. Other concessionaires sold out to either GPI or other merchants.[14]

Ironically, park visitation steadily rose throughout the 1930s, from 22,499 to 177,307 by 1940, due in part to the work of the CCC along with the availability of auto facilities and roads.[15]

Newly arriving CCC enrollees, numbering 1,278, would grow to 1,500 at the CCC's apex in 1935. During those years, they cleared burned-out fire areas, removed debris, graded roads, and constructed tents and car campsites. They cleared a 30-mile boundary cut to delineate the park and the Blackfeet Indian Reservation. They built a sawmill to produce fence posts and telephone poles. They strung telephone lines throughout the park and built water and sewage systems. Roads were banked, bridges were constructed, and reforestation took place throughout the park. And to protect it all, they fought forest fires from small burns to a furious giant in 1936.[16]

As was the case with the Forest Service 1910 conflagrations that threatened the entire northwest, including the newly established Glacier Park, the firefighting bravery of the untried CCC boys established a positive

FIGURE 8.2. Lunch hour at Many Glacier Camp, Civilian Conservation Corps, July 4, 1933. Courtesy of the Glacier National Park Archives; George A. Grant, photographer.

reputation and respect, particularly among the locals where initial suspicion and open hostility had reigned. By the end of the CCC's time in Glacier, it had supplied the area with 84,000 days of fire suppression.[17]

Because of its work and manpower availability, the CCC gave the park service the opportunity to develop a comprehensive fire control plan, with fire lanes and trails extending through practically every area of the park. Additionally, fire lookouts, telephone systems, and patrol cabins sprang up.[18]

On a personal note, I witnessed and reworked with my trail crewmates of 1961 and 1962 those fire trails in the Many Glacier Valley. Since there were only six or seven of us, I can also state that it would take a renewed program numbering in the hundreds, as was the case in the 1930s, to accomplish anywhere near that massive backwoods remote routing of the CCC. Our primary work was clearing and repairing the more heavily used tourist trails along with rescue and firefighting duties. We only chipped away at the absolutely necessary parameters of fire trails. As a practical matter, save for the manned fire lookouts, the ambitious fire suppression program of the Depression years ended with the onset of World War II. Ample argument can be found within the National Park Service and among fire control experts that much of the suppression practices motivated by the 1910 disaster were overkill, particularly in the remote wilderness areas of parks and forest. But that is a book for others to write and read.

While the CCC boys' work ethic and bravery were admired, problems existed in Glacier as well as throughout the system. All of these problems were recognized and addressed going in and, fortunately for the programs, were dealt with by leaders from the president on down, who, for the most part, handled each with firmness coupled with recognition of the reality of the moment. Of all the experiences of Glacier National Park's participation in the CCC's eight years of existence, I wish to address three that impacted its practices between 1933 and 1942.

While Roosevelt's belief that a necessary ingredient for the success of the program was to take young men out of their Great Depression environments of poverty and unemployment and into the beneficial atmosphere of nature and fresh air, it was not happily received by all the locals who were about to host these "street-slum foreigners." Fortunately, the right man for the job appeared again. Robert Fechner, a respected labor leader, was appointed by FDR to coordinate the agencies that would be involved in this as-yet-to-be-defined plan to meld together "two wasted resources, the young and the land in an attempt to save them both."[19] The plan was noble after the fact but frightening at the outset to those who saw potential loss of jobs taken by hordes of unsuitable, untrained ruffians. Because he was a labor man and politically sensitive, Fechner recognized the flashpoint potential immediately and expressed his concerns to Roosevelt. Importing nonresidents into regions in the West was sure to stir up resentment unless consideration was given to those locals who were also unemployed.[20]

An accommodation was immediately implemented. Local hiring of skilled workers placated three groups: national and local unions, local newspapers and critics, and the local skilled workers themselves. By the time FDR arrived at Glacier in August 1934, much of the criticism and discontent was muted, particularly when local merchants discovered that money from the camps flowed directly into their stores and businesses. Economic benefits for local merchants often made the difference not only for heightened local support but also for congressional or state legislative appropriations. Clanging cash registers often improve morale and morality.

In addition, other subsets of the CCC helped lessen criticism: separate programs were established for Native American tribes and veterans. The veterans were incorporated throughout most of the Glacier Park camps. The tribes had their own programs on their own lands; however, the Blackfeet did fight against fires throughout the park, fighting side by side with foreigners and veterans.[21] Disaster can also improve acceptance as firefighting funds flow into communities.

But acceptance was not the norm for two other groups that played roles in Glacier's CCC and conservation experience. The easier of the two assimilated groups were the conscientious objectors of World War II. The conscientious objectors were housed in one camp—Camp 55—that was small in numbers, but its residents provided the only available labor for the park since most young men and skilled workers in the area and across the nation were off at war. Thus, the pressure to hire local was no longer a problem. Throughout the war, the conscientious objectors would number only about five hundred total. Furthermore, they were selected, vetted, and supervised by the Peace Church committee whose members, in the case of Glacier's camps, were Mennonites.[22] Finally, they were all white.

Up to and through World War I, no fallback position existed for conscientious objectors. Conscientious objectors during that war still had to serve in the military, although as noncombatants. For those who could not accept even that form of service, the option was prison, with poor conditions that often led to death.

Following the war, the traditional Peace Churches (Amish, Mennonite, Church of the Brethren, Hutterite, and Quaker) met to fashion humane policy. As the prospects of another war loomed, they took their concerns to President Roosevelt. By the time the National Conscription Act of 1940 passed, a plan for national service performing work of "national importance" had been negotiated. Although FDR was skeptical, perhaps suspicious, of their motives, when that act passed, it included language that partially addressed the problem. It also specified that, true to FDR's history and conservation ethic, priority be given to soil and forestry restoration. But the enrollees would receive no pay!

By executive order, Roosevelt placed the ultimate authority under the umbrella of the Selective Service, which set standards for classification and the draft. The Peace Church committee helped identify acceptable campsites and projects.

Fortunately for all concerned, General Lewis B. Hershey, who was a firm and just administrator, defended the right of the conscientious objectors and their need for work alternatives, including the Peace Church–negotiated acceptance of "work of national importance." He stated the case at the outset in 1941: "The Civilian Public Service is an experiment in democracy to find out whether our democracy is big enough to preserve minority rights in a time of national emergency."[23]

The number of Civilian Public Service (CPS) enrollees stationed in and around Camp 55 near Belton/West Glacier, Montana, stabilized at around 150 members at any one time (with the addition of some spouses) by the end of 1942. The number would grow to more than 200 in 1945 when fire danger was extreme.

Fire suppression and fire hazard reduction were primary duties of those conscientious objectors. From June 1945 to June 1946, nearly 2,000 person-days were spent fighting fires.[24] (It appears that the term "person-days" was used because women were allowed to participate in the national system. That any women were enrolled at Glacier seems not to have been the case.)

In addition to fire-related assignments, the conscientious objector enrollees performed tree disease control and campground, trail, road, and building maintenance. In the winter, they cut down burned trees and produced more than 100,000 board feet of timber for use in repairing and building trails and bridges.

While constructive in what they accomplished in some of their tasks, such as the forging of the trail to and erection of Heaven's Peak Lookout, the impact of the conscientious objectors in Glacier National Park was mixed. The reasons vary, but there are some constants. Primarily, we were at war on two fronts, and the focus of the nation and its leaders was singular. Also, conflict could be found throughout the war between the Selective Service and the Peace Churches. Left unresolved, the churches pulled out of the agreement late in the war.[25]

Finally, because enrollees were allowed after six months to seek other work, many chose meaningful work in mental health facilities elsewhere. Perhaps their greatest contribution was that they kept the lid on fire and other distractive forces and acts. Whatever the final reckoning, they too served and most, as was the case with our fighting men and women, honorably.

FIGURE 8.3. In this August 5, 1934, file photo, President Franklin D. Roosevelt and Mrs. Eleanor Roosevelt were inducted into the Blackfeet tribe near Two Medicine Chalet, Glacier National Park, Montana. After the president had been installed as "Lone Chief," Mrs. Roosevelt received the title of "Medicine Pipe Woman." Courtesy of the Associated Press.

Leaving Many Glacier, the party retraced its route to St. Mary and thence on down the Blackfeet Highway to Two Medicine Chalet, arriving there at 5:45 o'clock. There, the President was greeted by a group of about 40 Blackfeet Indians in full regalia and a like number of Civilian Conservation Corps workers. The CCC chorus entertained with several songs, and the quartet of Negro boys offered a number. Favorites of the president were included.

— Excerpt from GNP Report on Presidential Visit to GNP, August 5, 1934[26]

It is only conjecture on my part as to where the groups honoring FDR on that sunny August day returned after the ceremonies ended and the president reboarded his train. We can assume the tribal leaders left for the reservation and the white CCC enrollees went to their various camps. But what of the four young African Americans?

While there appeared to have been African American CCC camps within Glacier National Park located at the farthest end of the North Fork Road in the northwest corner of the park at Anaconda Creek and Bowman Lake, two camps were located near Libby and Troy, Montana, within the National Forest Service's jurisdiction. From one called the Pipe Creek Camp would emerge a quartet that became popular throughout the region, performing for audiences and on radio.[27] Therefore, we can assume that it may have been this highly touted quartet that traveled to Two Medicine to serenade the president.

For this writing, it matters little which camp provided the entertainment. What is important is that they were in Montana in 1934 and that they were blacks from, like many of their white counterparts, the big cities back East and, perhaps, the South. They were, at once, isolated and segregated. Yet it appears that their isolation was no different than that of the white enrollees. Both had been transported long distances from home, set down in a remote area of the country, disciplined and governed by military personnel, and asked to do work they had never before experienced.

The difference in the two sets of camps was that the Glacier Park camps appear to have been isolated and totally segregated, with white camps completely separated from black camps and with only white supervisors, while the Forest Service camps near Libby and Troy, Montana, were isolated but segregated only within the camps themselves, with whites and blacks living in separate tents within the same camp.

The act establishing the CCC and the regulations that followed forbade any discrimination based on color, race, or creed. Yet due to conflicting laws, such as Army rules that condoned segregation on bases and camps, de facto segregation was allowed to occur in barracks and dining halls. Furthermore, the "Local Experienced Men" program allowed the hiring of local whites to fill better-paying, skilled, and supervisory jobs.[28] Due to levelheaded officials, some blacks were hired as supervisors and assistant supervisors. Within the Kootenai camps as well as in the totally segregated camps in Glacier National Park, the races seemed to have gotten along peacefully.[29]

It would appear that all enrollees, white and black, shared several characteristics. They were all isolated from home, family, and familiar surroundings. They all were furnished food, shelter, and clothing. They all had work. Many learned skills that would carry over for a lifetime, and they were sending money home to their mothers, fathers, wives, and siblings.

But it was the work that most certainly cemented a sense of camaraderie and purpose. Perhaps nature had more healing attributes than even FDR envisioned. Black or white, they rose at 6:00 AM and worked until 4:00 PM. Together or segregated, they built roads, trails, and even an airport near Libby. The Bowman Lake company built a trail to the Numa Ridge Lookout. If the shared hardship of work created a common bond, it was the sharing of song and sports that lessened racial animosity within and between camps.[30]

According to a historical interview with enrollee Francis Shekell,

> We had the Negro camp at Anaconda Creek (GNP), and I don't know where they came from. They always put on programs for us. They had kind of little skits that they put on, and boxing was their main thing. And they put on boxing exhibitions for us, and boy were they mean. They weren't grudge fights; they just practiced.
>
> They'd come down to our camp. We'd entertain them down there; we'd challenge them to a horseshoe game or something. We'd take them to the cleaners near every time.... Our camp was mostly local people around Flathead County or around Montana. We'd get together around once a week.[31]

However, despite the general aura of goodwill and common bond among the enrollees within the camps of the Forest Service and Glacier National Park as well as within some local communities, animosity and ill will were present. Enough so that even though Director Fechner had praised the work of the black enrollees and the goodwill they created locally with their responsible work ethic, he would do an about face and order "all Negroes in camps outside their home state ... to be repatriated as soon as possible, that they be replaced by white enrollees, and that strict segregation ... be maintained in all Corps areas."[32]

Clearly, the directive violated CCC policy. President Roosevelt's failure to uphold the policy was a blemish on his record of accomplishments in the CCC, specifically for African Americans. In the two years of their existence, the African American camps constructed an airport and built roads, trails to lookouts, and other good works in the northwest wilds of Montana and Glacier National Park.[33] Most importantly, through their CCC work, they gained marketable skills.

For all its flaws and failings, the CCC (and, to a lesser degree, the CPS) experience was a monumental achievement of organization, mobilization, and accomplishment nationally and within Glacier National Park. From 1933 to 1942, more than 3 million young men between the ages of seventeen and twenty-eight passed through the program. They were given a job. They were given a small stipend, most of which was sent home. They were provided shelter, clothing, and food. Equally important, they were given a lifetime experience in the great American outdoors coupled with the opportunity to learn a trade. And they were given hope.

During their time, the enrollees planted nearly 3 billion trees (more than half the nation's reforestation), constructed more than 800 parks nation-wide, restored many state parks, fought fires, established a series of new firefighting methods, and built service buildings and roads.

Nearly $220 million was spent within the national parks, including Glacier. But FDR's conservation policies for national parks did not end with the CCC. Seven national parks were added to the system, including the Great Smoky Mountains and Shenandoah in the East. Furthermore, he created by executive order numerous national monuments, many of which caused immediate transformation and enlargement of the park service in 1933.[34] Military parks, historic battlefields and monuments, the Statue of Liberty, Mount Rushmore, the Washington Monument, and Lincoln Memorial were transferred to the National Park Service. Now the park service not only encompassed the great vistas of natural America but also its history and shared ideas.

World War II, combined with the amazing rise of the auto-tourists, sealed the fate of passenger traffic on the Great Northern Railway and the hotels and completed what the Great Depression had failed to do. It was not apparent at first because visitation actually increased during the Depression due to several factors. The Going-to-the-Sun Road was dedicated on July 15, 1933, and Highway 2 connected East Glacier and Belton (West Glacier) in 1930, thus ending the railroad's automobile transportation between the two points. And in 1932, the much-publicized Waterton-Glacier International Peace Park was dedicated through the efforts of the Rotary Club of Canada and Montana.[35] Roosevelt's visit to the park and his nationally broadcast "National Parks Radio Address" was a clarion call to come and honor the parks. The CCC was improving and creating campgrounds and other facilities.

But the Great Northern without Louis Hill's leadership was beginning to tire of the Glacier Park experience. In doing so, they either missed the significance of the automobile or purposely chose to ignore it. Whatever

FIGURE 8.4. Dedication of Waterton-Glacier International Peace Park, 1932. Horace M. Albright accepts Peace Park expressions sent by President Hoover, which U.S. Congressman Scott Leavitt (R-MT) had framed and hung in the Glacier Park Hotel in Glacier National Park and in the Prince of Wales Hotel in Canada. *Left to right*: Horace M. Albright, unidentified individual, Eivind Scoyen, and another unidentified individual. Courtesy of Harpers Ferry Center, West Virginia; National Park Service photograph, negative number WASO-G-373.

combination of these reasons, by the start of the war, red flags were beginning to fly. Between 1941 and 1943, visitation dropped from 180,000 to 23,000.
From 1939 forward, a growing shortage of young hotel employees became a
problem. That was also true for park staff and other employees, so much so
that the hotels posted signs apologizing for poor service. In 1942, the last of
the CCC boys left, shuttering the camps and the great experiment of meld-
ing desperate lands and forests with the desperately unemployed youth of
America.[36] The small contingent of conscientious objectors could not take
up the slack.

By 1943, the Great Northern no longer stopped at the Glacier stations.
As previously mentioned, all hotels except Rising Sun Motor Lodge were
closed. The Prince of Wales did not operate between 1942 and 1946. In 1944,
the St. Mary Chalet was destroyed. Cut Bank and Sun Point chalets were
determined to be beyond repair and were destroyed in 1949. Belton, Sperry,
and Granite Park chalets were closed then sold in 1945. The Saddle Horse
Company failed.[37] Without visitors to ride to chalets that were destroyed or
closed, there was no need for the horses or wranglers, many of whom had
also gone to war.

Even if visitors had been available to travel to Glacier and other parks,
they were stymied by rationing of gas and tires. And even if they had considered travel by rail, they would have been turned away because the passenger
trains were in the business of hauling soldiers to and from training camps
and points of embarkation.

The one apparent bright spot during the war was that servicemen stationed near Glacier and other national and state parks spent time in them
on their leaves. It can be assumed that those men wanted to return with
their families after the war. Visitation numbers for 1946 to 1947 and thereafter would prove this out.

However, the problem for the Great Northern remained. Glacier visitor
numbers climbed from 300,000 in 1946 to 500,000 in 1951, but only 2 percent
came by rail. Regardless of the bleak existence of Glacier and other parks
during World War II, something monumental had occurred during its first
thirty years of existence. True to Stephen Mather's vision as well as others
who laid the foundations, there was now a national recognition of the need
for places to recreate and renew. So much so that during the Great Depression and the war to follow, Franklin D. Roosevelt was able to continue to
authorize new parks and create national monuments. With the war's end,
Americans were ready to enjoy their shared natural and historic treasures.

NOTES

1. C. W. Guthrie, *Going-to-the-Sun Road: Glacier National Park's Highway to the Sky* (Helena, MT: Farcountry Press, 2006), 8.

2. Guthrie, *Going-to-the-Sun Road*, 6–8.

3. Franklin D. Roosevelt, "Franklin D. Roosevelt: Radio Address from Two Medicine Chalet, Glacier National Park," The American Presidency Project, August 5, 1934, accessed September 18, 2014, http://www.presidency.ucsb.edu/ws/?pid=14733.

4. Joseph M. Speakman, "Into the Woods: The First Year of the Civilian Conservation Corps," National Archives, Fall 2006, accessed September 3, 2016, http://www.archives.gov/publications/prologue/2006/fall/ccc.html.

5. Arthur M. Schlesinger, *The Coming of the New Deal* (Boston, MA: Houghton Mifflin, 2003), E-book, 335.

6. Douglas Brinkley, *Rightful Heritage: Franklin D. Roosevelt and the Land of America* (New York, NY: HarperCollins Publishers, 2016), 3.

7. Brinkley, *Rightful Heritage*, 67–68.

8. Brinkley, *Rightful Heritage*, 109–12.

9. National Park Service, "The CCC and the National Park Service, 1933–1942: An Administrative History," National Park Service, April 4, 2000, accessed September 3, 2016, https://www.nps.gov/parkhistory/online_books/ccc/ccc2a.htm.

10. Michael J. Ober, "The CCC Experience in Glacier National Park," *Montana: The Magazine of Western History*, Summer 1976, 30.

11. Ray Djuff and Chris Morrison, *View with a Room: Glacier's Historic Hotels & Chalets* (Helena, MT: Farcountry Press, 2001), 122.

12. C. W. Guthrie, *All Aboard! for Glacier: The Great Northern Railway and Glacier National Park* (Helena, MT: Farcountry Press, 2004), 69.

13. Donald H. Robinson, "Glacier National Park: Through the Years in Glacier National Park: An Administrative History (Chapter 3)," National Park Service, May 1960, accessed September 01, 2016, https://www.nps.gov/parkhistory/online_books/glac/chap3.htm.

14. Djuff and Morrison, *View with a Room*, 24–25.

15. National Park Service, "Glacier National Park: Fact Sheet," National Park Service, accessed September 16, 2015, http://www.nps.gov/glac/learn/news/fact-sheet.htm.

16. Ren Davis and Helen Davis, *Our Mark on This Land: A Guide to the Legacy of the Civilian Conservation Corps in America's Parks* (Granville, OH: McDonald & Woodward Publishing Company, 2011), 326.

17. Ober, "The CCC Experience in Glacier National Park," 35.

18. Forest History Society, "U.S. Forest Service Fire Suppression," U.S. Forest Service History, March 17, 2015, accessed September 4, 2016, http://www.foresthistory.org/ASPNET/Policy/Fire/Suppression/Suppression.aspx.

19. Ober, "The CCC Experience in Glacier National Park," 32.

20. Speakman, "Into the Woods."

21. Ober, "The CCC Experience in Glacier National Park," 35.

22. Robert Kreider, "CPS Unit Number 055-01: The Civilian Public Service Story," The Civilian Public Service Story, accessed August 26, 2015, http://civilianpublicservice.org/camps/55/1.

23. Johnson-Humrickhouse Museum, "Civilian Public Service: An Experiment in Democracy," Johnson-Humrickhouse Museum, accessed August 8, 2016, http://www.jhmuseum.org/ourstory/community-stories/256-civilian-public-service-an-experiment-in-democracy.

24. Robert Kreider, "CPS Unit Number 055-01."

25. Robert Kreider, "Selective Service: The Civilian Public Service Story," The Civilian Public Service Story, accessed August 8, 2016, http://civilianpublicservice.org/storybegins/krehbiel/selective-service.

26. Eivind T. Scoyen, *Superintendent's Annual Report: 857-09 Presidential Visit*, report no. GLAC Nbr: 01.09, File Unit: 026, Folder: 2, National Park Service, U.S. Department of the Interior (Glacier National Park Historical Records and Central Files, 1934).

27. Dwayne Mack, "May the Work I've Done Speak for Me: African American Civilian Corps Enrollees in Montana, 1933–1934," *The Western Journal of Black Studies* 27, no. 4 (2003): 239–40.

28. Ober, "The CCC Experience in Glacier National Park," 36.

29. Mack, "May the Work I've Done Speak for Me," 240–41.

30. Mack, "May the Work I've Done Speak for Me," 242–43.

31. Francis Shekell, "Walton Historical Interview," interview by Janet Panebaker, *Glacier National Park Archives, Oral History Collection*, March 5, 1979.

32. Mack, "May the Work I've Done Speak for Me," 242.

33. Mack, "May the Work I've Done Speak for Me," 243.

34. Gary Scott, "The Presidents and the National Parks," White House Historical Association, accessed September 6, 2016, https://www.whitehousehistory.org/the-presidents-and-the-national-parks.

35. Parks Canada, "Waterton-Glacier International Peace Park," Parks Canada, February 19, 2015, accessed September 4, 2016, http://www.pc.gc.ca/eng/pn-np/ab/waterton/natcul/inter.aspx.

36. National Park Service, "Civilian Conservation Corps (CCC)," National Park Service, accessed September 4, 2016, https://www.nps.gov/glac/learn/historyculture/ccc.htm.

37. Robinson, "Glacier National Park: Through the Years."

CHAPTER NINE

Post-War America
A Renewed Love Affair Creates a Dilemma

By war's end, the Civilian Conservation Corps (CCC) boys had been gone for years, and the Civilian Public Service (CPS) pulled up stakes in 1946. Meanwhile, seemingly every ship and airplane at America's command brought the troops home. After disembarking, they fanned out across the land to farms, cities, and families. Some went back to jobs, but many (more than 9 million veterans between 1944 and 1949) received $4 billion in unemployment benefits to foster college and trade school education. The Serviceman's Readjustment Act of 1944 also established hospitals and low-interest mortgage loans.[1] It was one of the most visionary programs passed during America's history. It not only created educational opportunities for millions of returning GIs, it also took those millions of young men and women off the job market until the country could convert from a wartime footing to a renewed and vibrant peacetime economy. When coupled with the low-interest mortgage and hospital programs, billions of additional dollars flowed into people's communities and pockets, which hugely increased demand for goods and services.

Within a short time, many of those same returning servicemen and women sought to go out again into the America they'd fought to defend. Among their highest priorities was the desire to visit or revisit their parks, including Glacier National Park. In 1946, more than 200,000 would enter and experience the "Crown of the Continent."[2] By the early 1950s, that number had tripled. But as was the case at the beginning of the war, most of them arrived by automobile.

The swelling number of visitors throughout the national parks system was estimated to reach 80 million by the mid-1960s. Again, this was a major confrontation between people and preservation in the making. Glacier's growing quandary was no exception. For all the good works of Louis Hill and his railroad, Mather's sweeping highway to the sun, the CCC's hundreds of thousands of man-hours of renewal and expansion of trails and facilities, there were not enough hotels, motor lodges, and campgrounds to meet the demand.

That became even more critical since, it must be remembered, a number of chalets and camps were shuttered and destroyed either before or shortly after World War II. And no new hotels or chalets were contemplated as the railroad began to look for ways to get out of the lodging business, which had been losing money for years.

Ironically, even as they looked for ways to terminate their hotel experience, Great Northern executives were stepping up equipment expenditures in an attempt to capture more passenger business. Thus, when passenger traffic to Glacier National Park reopened in June 1946, the Great Northern, featuring its passenger trains the Oriental Limited and the Empire Builder, resumed its passenger service. By 1947, new streamliners were introduced with innovations and enhanced passenger comfort, including roomettes and coffee shops. Late in 1955 (and later than the competition), scenic dome cars were added for coach and luxury cars alike. Advertising was revamped to focus on train travel rather than Glacier as the destination. "Go Great … Go Great Northern" replaced "See America First," and the excitement of train travel supplanted mountains, waterfalls, glaciers, and Native Americans.[3]

Glacier Park, Incorporated, and the railroad turned a profit, and, for a short time, it worked, but not for long. For all its innovations and investments, the Great Northern (as well as other lines) could not compete with the automobile, the newly inaugurated interstate highway system that zipped families to and from their favorite vacation destinations easier and faster, and a rapidly expanding airline service. Airplanes could whisk visitors from all sections of the country to their park destinations in less than a day's time.[4]

It is interesting to note here that in 1915, at Mather's first national park conference, Orville Wright predicted that airplanes would soon be taking passengers to national parks, among other destinations. His pronouncement was met with disbelief for the most part.[5]

But if passenger railroads were faced with declining customers, rising costs, and insurmountable competition from cars, highways, and airplanes, the parks, certainly Glacier, were confronted with the rising tide of humanity. Not all those pressures would be visitor or interpark related.

Just as demand for more goods and services was on the rise as the economy righted itself, so was the demand for additional water power for electricity. Proposed as early as 1943 by the Corps of Engineers and the Bonneville Power Administrators, the Glacier View Dam would have been built on the North Fork of the Flathead River between Huckleberry Mountain and Glacier View Mountain, encompassing nearly 10,000 acres. It would have flooded Camas Creek, raised the level of Logging Lake, and destroyed the wintering grounds for deer, elk, and moose. It would have cost $95 million. It had the support of newly elected representative Mike Mansfield. Fortunately, it was opposed by former Senator Burton Wheeler, ranchers, the Glacier Park Hotel Company, the Sierra Club, Society of American Forests, Audubon, and the National Park Service. Looming above them all was the ghost of John Muir and the Hetch-Hetchy experience. This conservation battle royal pitted Muir (pure preservationists) against Gifford Pinchot (utilitarian conservationists):

> The Progressive Era's most controversial environmental issue was the 1908–1913 struggle over federal government approval for building the Hetch-Hetchy dam in a remote corner of federally owned land in California's Yosemite National Park. The city of San Francisco, rebuilding after the devastating 1906 earthquake, believed the dam was necessary to meet its burgeoning needs for reliable supplies of water and electricity. At Congressional hearings on Hetch-Hetchy held in 1913, supporters of the plan such as Gifford Pinchot, the first chief forester of the United States and a noted environmentalist, argued that conservation of natural resources was best achieved through management of the wilderness. Preservationist and Sierra Club founder John Muir did not testify before Congress, but he argued against the Hetch-Hetchy plan in his 1912 book, *The Yosemite*. In the end, Congress chose management over aesthetics, voting 43 to 25 (with 29 abstentions) to allow the Hetch-Hetchy dam on federal land.[6]

While debating the Glacier View Dam's construction in 1949, Secretary of Defense James Forrestal and Secretary of the Interior Julius Krug decided that if both departments did not agree, it would not be built.[7] The dam's plans are still gathering dust in some government warehouse.

Although the threat of the Glacier View Dam was removed, other threats arose and exist today. All external threats aside, there were internal problems aplenty, which prompted the National Park Service to reexamine where and how it would proceed in the future.

Tourism at Glacier stood at between 500,000 and 600,000 annually and was estimated to reach 1 million by sometime in the 1960s. Nationally, the estimate predicted 80 million visitors annually by the mid-1960s. The dual purpose of the "Organic Act" of 1915 would be stretched to the limit.

The answer was the brainchild of National Park Service Director Conrad Wirth—Mission 66.[8] Wirth rightly saw the popularity of President Dwight Eisenhower's massive $25 billion interstate highway system, which was to be completed over ten years. Wirth sensed he could link his own Mission 66 ten-year plan to improve the parks, making them ready for the onslaught of visitors who would surely be traveling over America's new road system. He called for an appropriation of $787 million over the ten years to be completed in 1966—the fiftieth anniversary of the National Park Service. Both programs passed Congress with overwhelming support.[9]

Work started immediately. New roads and repairs, water and sewage system upgrades and expansions, new and expanded campgrounds, bathrooms, trails, and 110 "visitor centers," the signature and centerpiece of Wirth's grand design, were completed. Three such facilities were designated for Glacier National Park.

By the end of the program, the arriving public and the park would have use of 584 comfort stations, 221 administrative buildings, 36 service buildings, 1,239 employee housing units, and those 110 visitor centers. The National Park Service would also acquire 78 additional park units.[10]

While much good and some greatness were contained within the plans and accomplishments of the program, it was from the outset weighted heavily in favor of "providing for the enjoyment" of the users rather than conserving and preserving the parks' natural historic wildlife.

The outcry was immediate from preservationists. They had every good reason to protest. They had little impact, at least not for the moment. It must be recognized that building, rebuilding, and expanding was the order of the day—an extension and continuation of the popular public works projects of the 1930s. However, their combined voices of concern and protest would, like those on the losing side of the Hetch-Hetchy debate, be carried on the winds into the next decade, resulting in the passage by Congress of the Wilderness Act of 1964. To this day, it is listed as one of President Lyndon Johnson's most cherished accomplishments.

Although the protests would continue, Mission 66 continued apace throughout the late 1950s into the 1960s. Glacier National Park received its share of funding—some $23 million over the course of the program, including plans for three new visitor centers at St. Mary's Going-to-the-Sun entrance station, Logan Pass, and Apgar in West Glacier. A stand-alone replacement for an aging and inadequate visitor center at Apgar never materialized. There were meetings and discussions aplenty, particularly as 2010—the hundredth anniversary of the park—approached, but nothing happened. Finally, in a spirit of making something new and fresh available for west side visitors, the recently completed Transit Bus Center was upgraded and renamed the Apgar Visitor Center in 2014. However, there are those who still hold out hope that a more expansive and educational complex will eventually become a reality—even if the center is located outside the west entrance of the park. Additional restaurants were built at Lake McDonald Lodge and Rising Sun, a new administration building was completed, and more housing for employees was constructed. Campgrounds were expanded with new fire pits and restrooms, along with improvements in signage, sewage lines and water systems, bridges, roads, and trails. A new ranger station was added at the American end of Waterton Lake.[11]

Of particular interest is the largest project completed in Glacier National Park during the Mission 66 program: the Camas Road. Constructed between 1960 and 1967 at a cost of $2.5 million, the road runs east to west from a junction with the Going-to-the-Sun Road for 11.7 miles to the North Fork Road. Its announced intent was to provide access to the North Fork of the Flathead River, connecting to the never-completed Loop Road to Canada in the Waterton Lakes portion of the Waterton-Glacier International Peace Park. It was also hoped it would relieve pressure for the Going-to-the-Sun Road, which was carrying more traffic year after year.[12]

Not so highly touted was the National Park Service's hope that more traffic up the North Fork would block any renewed effort to resurrect the Glacier View Dam project. It must be noted here that then-Senator Mike Mansfield was rising through the leadership ranks of the Senate and would become Senate Majority Leader in 1961—a force not to be ignored. It was Mansfield who as a congressman in the early 1950s had championed the dam. Even after it appeared to have been successfully blocked, he continued to introduce bills to bring it back to life for several years thereafter.

By improving access and visitation, numerous park administrators hoped to make the case that the area's wilderness appeal would become an alternative to the more-crowded venues within the park. While the present Camas Road is a beautiful drive, it is vastly underutilized. Without the Canadian connection, it is simply a road, not quite to nowhere, but nothing like the envisioned purpose of its 1950s champions. For years, its lonely, unoccupied entrance station, which was finally demolished in 2006, stood as an untold story of why a beautiful road dead-ends into the unpaved North Fork Road. To those who cherish the wilderness of the backcountry, that is a blessing. Unfortunately, for the rest of the park, it has produced little meaningful travel or viewership alternatives. But fortunately, with the national change in big-project philosophy and extreme cutbacks in appropriations, the Glacier View Dam will remain in that warehouse collecting dust.[13]

For all Mission 66's work, controversial or not, a number of its accomplishments, along with many others within the park and throughout northern Montana, would fall victim to one of the mid-1960s' three calamities: flood, fire, and gruesome fright. All weather conditions of early June 1964 were poised to come together in a perfect storm sequence.

Already, heavy snowpacks registering 75 percent above normal on May 1 lay unmelted in cooler-than-normal weather. An additional 13 inches blanketed Glacier and the western half of the state. Temperatures remained cold. But shortly before Memorial Day, it climbed above 70°F. Then the rains came. Not a gentle spring rain, but torrential storms producing 10 to 15 inches of precipitation that fell in little more than a day's time. Apparently, three storms collided at the wrong time and place. The rains were not only torrential—they were warm. The snowpack began to thaw, and the resulting torrents of water thundered down mountainsides, scouring all before them. Boulders broke away, dams burst, bridges collapsed, valleys flooded, and trails, roads, and railroad tracks buckled, then were swept away. Lakes rose, campgrounds disappeared, and hotels took on water up to several floors in some cases. Twenty-eight people died; thousands of homes were gone. The damage was estimated at $63 million. President Lyndon B. Johnson declared nine counties disaster areas.

Not only were some Mission 66 projects damaged or destroyed, several projects, such as the extension of the Camas Road to Canada and the visitor center at Apgar, were shelved. All park resources and manpower were dedicated to flood repairs. It was a massive undertaking. Gone were essential bridges and roads into and within the park. Both bridges at West Glacier were fractured and twisted, making them impassable. Highway 2 and the Great Northern Railway tracks running alongside were eaten away, closing automobile and train traffic.

The Going-to-the-Sun Road was destroyed along several sections. The only road to the Many Glacier area was washed away, and the hotel was flooded. The Two Medicine River joined with the flooding caused by the breached Swift Dam, producing a combined river two miles wide that washed out onto the plains and the Blackfeet Reservation.

That river and others destroyed hundreds of homes, farmland, dams, and roads. By some accounts, the Blackfeet Reservation suffered the worst damage within the far-reaching sweep of the flood.[14] Great Falls, Montana, was inundated to its rooftops, as were towns throughout the Flathead Valley. As soon as the flood subsided, federal, state, railroad, and park personnel and contractors sprang into action. Within weeks, most roads and bridges were made functional. Flood reconstruction was the order of the day for the remainder of the 1960s.[15]

Mercifully, many of the Mission 66 projects were completed and, for the most part, went unscathed. Today, the two visitor centers are at full capacity in high season.

If the premier twin sculptors of mountains and ice took millions of years to work their magic to form Glacier National Park's natural wonders, flood and fire are their mischievous partners who, from time to time, rearrange, transfer, and renew the landscape in the blink of an eye. While destructive, even deadly, they are essential to the natural order. The problem is that mankind is the uninvited interloper who often tragically stands in their path, perfecting policies and infrastructures that lead to imperfect consequences. The cures too often are more disastrous than the disease.

From time to time, river and floodplains need a good flooding to renew and replenish. If allowed to follow their natural course, floods give rivers and floodplains the means to fulfill their mission: to replenish nutrients, deposit new ones, drop seeds, and reoxygenate the area. In short, the surging rivers maintain and reinvigorate their ecosystems. And the system in its entirety can withstand and benefit from those periodic overflows. Roads, bridges, and buildings cannot, and manmade diversions and channeling often exacerbate the problem.

Forest fires are similarly beneficial, even as they wreak havoc on humans, their livelihoods, and structures. Again, the problem is that we have chosen to live and recreate in an area teaming with flora, fauna, and the real possibility of fire. Ironically, those very plants and animals have enjoyed renewal as a result of fires that have sprung up over the centuries. For the purpose of this writing, the fires during and since the great fire of 1910 that occurred within months after the creation of Glacier National Park will serve to make this point on several levels.

The 1910 fire was the largest in the park's history (some 100,000 acres) until the combined fires of 2003, which destroyed 136,000 acres, more than 13 percent of the park's total acreage. The enormity and severity of the 1910 calamity, which burned more than 3 million acres across sections of northern Washington, Idaho, and Montana, killed eighty-five people, many of whom were Forest Service firefighters. Because of their deaths and the monstrosity of the wreckage, the Forest Service and the government developed a "no-burn" strategy, which led to unintended consequences that defied the natural order by preventing fire from performing its role in the ecological balancing act within forests. In a tragic irony, due to the publicized bravery of the firefighters, it gave legitimacy to the Forest Service nationally and among congressional appropriators.[16]

Unfortunately, it also gave rise to the no-burn rule (which later became the 10:00 AM rule, whereby all fires were to be suppressed by the next morning after being identified). To take the policy that all fires were detrimental to the people, a cartoon black bear named Smokey was introduced in 1944 on billboards and posters to drive home the message that "only you can prevent forest fires."[17]

For decades, the policy seemed to work. Annual burn acreage was reduced from 30 million acres during the 1930s to roughly 4 million acres in the 1960s.[18]

Unfortunately, it was seriously flawed. Over those decades, millions of acres of forest in national forests and parklands were filled with dead trees that piled up like giant, dry matchsticks from windfalls. Without periodic fires to clean out the dead wood, living trees and plant species more beneficial to the forest were choked out. This denied groundcover plants and brush to sustain deer, elk, and even the bears. Like Grinnell, Smokey and his friends were also being hoisted on their own petard.

But early on, some, like the premier environmentalist Aldo Leopold, began to recognize that wildfires were essential to the health of ecosystems and were necessary to enrich future growth. By the 1960s, those few early harbingers of no-burn-policy dangers were joined by more and more who saw fire as an integral part of a forest's lifecycle. In 1962, Secretary of the Interior Stewart Udall stepped in and commissioned a study group to refine and define wildfire management within national parks. Part of the findings that gained almost immediate acceptance was that parks should be managed as ecosystems. Shortly thereafter, within the 1964 Wilderness Act, encouragement to allow the natural order to occur, including fire, was written into the language.[19]

By 1968, the National Park Service adopted new policies, recognizing fire as part of the ecological process. The Forest Service followed suit in 1974. Fire control became fire management in wilderness areas of parks and forests. Controlled burns were added to the equation. Slowly but surely, the services and Congress were moved to tip the scales back toward the fine balancing act of "enjoyment" versus "preservation."

At this point, I turn back to Glacier National Park in 1967. Two highly publicized occurrences focused on the failure of park management to give equal attention to both parts of the 1916 Organic Act's dictates.

Although small in size compared to earlier Glacier fires in 1910, 1926, 1936, and those to follow in 2003 and 2006, the 1967 fires (some twenty of them), ignited by lightning throughout the powder-dry forest, focused renewed attention on the lack of progress in complying with policies set forth under the Wilderness Act. Of particular interest and publicity was the Garden Wall Fire, which threatened the Going-to-the-Sun Road but, to the best of my knowledge, little else. Only 6,700 acres burned, but nearly 3,500 firefighters were called in to suppress the blaze.[20] In and of itself, that fire may not have reached the level of importance to warrant a review of park management practices for lack of compliance. But another tragedy in 1967 would call down the wrath of preservationists, policymakers, and the public.

Even as crews battled the fire that erupted out of the lightning storm of August 11, 1967, two other horrific events occurred the night of August 12–13. These dual incidents, chronicled in Jack Olsen's definitive 1969 book, *Night of the Grizzlies*, set forth facts and failures that were bound to have collided at some point.[21] The facts were failures and the failures became facts.

On the day before the events, young women and men, park concession employees, set out on separate hikes to the Granite Park Chalet area near the top of the Garden Wall and toward the Trout Lake campsite, which was over Howe Ridge looking down on Lake McDonald. Although ten miles apart, both parties were moving toward a common catastrophe.

Within hours of one another, both parties were attacked by two grizzly bears. Two young women were mauled and died from their wounds. A fellow employee at the Granite Park site was attacked but survived. Within hours, the attacking bears were tracked down and killed. The media reaction was immediate and none too good. Finger pointing from every direction abounded. Some thought the bears were drunk on huckleberries. Others stated that the hikers had not followed proper backcountry practices, while some exclaimed both young women were in their menstrual cycle, attracting the bears. Jack Olsen would write that after decades of peace between man and bears, enough factors were present to arrive at the conclusion that it was inevitable.[22] These twin tragic deaths were the first to occur by grizzly attack in the park's history.

What is irrefutable is that park visitation reached nearly 1 million during that summer. More and more, with the introduction of lightweight hiking equipment coupled with the growing desire of many to enjoy the wilderness in its purity, users were marching toward one species that could, when angered and cornered, push back with terrifying results.

It did not help that park management practices in Glacier and in other parks encouraged close encounters by allowing, with disregard of state park policies, garbage to be dumped near hotels and chalets for the enjoyment of park visitors, who delighted in watching bears eat the garbage at close range. Furthermore, roadside photography was a fast-growing pastime of tourists, who snapped pictures of every animal they could attract, often by inviting them to partake of food offered up by small hands and smiling faces. For their enjoyment, visitors were allowed to create bears less fearful of encroaching humans. At that moment, they were setting the scene that led to that night in August 1967.

Park personnel were forced to immediately address the problem. Garbage dumping was prohibited. Trails were closed after bear sightings. Campers and hikers, through brochures and signage, were educated on how to avoid bears and make them aware of incoming human presence. Campers and hikers were also instructed to pack out what they packed in. Troubled and aggressive bears were transported deep into the remote areas of the park. Trail crews were commanded to maintain designated campsites to keep them clean and free of possible bear attractants.[23]

With these two back-to-back disasters of fire and bear attacks, the National Park Service and Glacier Park staff began to reorient. While the user would still have a place in the park, a wilderness "preserved and unimpaired for the enjoyment of future generations" according to the 1916 Organic Act began to receive equal billing. It was none too soon. Glacier's annual visitation count would rise from 1.2 million in 1970 to 2 million in 2007.[24] The number has grown every year since.

Although met with some begrudging resistance, the forces of the renewed conservation and preservation ethic began to take hold. Enforced by the Wilderness Act of 1964, park officials were forced to restore the delicate balance by setting forth in Glacier what was wilderness. Once established, this delineated area would be off limits to any "permanent improvements for human habitation."[25]

For a time, the foot draggers and old guard prevailed. But, as is often the case, their laxity would catch up to them. In 1969, it was revealed that the Logan Pass Visitor Center's sewage was being allowed to flow untreated into Reynolds Creek, winding up in St. Mary's Lake. The superintendent was transferred and a new one appointed. The new superintendent didn't fare much better. While addressing the sewage and bear problems, he fell, for the most part, on the side of more development and visitor pleasuring.

The general criticism was that Superintendent William J. Briggle was running Glacier as a recreation park rather than a natural wilderness setting. Specifically, he was called out for condoning waterskiing and snowmobiling in the park and supporting a proposal of a boardwalk from Logan Pass Visitor Center up to Hidden Lake Overlook. That confrontation grew so heated that the 1971 trail crew threw down their tools and refused to build the boardwalk. Their protest centered around the objection that the wooden walkway was chemically toxic and an environmental atrocity.[26]

A personal observation: the members of my trail crew in 1961 to 1962 would never have threatened to throw down their tools and walk off the job. We once complained to Don Hummel, owner of Glacier Park, Incorporated, when he proposed cutting hotel employees and trail crew food portions as a cost-cutting measure. But we made our case in simple terms, pointing out that we were working the trails for long hours in order to get the trails ready for his hotel clientele, that shoveling rock and snow was tough going, and that we were working up a great hunger and thirst. Hummel agreed, and our knapsacks and dining hall tables remained full.

But 1971 was a decade after that mild confrontation. During that ten-year span, the youth of America had taken to the streets, lunch counters, and platforms to take on the establishment over civil rights, the Vietnam War, and all manner of environmental atrocities. Protest had become the order of the day, often without regard to the consequences, job loss, or jail time. The trail crew of 1971 did lose their jobs, but after more criticism was leveled, the superintendent allowed that they would be evaluated for employment the following year.[27]

Over the next year or so, the boardwalk was completed, but untreated lumber was used. In my opinion, the boardwalk confrontation was one of the most public demonstrations of the growing dilemma between recreation and conservation.

There is no question that by the early 1970s, the number of hikers climbing to Hidden Lake was increasing at an alarming rate—often trampling the beautiful alpine flora and delicate soil to unsightly ruin. It has been apparent to me that on my annual treks to the park, the artificial pathway has cut down on the damage. But because of the publicity, other conservation steps were initiated. The wilderness began to take the upper hand.

Bus shuttle service to Logan Pass was established to cut automobile traffic. Some areas, including one below Logan Pass, were closed to foot traffic to restore vegetation. Campground and RV sites were established outside the park. Snowmobiles were banned in 1975, and the artificial treatment of animal life and fire was addressed. The introduction of non-native fish for the pleasure of fishermen was discontinued. Wolves and mountain lions were allowed to naturally return to Glacier.

In 1976 and 1979, respectively, Glacier National Park and then Waterton Lakes National Park were designated a Biosphere Reserve under the United Nations Educational, Scientific, and Cultural Organization's (UNESCO) Man and the Biosphere Program. This gave worldwide recognition and further legitimacy to the value of holding in place these uniquely intact diverse ecosystems. In 1998, the Waterton-Glacier International Peace Park was dedicated as a World Heritage Site.[28]

While the world and a great majority of Americans have come to cherish and honor the necessity for wilderness, Congress has failed to give Glacier its official blessing to permanent wilderness status. The National Park Service policy treats 93 percent of Glacier's acreage as wilderness to the best of its ability and funding. Fortunately, so much of those areas are so remote that they are protected by location. It is not perfect, but it is sufficient for now.

In the next chapter of this book, we will look at the future of Glacier National Park as it deals with climate change, increasing population, and the ever-present dilemma of the dual mandate arising out of the Organic Act.

But before moving on, I want to address my concept of giants, which has been the governing undercurrent of this book and why, with the passage of time through these pages, giants may seem to have faded.

Many giants, in whatever field of endeavor, are often hard to recognize and appreciate during their lifetimes, some only decades after their deaths, some never. Most are recognized by a definable accomplishment, although some, such as the Native Americans who held sacred the lands and mountains to be called Glacier, are heralded for what they did *not* do—plunder and despoil the landscape. Those are most difficult to discover and honor, but they are giants nonetheless.

Most are initiators, happy to champion and create, but are often not suited or positioned to run the organizations created or market and manufacture the product invented. Certainly, that applied to Muir, Teddy and Franklin Roosevelt, Grinnell, and Olmsted. James J. and Louis Hill and Stephen Mather are exceptions.

Most important in the flow of history is the fact that giants, with few exceptions, have happened on the scene at a precise moment when all the elements aligned with that individual's life purpose and connected them with others and the universe, allowing them to rise above the fray and fulfill their purpose.

That is why during the brief span of time from approximately 1850 through the early part of the twentieth century, a cauldron of conservation possibilities captured the imaginations of men and women who, likewise, were dedicating great portions of their lives to the concept and ethic of parks and who often went on to advocate for specific parks.

That movement would carry over into the 1920s and early 1930s, thanks in large part to the organizational genius of Stephen Mather, who also had a first-class grasp of public relations. But Mather died in 1930. Other voices for the parks were dead or removed from the field of battle. At that moment in time, with a horrific depression looming, the national park movement could have slowed or ceased, perhaps even receded.

But the election of 1932 forestalled those possibilities, fortified by Franklin D. Roosevelt, who, for all his forward-looking progressivism, was a disciple of the conservation and park ethic reverting to the turn of the twentieth century. His rural New York upbringing and abiding admiration of Teddy set him on his own conservation journey that would surpass the elder Roosevelt's accomplishments on many levels.

But FDR's gigantic achievements could just as easily have been over-shadowed, perhaps lost, in the enormity of the Great Depression's wreck-age and the all-consuming focus on winning World War II. But Franklin Roosevelt, Teddy Roosevelt, Stephen Mather, John Muir, Frederick Law Olm-sted, Louis Hill, and George Bird Grinnell had one thing in common. They all knew how to communicate their message and to whom. They courted potential advocates in the media, and they knew and liked the working press. And they all worked in simpler times when there were no television or cable networks, social media, and "talking heads" instantaneously inter-preting every speech and news release. They were all past masters of press and public relations and, yes, in instances such as the Roosevelts, they had a friendly, even admiring, working press with which to interact.

That era of goodwill and journalistic partnership lasted through Presi-dent John Kennedy's short time in office. But matters began to change almost from the day Lyndon Johnson took office. As the Great Depression and the good war faded from view, other more current issues would come into play that would permanently alter the relationship between the nation's leaders and the press: the fight for civil rights, the war on poverty, and, most important, the war in Vietnam. The war came to define LBJ's tenure, and, eventually, even civil rights and the Great Society would be pushed aside and drowned out by the anger and bitterness of Vietnam. As that conflict wore on, Johnson lost the confidence and trust of the press and other news media. They became cynical and eventually hostile. For the most part, that has been the case ever since. "Question everything" has become the domi-nant mantra.

I mention all of this because it has a direct bearing on the appearance and sustainability of "giants."

By any measure, Lyndon B. Johnson should have been a giant among con-servation giants. But he was defined both by his other accomplishments—civil rights, Medicare, education, and the war on poverty—and his monu-mental failure—Vietnam. In the end, the Vietnam War poisoned everything. It is sad because there was much in his administration to praise, particularly in his environmental and conservation accomplishments.

Lyndon Johnson, with the constant support and advice of his wife, Lady Bird Johnson, fashioned and passed almost intact his environmental pro-posals under the umbrella of his Great Society initiatives: the Clean Air Act of 1963, the Water Quality Act of 1965, the Endangered Species Act of 1966,

and the Wetlands Preservation Bill in 1967. Legislation was passed that ben-
efited the national parks as well: the Wilderness Act of 1964, the National
Historic Preservation Act of 1966, the National Park Foundation in 1967, the
National Trails System in 1967, and the Wild and Scenic River System in 1967.
In addition, he added fifty new park units and expanded existing ones as
well as created national recreation areas and other urban park sites.[29]

But whatever his accomplishments in the arena of environmental quality,
they were torn asunder by his disastrous policies concerning the war and
his secretiveness and duplicity in conducting that conflict. Only decades
later have those monumental achievements begun to receive a second and
often admiring second look. In my opinion, Lyndon Johnson has risen and
will continue to rise in stature as a giant for a better Earth, even if he must
remain a flawed giant, scarred by a war he could not win.

But it was not only Lyndon Johnson who was tarnished and crippled by
his disastrous war. His conduct, coupled with the tragic and ruinous presidency of Richard Nixon, has cast a permanent stain on the presidency and
the role of the media. That stain, running side by side with the rise of social
media and attack journalism, has left little room for giants.

Fortunately for us, there are those good and competent men and women
(and nonprofits that advocate for their ideas and causes) who, for the most
part, are able to rise to the top while making government and industry
run well.

And fortunately for Glacier and our national parks, we had giants when
we needed them in a time that would accept and honor giants.

NOTES

1. NOLO, "Servicemen's Readjustment Act (G.I. Bill)," NOLO, accessed September 4, 2016,
https://www.nolo.com/legal-encyclopedia/content/gi-bill-act.html.

2. C. W. Buchholtz, *Man in Glacier* (West Glacier, MT: Glacier Natural History Association,
1976), 70.

3. C. W. Guthrie, *All Aboard! for Glacier: The Great Northern Railway and Glacier National
Park* (Helena, MT: Farcountry Press, 2004), 88.

4. Guthrie, *All Aboard! for Glacier*, 88.

5. Horace M. Albright and Robert Cahn, *The Birth of the National Park Service: The Founding
Years, 1913–33* (Salt Lake City, UT: Howe Brothers, 1985), 49–50.

6. History Matters, "'Dam Hetch-Hetchy!': John Muir Contests the Hetch-Hetchy Dam," History Matters, accessed September 5, 2016, http://historymatters.gmu.edu/d/5720/.

7. C. W. Guthrie, *Glacier National Park: The First 100 Years* (Helena, MT: Farcountry Press,
2008), 99.

8. Ethan Carr, *Mission 66: Modernism and the National Park Dilemma* (Amherst, MA: University of Massachusetts Press, 2007), PDF.

9. Dayton Duncan and Ken Burns, *The National Parks: America's Best Idea: An Illustrated History* (New York, NY: Alfred A. Knopf, 2009), 334–49.

10. Carr, *Mission 66*.

11. Buchholtz, *Man in Glacier*, 74.

12. Vince Devlin, "Short Glacier Road Has Long Connection with Turning Points in Park History," *Missoulian*, June 2, 2015, accessed August 8, 2016, http://missoulian.com/news/local /short-glacier-road-has-long-connection-with-turning-points-in/article_2ceabe1c-49f9-522c -89bc-4888b520a678.html.

13. Buchholtz, *Man in Glacier*, 75.

14. Guthrie, *Glacier National Park: The First 100 Years*, 110.

15. Buchholtz, *Man in Glacier*, 76.

16. Forest History Society, "U.S. Forest Service Fire Suppression."

17. Smokey Bear, "About the Campaign," Smokey Bear, accessed September 4, 2016, https:// smokeybear.com/en/smokeys-history/about-the-campaign.

18. Natural Resources Defense Council, "Wildfires in Western Forests," Natural Resources Defense Council, May 2003, accessed July 27, 2007, www.nrdc.org/land/forests/pfires.asp.

19. National Park Service, "Wilderness: Frequently Asked Questions," National Park Service, accessed September 16, 2015, http://wilderness.nps.gov/faqnew.cfm.

20. Guthrie, *Glacier National Park: The First 100 Years*, 111–12.

21. Jack Olsen, *Night of the Grizzlies* (Moose, WY: Homestead Publishing, 1996).

22. Olsen, *Night of the Grizzlies*.

23. Olsen, *Night of the Grizzlies*, 219.

24. National Park Service, "Glacier National Park: Fact Sheet."

25. Buchholtz, *Man in Glacier*, 77.

26. Buchholtz, *Man in Glacier*, 69.

27. Buchholtz, *Man in Glacier*, 69.

28. Guthrie, *Glacier National Park: The First 100 Years*, 147.

29. National Park Service, "Lyndon B. Johnson and the Environment," National Park Service, accessed July 29, 2016, https://www.nps.gov/lyjo/planyourvisit/upload/EnvironmentCS2.pdf.

CHAPTER TEN

Looking Ahead

Practically from the outset of the establishment of Glacier National Park in 1910, Grinnell began to have regrets about the results he had championed. From 1911 forward, he would express those feelings. In 1917 in a letter to his friend and supporter, L. O. Vaught, he voiced his resentment over the years but concluded that such "crowds" were a necessary evil to ward off destruction by "a lot of vandals."

"After the vandals had got through with it, it would be no good to any of us, while if made a park, and protected, it would give a great number of people a deal of pleasure. I made up my mind that my small feelings and the feelings of a small number of people who felt as I did ought to be sacrificed for the good of the public, as they have been."[1]

When George Bird Grinnell wrote that letter in 1917, despairing of the crowds, approximately 18,000 visitors came to the park each year. In 2015, even with disruptive fires in August, more than 2 million visited the park! Running alongside that number was the announcement in June 2015 that the 100 millionth visitor since 1910 had entered the park.[2]

Today, Grinnell and Muir might have caught the next plane out. Louis Hill would throw up his hands at all the vacationers coming by automobile and airplane. Mather and Albright might have admired the Going-to-the-Sun Road while at the same time worrying whether they'd been too successful in promoting the automobile. The Roosevelts might well have worked the crowds at West Glacier or St. Mary's, hopefully giving a joint radio chat on the continuing relevancy of parks—particularly Glacier—and the immediate need to harness the ravages of global warming.

Those 2 million visitors are but an infinitesimal representative of the other 7 billion people on Earth, most of whom will never visit Glacier Park but are having and will have direct and indirect effects on practically every

aspect of Glacier's present and future. So many variables could and will confront Glacier that it's impossible to fashion silver-bullet solutions for one or
a number of the problems that are imminent or just over the horizon. All we
as owners of the shared treasures can do is recognize the issues and support
those who are charged with the tasks of attempting to stem the various tides
that threaten.

Unfortunately, one change appears to be unavoidable: the rapid melting
of the glaciers due to excessive warming from climate change that is the
fault of all of us. At the present rate of melting, the remaining twenty-five
glaciers (if there are twenty-five left) will vanish by 2030—give or take a
decade.[3] Only the onset of a new ice age could correct this calamity. Yet,
even as I write this chapter, most of the countries of the world are meeting
in Paris to attempt to hammer out meaningful solutions to correct our self-
inflicted abuses. No matter their results, they cannot save the glaciers in
Glacier National Park. Hopefully, their actions can salvage other diminishing ice sheets to keep large parts of the world populations from drowning
or burning in their own neglect. We can only hope that the urgency of the
mounting evidence can stem this literally growing tide.

To that end, the dramatic and rapid demise of the park's glaciers should
be held up as the "poster child" to the delegates. All the issues are in place:
dying glaciers, wildlife in adaptive motion, tinderbox forests, drier and longer warm seasons, and less snowpack with less moisture.

Fortunately, on the positive side, the National Park Service has long recognized the pending crisis and has for the last decade or so continuously
gone about making the case for solutions and alternatives within the system and without, in the broader national and local communities. As of this
writing, the director of the National Park Service, Jon Jarvis, is committed
to carrying the message and expanding the audience, particularly to those
young Americans of the next generation. It is a daunting task, but it is absolutely essential.

In no particular order because circumstance seems to change daily, chal-
lenges can be found at every level. Compounding the problem is the constant distracting chatter of our noisy world where media's talking-heads,
politicians, and demagogues drown out consequential thought and dis-
course.

For all their original thought and advocacy on the national stage, John
Muir, George Bird Grinnell, Stephen Mather, and even Franklin D. Roosevelt

had only a truly small audience and small number of decision makers to reach and convince in the mid-twentieth century.

Grinnell, for example, had to write to no more than a few hundred conservation-minded individuals, who would, in turn, solicit the support of their friends, fellow members, and elected officials. His *Forest and Stream* magazine was very influential, respected, and widely distributed, but, again, its subscription numbers would be dwarfed by today's e-blasts from causes and candidates.

Furthermore, even though opposition to these giants and others was present in the vanguard of the conservation movement, it was not answered by instantaneous political rhetoric and "news analysts," who seldom know what they are talking about. If it's climate change, they've been preprogrammed to be against solutions, even though glaciers are disappearing before our eyes.

Fortunately, a growing number of influential individuals and organizations within the media are fighting back with arguments and facts demonstrating the devastating consequences that are happening in real-time: islands and shorelines are disappearing; polar bears are becoming stranded on smaller and smaller ice floes; extreme, changing weather patterns are becoming commonplace; and, yes, the glaciers of Glacier National Park are fading toward extinction.

According to the *Washington Post*, "The glacier's [Grinnell's glacier] steep decline mirrors that of hundreds of other U.S. glaciers, from California's Sierra Nevada to the North Cascades to the Central Alaska Range. All are in retreat, yet nowhere are the effects so profoundly felt as in Glacier National Park, which experts say could be glacier-free by mid-century."[4]

Happily, standing behind those individuals and organizations is the positive attitude of the American people toward their parks. In a June 12, 2012, national public opinion survey commissioned by two highly respected and nonpartisan organizations, the National Parks Conservation Association and the National Park Hospitality Association, it was clear that our national parks are highly revered.

Ninety-five percent of voters in the national public opinion survey want the federal government to ensure parks are protected for our future. Eighty percent of American voters have visited at least one national park, and 90 percent hope to visit a park in the future. Ninety percent think that candidates who prioritize national parks are seen as caring for the environment,

FIGURE 10.1. Vice President Al Gore visits Grinnell Glacier in Glacier National Park, September 2, 1997. *Left to right*: Ranger Naturalist David Casteel, USGS Research Scientist Dr. Daniel Fagre, Vice President Al Gore. Courtesy of the White House; official White House photo number 02SEP97 PH VO15524-013.

are patriotic, and are good stewards of our natural resources. Seventy-seven percent feel that the next president (to be elected in the centennial year of the National Park Service) should ensure that parks are fully restored to be ready to serve all Americans (and visitors) in their second century.[5] This survey is reaffirmed by the Yale/George Mason 2015 Six Americas study on America's attitudes on climate change. Here, 72 percent were "much more" to "somewhat more likely" to vote for a pro-park presidential candidate as opposed to 32 percent who were "much less likely" to "somewhat less likely" to support that candidate.[6]

And the aforementioned 2012 survey went on to convey that 80 percent expressed concerns that funding shortages are damaging national parks. Conversely, few voters opined that appropriations should be cut for our parks.[7] This overwhelming support by American citizens is fortified by a number of recent studies on the economic benefits of our parks.

In a 2006 study, *The U.S. National Park System, an Economic Asset at Risk*, ample proof can be found that our parks generate at least $4 in value for every $1 invested. They also support $13.3 billion of local private-sector economic activity and 267,000 private-sector jobs. Furthermore, they attract businesses and individuals to local areas.[8]

Glacier National Park is a case study of one park and its contributions to the local economy. A 2013 survey showed that 2.2 million visitors to Glacier spent nearly $179 million in the communities near the park, which supported 2,824 jobs in the area as well as gasoline, lodging, sporting goods, and other businesses.[9]

On a personal note, I can attest to the findings of both the National Park Service public opinion and economic surveys. Throughout our fight in Texas for our state parks, we utilized polls and economic benefit studies to make our case that state parks not only had the broad and deep support among Texans of all political persuasions and demographic categories, but also that parks made sense at all levels: spiritual, mental, and physical well-being as well as in the pocketbook.

But even with these consistent demonstrations of significant support and benefit, it took a decade to convince the Texas Legislature to do the right thing. In 2015, they finally acted and gave Texas state parks not only a tremendous increase in funding but also made that funding permanent. All of this is to say that even with support of the people and positive economic benefits as proof, those dedicated advocates such as National Park Service Director Jon Jarvis, Superintendent Jeff Mow of Glacier Park, the entirety of the National Park Service, and its supporting organizations must continue to press the message over and over again. Parks must be repositioned as essential to our democracy and national shared pride.

It will not be easy, and results will not be immediate, but time is of the essence. Glacier is the perfect laboratory to make the local, national, and worldwide case for action. Again, it has dying glaciers, wildlife in adaptive motion, tinderbox forests, drier and warmer seasons, and less snowpack with less moisture. Add to that 2 million visitors annually, even with the real possibility of confronting raging wildfires, and all the ingredients for corrective measures and positive changes are there as opposed to unchecked catastrophes.

But even with the institutional commitment of the NPS system, its leaders, and support organizations such as the National Parks Conservation Association, the National Park Hospitality Association, the Sierra Club, and others, equally strong counterbalancing forces can and often do stymie change and scientific research. Even within the government itself, our parks are subject to the dictates and sometimes whims of three masters: the White House, Congress, and the Department of the Interior.

Even if two of these share in the commitment to inspire a new generation, reestablish a new national conservation ethic, and, perhaps, foster meaningful, breakthrough research, the other can apply the brakes or scuttle grand plans. To compound the challenge, it must be noted that the Department of the Interior is an agency that must attempt to plan and protect in perpetuity on an annual budget cycle. This can stifle, if not torpedo, long-term planning. It is no way to successfully run a business or an agency.

At the park level—in this case Glacier—the challenge of trying to address the future while planning and having to adjust to the immediate when the now is changing so rapidly is also a consideration. The year 2015 was a case in point. For most of the winter and spring, little to no snowpack or late rains harbingered dry conditions and fire potential for the upcoming summer at Glacier. In early June, tremendous rains fell, and the park leaders breathed easier. Then, not a drop of rain for two months; grasses, brush, and trees baked then totally dried out. In August, fires broke out in various areas of the park, including near and over the Going-to-the-Sun Road. Traffic and tourism were disrupted. The road closed, and choking smoke filled the valleys. Almost simultaneously, a remote area of fire threatened Highway 2 and the township of Essex, Montana, at the southern edge of the park. Evacuation was ordered, and, for a few days, the highway was closed.[10] When fires (or floods) threaten the entire park, planning and research are set aside or at least temporarily placed on hold until the dangers pass.

But there is less and less time to put research and planning on hold. The natural order, prompted by the unnatural, is rapidly changing, not just in Glacier National Park but also in entire ecosystems and beyond. Those changes, if left unchecked, will have dire consequences from the Yukon in Canada to the Missouri and Columbia River watersheds, which are the lifeblood of downstream farmers, ranchers, small towns, and great western cities. That would be a calamity in and of itself, but the same phenomenon is taking place throughout the American West. From the Rockies to the Cascades, rapidly melting and diminishing snowpack, coupled with longer periods of drought, is a menacing prospect for the future in an area that contains 40 to 50 million people who depend on water, 80 percent of which comes from the mountains.

All of these changes are why we as a nation must turn more of our attention to one of the remaining pristine and intact ecosystems—the "Crown of the Continent" ecosystem—of which Glacier National Park is at the center. The National Park Service Centennial is a window of opportunity. During the period of 2016 and the immediate years beyond, at least some additional attention will be paid to our nation's natural and historic treasures. Hopefully, those speeches, media events, ceremonies, and White House and congressional actions will also focus on the plight of our parks and the fact that we have within the system a park that remains a laboratory fully intact—at least for the moment.

What follows are a few of my thoughts and observations that have been developed over nearly fifty-five years of time spent in Glacier, brought into sharpened focus over the past two years of research and conversations for this book. From the geological actions that set in motion the formation of the mountains and glaciers to the men and women who heeded the call to preserve and then protect the landscapes that, by accident or grand design, are truly one of the few intact ecosystems remaining, there is an imperative to honor by action. Hopefully, time still remains to build on the research that is ongoing and then use the results of those findings to reserve or slow the threatening trends while giving additional proof to the voices for the future that there is, to paraphrase Wallace Stegner's monumental Wilderness Letter (1960), still remaining a landscape that can be a beacon for the "geography of hope."[11]

Glacier Park is not a designated Wilderness Area, but, fortunately, arising from a 1974 wilderness study prepared for Congress, 95 percent of the park was identified as qualifying for wilderness designation. Unfortunately, Glacier has not received congressional approval for full wilderness status. However, as mentioned previously, 93 percent of Glacier is managed as a wilderness under a directive from the National Park Service. That, combined with its designation as an International Peace Park, a Trans-Boundary Biosphere Reserve, a World Heritage Site, and the core of the Crown of the Continent ecosystem, has given it de facto status as wilderness. While not permanent, it is protection enough to allow it to continue to be an ecologically intact area. As a consequence, it truly remains a laboratory for the present and our future.

Because it has just been mentioned, I would hope that the good intentions and work set in motion in recent years to protect and sustain the Crown of the Continent ecosystem will be encouraged and enhanced. The ecological importance of this ecosystem cannot be overstated. The plants and animals within Glacier's 10-million-acre span remain unchanged since

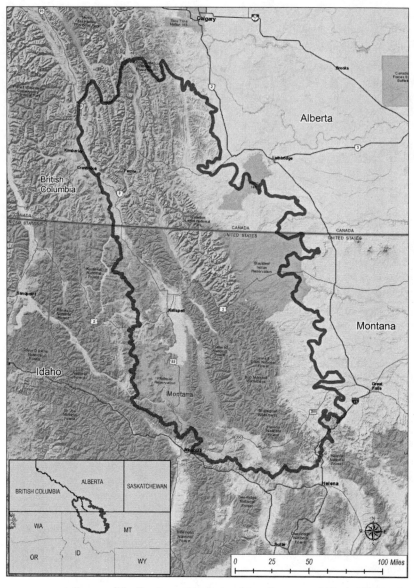

FIGURE 10.2. Crown of the Continent Ecosystem Map. Courtesy of Glacier National Park/U.S. National Park Service.

the explorations of Lewis and Clark. It harbors 71 species of native mammals, 276 species of birds, 27 native fish, and 12 species of reptiles and amphibians.[12] Glacier National Park, Waterton Lakes National Park, The Bob Marshall Wilderness, national forests, and the headwaters of three great rivers lie within the ecosystem's boundaries: the Columbia River flows to the west, the Mississippi River to the east, and the Saskatchewan River to the north.

The ecosystem is also vitally important to its human inhabitants. It is the home of two major Indian reservations: the Blackfeet to the east and the Confederated Salish and Kootenai Tribes to the west and south. It is also home to several million non–Native American humans, whose demand for more water, land, industry, and amenities (recreation) continues to escalate. Population increases in the system are some of the fastest growing in the United States. It is inevitable that the very reasons people seek the pleasures and peace of the mountains, rivers, valleys, and wildlife of the region are causing them to push up against and, in some cases, overwhelm the objects of those affections. The need to protect this rugged, yet vulnerable, ecosystem has never been greater.

It is recognized that this area is a mosaic of national, tribal, state or province, local, and private holdings and jurisdictions, all grounded in rules, regulations, and traditions that often are in conflict when it comes to cooperation and resolution for the common good. However, it is also recognized that those various agencies, landowners, and nongovernmental organizations (NGOs) have been and are continuing to seek answers and collaborative projects to compliment the whole of the ecosystem and beyond.

All of that is worthwhile and needs to be supported with additional research funding, cooperation at all levels, and publicity of the present circumstances and future consequences within and far beyond the ecosystem. Of these, it is my opinion that publicity on a scale that reaches beyond the immediate confines of the Crown of the Continent is most imperative.

And the time to strike is at hand. In the space of writing these last pages, the 196 countries meeting in Paris have reached a monumental accord to individually and collectively address the threats of climate change. That achievement can be complemented by the heightened awareness of the contributions of our national parks during the 2016 centennial of the National Park Service. Surely, the examples of Glacier National Park's ongoing research and planning can continue to be highlighted to demonstrate the need for immediate action to at least mitigate the circumstances which threaten to shut off water from Glacier's frozen reservoirs, extend and fuel more consuming forest fires, and cause flora and fauna to go extinct or move to higher and distant grounds. In fact, I am confident that by putting the straits of Glacier before those still-somewhat-doubtful sections of the population, even the naysayers will be moved to act on behalf of Glacier.

To be effective, that message must be sustained, sustainable, and global. It must be more than a passing admonition. It must reach into all corners of the world where greater glacier reservoirs are in retreat but might be saved or slowed by reversing the ominous trend lines.

At the same time, we must strive to extend the wonders of our parks and nature to younger generations. National Park Service Director Jon Jarvis and his successors must be supported to do everything within their power to reach those youths who by an early age become afflicted with "nature deficit disorder." (Research shows children today spend between seven to eleven hours per day indoors doing sedentary activities involving electronic media and spend only minutes per day outdoors playing in nature.) Adults are not far off that trend. Let one or more decades go by without meaningful reintroduction to a conservation ethic, and we will have a nature-ignorant America—indeed, world.

But there are always trade-offs that must be addressed. For example, I have long concluded that extending the opening and closing of the hotels and other visitor accommodations from early June to November might help alleviate the crush of visitors in the months of July and August. The period after Labor Day is a beautiful time in the park—a time that could be made attractive to seniors and young professionals. Fewer people are there at that time, and the autumn colors are spectacular. However, such increased visitation might run up against the final movements of grizzlies and other large animals as they prepare to hibernate. Nonetheless, such a solution should be considered, studied, and acted on.

These undertakings in the present and future should be amply funded in the United States by a Congress that needs to be reeducated on the benefits of nature and inspired by the national recommitment to perpetration of our best ideas. But given the present mood of Congress and the toxic noise that drives its determinations, we must turn to ourselves and those organizations and individuals who have historically given of themselves and their treasure in support of our parks.

Like the ongoing research, collaboration, and messaging that have been identified, much has been and is being done to encourage and enhance private philanthropy for the benefit of parks at the national and local levels. The National Park Foundation and the Glacier National Park Conservancy have played significant roles in supplementing programs and initiatives not covered by congressional appropriations, fees, or other revenues. In anticipation of the National Park Service centennial, the National Park Foundation has instituted, in partnership with the National Park Service, several major initiatives: an aggressive fundraising plan with an initial goal of $250 million, a national study of park philanthropy, and a companion study on the Total Impact Valuation of our parks.[13]

The results to date are comforting, if not surprising. The March 2016 Potrero Group study on park philanthropy found that National Park Service philanthropic organizations combined generate in excess of $300 million annually.[14] The National Park Foundation has played, and is continuing to play, a major role in promoting giving, not just through the foundation, but among all friends groups.

As proof of that renewal and enhanced dynamic, the National Park Foundation board of directors recently increased the Centennial Campaign goal from $350 million to $500 million. As of this writing, the foundation has some $355 million in hand or pledged.[15]

The joint Colorado State University and Harvard University study *Total Economic Valuation of National Park Land, Water, and Programs* (June 2016) found that those park lands, water, and historic sites were valued at $62 billion, and park programs account for some $30 billion in investment.[16]

Even Congress, to a degree, has joined in the spirit of the moment of the centennial, passing the Centennial Grants Program, the National Parks Commemorative Coin Program, and other funding solutions, all of which could bring in significant additional funding. There is a long way to go, but signs are encouraging. Comforting, but not surprising. Throughout our parks' history, Americans have supported our parks and have come to appreciate their value, not only in terms of dollars but also those connected to individual and national well-being. If Congress can continue to grow in the recognition of parks' worth and Americans' support of parks by huge majorities, the centennial will be more than a hundred-year celebration.

In the meantime, the Glacier Conservancy, in partnership with Glacier Park staff, has published a new "2017 Field Guide to Centennial Park Project

Priorities," which includes education, preservation, and research projects to ensure the highest and best use of private support and full leverage of federal dollars. Among them are a variety of projects aimed directly at the effects of climate change, including support for the Crown of the Continent ecosystem and Trans-Boundary Conservation initiatives. Given past performance and current status, there is every reason to anticipate those goals will be met or exceeded. In fact, the Conservancy board has recently raised its budget goals from $1.1 million in 2015 to $2 million for the 2016–2017 fiscal year![17]

But no matter the level of successes, there will be continuing need for private philanthropy. And that poses two questions that are often raised: Why private philanthropy at all? Isn't this the responsibility of the national government?

The simple answer is that the needs of our parks have historically exceeded the willingness of Congress (or state and local elected bodies) to appropriate funds. It was true with the first park—Yellowstone—and it is a compounded truth today. But a deeper reason flows to the very core of Teddy Roosevelt's "essential democracy."

In an undated tract, Freeman Tilden of the National Park Service wrote a thoughtful piece for the predecessor to the National Park Foundation, the National Park Trust Fund, titled *The Fifth Essence*. His premise was that after the early Greek philosophers decided there were four elements, or essences—fire, air, water, and earth—they began to perceive there was something else: a soul of the elements—"behind the thing seen must lie the greater thing unseen"—the fifth essence.

Tilden went on to explain that each individual could find this essence in his or her own backyard, but the "consummate expression of this ultimate wealth of the human spirit can be found in the National Park System."[18] Over the years, I have thought much about this and have come forth with some thoughts on Tilden's musings.

It does not matter which park you are considering within the system. From the great western panoramas to the silent sites of our American struggles, each carries with it a spiritual element of the American story about the places through which our ancestors passed until culminating in those unique triangulations of the present—you and me. So when we stand at those awesome vistas next to the silent guns or, yes, at cliff dwellings of people who came long ago and disappeared before modern man set foot on this continent, we are at once looking into the face of the past, the mirror of our present, and an absolute necessity for our future.

In doing so, we need to contemplate that greater thing unseen and ask ourselves how we can be a part of the "first essential" in protecting this ultimate wealth of the human spirit. To not do so will ensure that this most original American idea will have a diminished future. In turn, our children and their children will be a diminished people. For the national parks, like all great institutions, require the dedicated commitment of each and every citizen if they are to be more than distant objects without soul or relevant meaning.

From the outset, men and women recognized this remarkable responsibility and went about ensuring these places would be saved for visitation, contemplation, and inspiration for future generations. In many instances, they paid for the lands out of their own pockets or deeded over to the government lands already owned. Indeed, the early explorers and advocates of Yellowstone—our first national park—banded together to preserve and protect that incredible area by ensuring the land went to the government and then championing national park status to protect its wondrous natural gifts rather than buying it up and exploiting it for personal use.

That has continued without abatement since 1872. We Americans are a generous people. From church to exploration, from museums to medical research, we find ways to find an extra dollar to donate to worthy causes. That is as it should be! Our form of governance and interdependence requires citizen participation—at the ballot box and the collection plate. That generosity has often reached spectacular heights when it comes to our national parks. One family, the Rockefellers, has been instrumental in helping create or preserve many of our national treasures, including the Grand Tetons, Great Smoky Mountains, Acadia, the Blue Ridge Parkway, and the Virgin Islands National Parks. Laurance Rockefeller was the embodiment of that grand tradition, continuing to think of and give to us gifts of parks up until his death in 2004.

Yet the Rockefellers are but one among many families and individuals who have recognized the importance of private philanthropy as a means to initiate or continue the preservation of our most cherished natural and historical possessions. The Mellon family has contributed greatly to the creation of many of our national seashores. The Roosevelt Memorial Association donated Theodore Roosevelt Island. In California, the Muir Woods were given by Congressman William Kent and his wife. Many foundations, corporations, and individuals contributed to the rehabilitation of the Statue of Liberty and restoration of Ellis Island's Great Hall. Those generosities are matched yearly by other gifts in every park. Perhaps not all are great in financial or even monetary terms but are just as important. Surely, a volunteer trail crew worker is every bit as important as the gifts of the Rockefellers. For what good are Glacier's trails if they are allowed to fall into disrepair or unsightliness? There is room for every citizen to support the park(s) of his or her choice. In fact, that is a necessity regardless of whether or not there is an unending flow of generosity from major benefactors or congressional appropriations.

Because the first essential of the fifth essence is that every citizen does more than dutifully pay taxes and pray that some small part will support the parks. Just the name alone should be prompting enough — The National Parks. They are not just government's properties, although, I must say, the National Park Service is staffed with dedicated people who have done us great service over the years since its creation. They are our parks.

Thus, the ultimate gifts of the first essential cannot be measured or sustained by sterile numbers on a balance sheet or the generous support of others. Every citizen must approach them with the thought that those who have given in the past did so for the benefit of the present, and, in turn, those who will stand in your place at some future time will be able to sense that behind the thing seen, you, through your generosity of self and means, became part of the greater thing unseen, forever present.

All of this is to say we have a national imperative — indeed a global imperative — to reverse the damage we have caused in the last century or so to a work of natural artistry which has been in progress for a billion-plus years. To quote Dan Fagre of the U.S. Geological Survey, "It is a moral issue, not a scientific one. Science is like the navigator of a ship. It can point the way. It can enlighten people on the direction to take. That is all. The crew has to do the heavy lifting out of some sense of responsibility. If we are enlightened, the way forward becomes obvious. To halt climate change, we will have to rely on the better angels of human nature."[19]

Throughout the history of Glacier, we have had the giants of Earth and humankind as our better angels to form and then protect and preserve a landscape that is the epitome of the "geography of hope." We must summon from within our own better angels to ensure that those who will come after we have gone can see and then sense the greater unseen. In doing so, we will have collectively assumed the role of those giants who came before and laid the groundwork. We are the culmination of Stephen Mather's vision. We are the visitor advocates that he foresaw, and we must become the next wave of giants.

In the meantime, the Glacier National Park of today waits to inspire renewal and discovery of the visual and unseen with the realization that the main thing is greater than the whole thing. In doing so, note and hold National Park Service Director Jon Jarvis's most simple and direct call to action: "We are in the forever business."[20]

NOTES

1. George Bird Grinnell, "Letter to Lawrence O. Vaught," George Bird Grinnell to Lawrence O. Vaught, 1917, Lawrence O. Vaught Papers: File Unit 82: Correspondence, George Bird Grinnell: Glacier National Park Archives, Montana.

2. Vince Devlin, "Glacier National Park Welcomes 100 Millionth Visitor: '#WINNER,'" *Missoulian*, June 11, 2015, accessed August 30, 2016, http://missoulian.com/news/local/glacier-national-park-welcomes-millionth-visitor-winner/article_9692204b-8804-544d-8d5d-818 93cb54d24.html.

3. National Park Service, "Glaciers," National Park Service, accessed August 30, 2016, https://www.nps.gov/glac/learn/education/glaciers.htm.

4. Joby Warrick, "The Great Thaw: As Temperatures Rise, Many American Glaciers Could Vanish in a Few Decades," *Washington Post*, November 26, 2015, accessed August 30, 2016, http://www.washingtonpost.com/sf/national/2015/11/26/ice-worlds/.

5. Amy Hagovsky, "New Poll of Likely Voters Finds Unity in Public Support for National Parks," National Parks Conservation Association, August 7, 2012, accessed November 26, 2015, https://www.npca.org/articles/693-new-poll-of-likely-voters-finds-unity-in-public-support-for-national-parks.

6. Connie Roser-Renouf et al., "Global Warming's Six Americas' Perceptions of the Health Risks," Yale Program on Climate Change Communication, March 16, 2015, accessed February 20, 2016, http://climatecommunication.yale.edu/publications/global-warmings-six-americas-perceptions-of-the-health-risks/.

7. Hagovsky, "New Poll of Likely Voters Finds Unity in Public Support for National Parks."

8. Jared Hardner and Bruce McKenney, "The U.S. National Park System: An Economic Asset at Risk," National Parks Conservation Association, May 30, 2006, accessed February 20, 2016, https://www.npca.org/resources/1109-the-u-s-national-park-system-an-economic-asset-at-risk.

9. Denise Germann, "Glacier Creates $179 Million in Economic Benefit," National Park Service, July 21, 2014, accessed July 21, 2014, https://www.nps.gov/glac/learn/news/glacier-creates-179-million-in-economic-benefit.htm.

10. Tia Troy, "Reynolds Creek Fire Update: Montana's Glacier National Park," Glacier Country Montana, July 23, 2015, accessed August 7, 2016, https://glaciermt.com/blog/reynolds-creek-fire-update-montanas-glacier-national-park/.

11. Wilderness Society, "Wallace Stegner," The Wilderness Society, accessed August 7, 2016, http://wilderness.org/bios/former-council-members/wallace-stegner.

12. National Park Service, "Glacier National Park: Fact Sheet," National Park Service, accessed September 16, 2015, http://www.nps.gov/glac/learn/news/fact-sheet.htm.

13. Will Shafroth, "Your Book Chapter Review," e-mail, July 29, 2016.

14. Potrero Group, *National Park Partners: Status and Trends*, report (National Park Foundation, 2016).

15. Shafroth, "Your Book Chapter Review."

16. Michelle Haefele, John Loomis, and Linda J. Bilmes, *Total Economic Valuation of the National Park Service Lands and Programs: Results of a Survey of the American Public*, report, Colorado State University and Harvard University (2016), 3.

17. Nikki Eisinger, "Glacier National Park Conservancy Interview," telephone interview by author, August 11, 2016.

18. George Robinson, "Biographical Vignettes: Freeman Tilden, 1883–1980," National Park Service, December 1, 2000, accessed August 7, 2016, https://www.nps.gov/parkhistory/online_books/sontag/tilden.htm.

19. Christopher P. White, *The Melting World: A Journey Across America's Vanishing Glaciers* (New York, NY: St. Martin's Press, 2013), 257.

20. Will Shafroth, "Jon Jarvis Quote," e-mail, August 7, 2016.

CHAPTER ELEVEN

The Main Thing
Is the Whole Thing

In one sense, it is the whole thing that makes Glacier the "Crown of the Continent," but the whole thing is divided into a number of main things, all of which could stand alone as a national park. That is a problem but also an opportunity. Few American or foreign visitors have the time or inclination to witness all of the parts in full or even in part. Therefore, they should be prepared to visit more than once.

The first time should take the form of a general scouting mission. If that is all the time to be had, so be it. But if there is room to return, come with a plan to open yourself to all you can witness in a few days, and, when possible, stop a while and let the landscape pull you in. For in a day within a season, those landscapes can change, taking on different colorations during various times of the day or at the whims of weather. A summer afternoon storm in Swiftcurrent Valley can wrap mountains that moments before sparkled in sky-blue sunlight into cloud-shrouded ghosts, occasionally lit by lightning. And at the end of its drama, the storm can encircle the peaks of Grinnell and Wilbur in a rainbow that causes viewers to forego having to search for its gold. Those peaks or others to the left or right wreathed in a crown of colors are treasure enough to last a lifetime.

In that split second of nature's sleight of hand, perhaps enough magic will draw you deeper into the mystery. Enough to make you stand an hour longer, rise earlier the next day to see what newness is revealed, forgoing morning lecture and then vowing to return.

While I have borne witness for fifty-plus years, I have not shared the whole of the thing or even something of all the parts. I will die with some grand detail left for others to experience and explain. But perhaps I can share enough of the main things to give the reader a sense of the natural magic that drew Grinnell, the Hills, others, and me into its parts that became surrogates for the whole.

Surely, if you only drive through or around the park, you will see the giants of the earth and their handiwork. Without effort, the mountains will be shoved and carved into shape by those forces unleashed so long ago. From the east side of the Going-to-the-Sun Road, Jackson and Blackfeet glaciers can, even in their diminished state, be seen. Or driving up the Swiftcurrent Valley toward the Many Glacier Hotel, the Salamander Glacier hangs from the Garden Wall, and looking up and to the left from Swiftcurrent Lake, Gem Glacier can be spotted atop Mount Gould. From here, if you can force your-self to stand in place long enough to drink in the scenery, you can find those telltale layers formed in the Belt Sea then thrust up and over the younger formations, and, in an instant, you can be transformed back 1.6 billion years. Without moving your feet, you can cast your eyes along the mountainsides rising up from the Swiftcurrent Road to perhaps spot a grizzly bear with cubs or bighorn sheep—though rarely at the same time or in the same space. Or maybe a bald eagle will float past your line of sight. Whatever magnificence you have come to witness will more than likely be enhanced by smaller players moving across the natural stages of Glacier.

It is here, without great detail, that I want to share some of those lesser players that give the grand things character, color, and texture. And I will do so from personal experience and observations. For regardless of the fact that I have not witnessed the entirety of the whole, I have, over my fifty-plus years of exploration, seen enough of the parts to comprehend the main thing.

Even though it is in the farthest northwest corner of one of our northern states, as mentioned previously, Glacier is home to more than 276 species of birds, 27 native and non-native species of fish, 71 species of mammals, and 1,132 varieties of plants as well as 855 species of mosses and lichens.[1] Something is moving and flying in every season, although winter has to be taken for its breathtaking solitude with an occasional stirring or startling to flight.

All are interesting in and of themselves (although some are so remotely located and secretive that they are hard to find), but together they give the park extra dimension. Once upon a time, when I began to go to Glacier in the autumn, I saw a phenomenon so spectacular that the usual October silence of McDonald Creek below Lake McDonald turned into a parking lot of observers who were there to watch some three hundred to four hundred bald eagles feed on kokanee salmon. It was a sight so exciting that visitors from as far away as Europe and Asia heard about the annual phenomenon and came to view for themselves the eagles diving from frosted tree limbs into the creek and returning with a fish. For as long as my family and I wished to stay, mature and young eagles would ply their trade. Sometimes, the young would sink their talons in more than they could lift. Only after a struggle would they disconnect. Occasionally, death would occur when the hooks were sunk too deep and the eagle was dragged under the water.

I point out this scene as much for the origins and unintended consequences as the moment of its happening. The kokanee were artificially introduced into Flathead Lake and River in 1916. Immediately, they displaced the population of cutthroat trout. Eagles took note and began to gather along McDonald Creek where the salmon came to spawn. By 1981, more than six hundred eagles were feeding on upwards of 100,000 salmon annually. Unfortunately, another unnatural occurrence was introduced that destroyed the kokanee population. Mysis shrimp were imported into the waterways in the 1950s. By 1981, they had become a deadly competitor for the salmons' zooplankton food source, and by the next year, the salmon population crashed. The eagles again took note of the vastly diminished count and left or overflew the area. What was most interesting to me is how did the eagles that, according to some accounts, ranged down to the southwestern United States and into Canada communicate the salmon catastrophe in a year's time? What is also noteworthy is how swift and total the devastation was. For sixty-odd years, man, bears, and eagles had fished the salmon without making a dent in their population. In twenty years or so, the small shrimp destroyed the kokanee.

While this catastrophe was occurring, another imbalance took place: the non-native lake trout began to displace the native bull trout. Today, some thirty years later, these non-native species introductions, whether planned or accidental, have wreaked havoc on the ecosystems. To combat the total destruction of the native bull trout, the park service has had to resort to non-natural artificial methods to thwart the advance of the lake trout into Glacier's waters. Perhaps in the not-too-distant future, humankind will wake up and understand that nature in its wildest form worked for billions of years to perfect the balance of the natural order and basically had it right by the time we came along to muck it up.

Be that as it may, eagles and osprey are still poised above the rivers, lakes, and streams, waiting for the shadows in the flow to ripple past. And in that moment, a spread of wings, a prong of talons, and a gliding flight path toward the unsuspecting prey are set in motion.

With little exploration, some of the more likely places for eagle and osprey viewing can be ascertained from locals and park personnel. Live "critter cameras" even allow wildlife enthusiasts from afar to enjoy the nesting, hatching, feeding, and first flights of some of the birds of prey in Glacier.

But if you want to come closer to witnessing a number of the parts of the whole, I suggest a float trip down the North Fork of the Flathead River—a designated Wild and Scenic river. From this vantage point, mountains can be viewed to the east, water flows over timeless rocks, shelves, and boulders shaped by the flow and silt from glacier runoff, and all manner of possibilities can be seen among the animals and birds, including eagles and osprey.

As I often do, once spotted, I ask the boat guide to back-paddle and hold with the hope of seeing piercing eyes and wings and talons lift off a branch, ready to gather in the next meal. And in that split second when bird, fish, river, and mountains topped by snow-white then blue merge, you will begin to sense the whole thing.

In most years, the Trail of the Cedars that joins the Avalanche Lake Trail is my family's favorite warm-up hike. The short one-mile trail with boardwalks for the first stretch connects with a paved section that loops back to the Going-to-the-Sun Road. Within its short stretch is one of the most peaceful strolls that still gives the observer a sense of timelessness. By entering on the east side of the trail, one is immediately met by towering western hemlock, red cedars, and cottonwoods. These giant trees and complementing ferns and mosses produce a rainforest that should by all circumstances be found farther west, specifically along the Pacific Coast.

Here again, a small twist of nature has added to the variety of the whole thing. These trees and plants stand on the easternmost edge of the maritime climate of the Pacific Northwest. This moisture encapsulation allows the cedars and hemlocks to grow to heights of 100 feet and some to live past five hundred years. Their location, tucked in between mountains along with the high moisture content, has also protected them from fires over the centuries.

If the short stroll is a complete natural sentence, Avalanche Gorge is an ending exclamation point. For most of the summer months, the snowmelt flows from Sperry Glacier, tumbling down waterfalls into Avalanche Lake, then Avalanche Creek, and finally compresses into the Gorge's narrow passage. There, in a very confined space, a thunderous scene of white water and rock carving occurs. Standing on the bridge looking into the cut, one can almost become hypnotized watching the water splash and smash through the narrow opening of the long-polished rocks. If time or circumstance prevents further exploration, take the paved path out to the road, but if possible, hike on to Avalanche Lake. It's an easy 1.6-mile walk past the upper Gorge, through old growth forests, ending at the mountain-encased Avalanche Lake where you can stand for a minute, an hour, or a day, watching the multiple waterfalls leap from the mountain rim. When facing the lake looking left and up, try to locate mountain goats performing what looks to be a death-defying balancing act on the cliffs.

While most visitors choose summer to visit Glacier, I prefer the fall. The reasons are numerous. There are few crowds. Wildlife is moving about in preparation for winter. With luck, snow powder can be seen on the peaks, the skies are autumn blue, and the yellow, orange, and red colors of fall abound.

A word of caution is needed here. There is, depending on the weather, a narrow window of opportunity. If early snows do not hinder road travel, the Going-to-the-Sun Road is open to Logan Pass until mid-October or early November. And it is to Logan Pass during this time you will want to go.

Simply stepping out of the car onto the visitor center parking lot in the fall is an experience I hate to miss. Off in every direction, mountains roll away toward Canada to the north and St. Mary's Lake and Valley to the east and rise in various glacier-shaped formations to the south and east. Mount Clements, the Garden Wall, Mount Oberlin, Mount Reynolds, Heavy Runner, and Bearhat mountains dominate the scenery in every direction. Among them are all the works of glaciers: arêtes, horns, cirques, hanging gardens, and U-shaped valleys. One alpine meadow surrounds the visitor center and trail. Perhaps it was here that Bill Gilbert found his inspiration to exclaim that the "main thing is the whole thing!"[2]

To me, every step of the trail leading to the Hidden Lake Overlook and then down into Hidden Lake is an affirmation of that observation. But like all other areas of the park, the small (and not so small) things also give the area added value. With my preference for autumn, one trade-off must be noted. It is a trade-off to the benefit of summer visitors. After snowmelt and throughout the summer, the hanging meadows are filled with wildflowers in an array of colors, and if the summer is the only chance to visit, the visitor will not notice that a trade has been made. The only problem is that they must share the parking lot and trail with hundreds of daily visitors—so come early in the day or stay for the evening light.

That aside, I opt for October. Down from the parking lot and across the road, mountain goats and bighorn sheep move about with little fear of humans. Up the trail, chipmunks scurry about, and hoary marmots bask in the sun. Off in the meadows—hopefully far enough away—a grizzly may be rooting around for a few extra pounds of bulbs before hibernating.

The entire hike to the overlook is an easy 1.3 miles. Near the top, particularly if there is a blanket of snow, begin to look off the trail among the crags for a most remarkable bird—the ptarmigan. The ptarmigan is a member of the grouse family that changes color with the season, grayish brown in summer to white in the winter. On more than one occasion, I've been startled by a mound of snow hurrying away as I approach.

If the timing is right, at the top in and around the overlook, mountain goats in their new winter coats of white move about, seemingly at ease with human intruders. As winter begins to set in, they will move farther down into the protection of Hidden Lake's glacier-carved depression, capped by Bearhat Mountain. Here again is one of those sites that offer up another dimension to the whole thing.

On the way back down the trail, stop for a while and take in all before you. In autumn, the season I have come to love, all things are beginning to slow, even as critters hurry about in anticipation of winter. It will be most rewarding to take your time coming off the top of the Continental Divide.

Although I have come to prefer autumn, I cannot turn my back on the other seasons of Glacier. Because I worked on the trail crew in the Many Glacier/Swiftcurrent Valley in 1961 and 1962, I will always have time for summer. Having made that exception, let me say that all seasons are rewarding in Glacier, although the dead of winter often prohibits entrance and exploration. But from May through November, there's awesome bounty to be experienced, weather permitting.

Although crowded, summer offers a riot of wildflowers along the road that follows Swiftcurrent Creek, then Lake Sherburne (actually a reservoir). From moment to moment, glimpses of mountains and waterfalls begin to reveal themselves until, rounding a bend, the panorama of massive mountains, lakes, waterfalls, and glaciers comes into full view. And with each turn or hill topping, something new presents itself. In early summer, bighorn sheep may be close by. In late summer, grizzly and black bears work the slopes, feeding on huckleberries. At road's end, within the walled confines, are all parts of Glacier's whole: the Belt formations, glaciers, sparkling lakes, an assortment of wildlife, and mountains sculpted into many of the recognized shapes.

To accommodate the visitor's need to explore these wonders, hiking trails fan out in all directions to Grinnell Glacier, Iceberg Lake, Ptarmigan Tunnel, and Swiftcurrent Pass, which leads to the top of the Garden Wall into Granite Park, where a hardy soul can hike out along the Highline Trail down to Logan Pass.

But even if confined to the lobby and porches of the Many Glacier Hotel, there's the satisfaction of sights in all directions. Perhaps a young moose will add to the moment, feeding across Swiftcurrent Lake along the alder-cluttered shoreline. A grizzly sow and cub might meander above the road in search of berries, while small chipmunks scamper from person to person in search of a handout.

If overnighting at the hotel, Swiftcurrent Motor Lodge, or in the campground, wake before sunrise and seek a place to view the mountains surrounding the lake as the alpenglow dawn paints the mountain faces in copper-gold. And if that is all that is allowed, it will be enough to satisfy. But there is the autumn when most visitors have gone. In that time of solitude, the first hints of winter's onset begin to creep into the forests and lakes and mountains. Perhaps the first sign is an early snowfall that covers the Garden Wall with a powdered-sugar blanket. Waterfalls become whispers, and aspen and larch begin to break out in brilliant colors against the arriving white crowned in blue.

Here again, if one will take the time to stand, listen, and observe, you will sense the flora and fauna of Glacier National Park shutting down for winter. But the shutting down period of mid-September through October is a crescendo of color that holds back the gray-white of winter. For those thirty days or so, nature is at its best, giving observers the opportunity to find solitude, even as their hearts race with the gladness of blues and golds.

FIGURE 11.1. Mountain goat on Sperry Trail,
1982. Courtesy of George Bristol; George Bristol
photo collection; George Bristol, photographer.

This chapter could go on through hundreds of locations and thousands of individual vistas, but, hopefully, it is enough to interest while trying to explain Glacier's essence within that sets it apart from the other grand experiences offered by other national parks.

Yet for all my years of discovery, I have never fully found an end to that exploration. Every part of the whole has meaning, and even those can change with weather, season, or time of day. Thus, I can only conclude that the main thing is the whole thing that visitors witness at a single moment. Then, as they move toward another rounding of a bend on road or trail, something different appears, and the reward experienced only moments before is renewed.

Perhaps the uniqueness of Glacier National Park is that there is no end to its diversity. And thus, any time spent, be it a day, a year, or lifetime, is the main thing—without ever knowing the entirety of the whole. After a near-lifetime of searching, I also have concluded it is not necessary. There is enough in the parts to make you whole.

But come—and come soon. Glacier National Park is changing, as it has for nearly a billion-plus years. And do not fret about the main thing or the whole thing. Again, to quote John Muir, "When we try to pick out anything itself, we find it is hitched to everything else in the universe."[3]

NOTES

1. National Park Service, "Glacier National Park: Fact Sheet," National Park Service, accessed September 16, 2015, http://www.nps.gov/glac/learn/news/fact-sheet.htm.

2. National Park Service. "Glacier National Park Press Kit: Glacier National Park and Other NPS Quotes," National Park Service, accessed April 22, 2015, http://www.nps.gov/glac/learn/news/upload/press_quotes.pdf.

3. Sierra Club, "Quotations from John Muir," The John Muir Exhibit, accessed September 1, 2016, http://vault.sierraclub.org/john_muir_exhibit/writings/favorite_quotations.aspx.

Franklin D. Roosevelt Radio Address from Two Medicine Chalet, Glacier National Park

August 5, 1934

I have been back on the soil of the continental United States for three days after most interesting visits to our fellow Americans in Puerto Rico, the Virgin Islands, the Canal Zone and the Territory of Hawaii. I return with the conviction that their problems are essentially similar to those of us who live on the mainland and, furthermore, that they are enthusiastically doing their part to improve their conditions of life and thereby the conditions of life of all Americans.

On Friday and Saturday I had the opportunity of seeing the actual construction work under way in the first two national projects for the development of the Columbia River Basin. At Bonneville, Oregon, a great dam, 140 miles inland, at the last place where the river leaps down over rapids to sea level, will provide not only a large development of cheap power but also will enable vessels to proceed another 70 or 80 miles into the interior of the country.

At Grand Coulee, in north central Washington, an even greater dam will regulate the flow of the Columbia River, developing power and, in the future, will open up a large tract of parched land for the benefit of this and future generations. Many families in the days to come, I am confident, will thank us of this generation for providing small farms on which they will at least be able to make an honest and honorable livelihood.

Today, for the first time in my life, I have seen Glacier Park. Perhaps I can best express to you my thrill and delight by saying that I wish every American, old and young, could have been with me today. The great mountains, the glaciers, the lakes and the trees make me long to stay here for all the rest of the summer.

Comparisons are generally objectionable and yet it is not unkind to say from the standpoint of scenery alone that if many and indeed most of our American national parks were to be set down anywhere on the continent of Europe thousands of Americans would journey all the way across the ocean in order to see their beauties.

There is nothing so American as our national parks. The scenery and wild life are native and the fundamental idea behind the parks is native. It is, in brief, that the country belongs to the people; that what it is and what it is in the process of making is for the enrichment of the lives of all of us. Thus the parks stand as the outward symbol of this great human principle.

It was on a famous night, 64 years ago, that a group of men who had been exploring the Yellowstone country gathered about a campfire to discuss what could be done with that wonderland of beauty. It is said that one of the party, a lawyer from the State of Montana, Cornelius Hedges, advanced the idea that the region might be preserved for all time as a national park for the benefit of all the people of the Nation. As a result of that suggestion, Yellowstone National Park was established in 1872 by Act of Congress as a "pleasuring ground" for the people. I like that phrase because, in the years that have followed, our great series of parks in every part of the Union have become indeed a "pleasuring ground" for millions of Americans.

My old friend, Franklin K. Lane, Secretary of the Interior in the Wilson Administration, well described the policies governing the national park administration when he said:

"The policy to which the Service will adhere is based on three broad principles: First, that the national parks must be maintained in absolutely unimpaired form for the use of future generations as well as those of our own time; second, that they are set apart for the use, observation, health and pleasure of the people; and, third, that the national interest must dictate all decisions affecting public or private enterprise in the parks."

The present National Park Service stands as an example of efficient and far-seeing governmental administration and to its former duties I added last year by transferring from other departments many other parks, battlefield sites, memorials and national monuments. This concentration of responsibility has thus made it possible to embark on a permanent park policy as a great recreational and educational project—one which no other country in the world has ever undertaken in such a broad way for protection of its natural and historic treasures and for the enjoyment of them by vast numbers of people. Today I have seen some of the work of the Civilian Conservation Corps boys in this Northwestern country. Of the 300,000 young men in these Camps, 75,000 are at work in our national parks. Here, under trained leadership, we are helping these men to help themselves and their families and at the same time we are making the parks more available and more useful for the average citizen. Hundreds of miles of firebreaks have been built, fire hazards have been reduced on great tracts of timberland, thousands of miles of roadside have been cleared, 2,500 miles of trails have been constructed and 10,000 acres have been reforested. Other tens of thousands of acres have been treated for tree disease and soil erosion. This is but another example of our efforts to build not for today alone, but for tomorrow as well.

We should remember that the development of our national park system over a period of many years has not been a simple bed of roses. As is the case in the long fight for the preservation of national forests and water power and mineral deposits and other national possessions, it has been a long and fierce fight against many private interests which were entrenched in political and economic power. So, too, it has been a constant struggle to continue to protect the public interest, once it was saved from private exploitation at the hands of the selfish few.

It took a bitter struggle to teach the country at large that our national resources are not inexhaustible and that, when public domain is stolen, a twofold injury is done, for it is a theft of the treasure of the present and at the same time bars the road of opportunity to the future.

We have won the greater part of the fight to obtain and to retain these great public park properties for the benefit of the public. We are at the threshold of an even more important battle to save our resources of agriculture and industry from the selfishness of individuals.

The Secretary of the Interior in 1933 announced that this year of 1934 was to be emphasized as "National Parks Year." I am glad to say that there has been a magnificent response and that the number visiting our national parks has shown a splendid increase. But I decided today that every year ought to be "National Parks Year." That is why, with all the earnestness at my command, I express to you the hope that each and every one of you who can possibly find the means and opportunity for so doing will visit our national parks and use them as they are intended to be used. They are not for the rich alone. Camping is free, the sanitation is excellent. You will find them in every part of the Union. You will find glorious scenery of every character;

you will find every climate; you will perform the double function of enjoying much and learning much.

We are definitely in an era of building, the best kind of building—the building of great public projects for the benefit of the public and with the definite objective of building human happiness.

I believe, too, that we are building a better comprehension of our national needs. People understand, as never before, the splendid public purpose that underlies the development of great power sites, the improving of navigation, the prevention of floods and of the erosion of our agricultural fields, the prevention of forest fires, the diversification of farming and the distribution of industry. We know, more and more, that the East has a stake in the West and the West has a stake in the East, that the Nation must and shall be considered as a whole and not as an aggregation of disjointed groups.

May we come better to know every part of our great heritage in the days to come.

Source: Franklin D. Roosevelt, "Franklin D. Roosevelt: Radio Address from Two Medicine Chalet, Glacier National Park." The American Presidency Project, August 5, 1934. Accessed September 18, 2014, http://www.presidency.ucsb.edu/ws/?pid=14733.

Report of Presidential Visit to Glacier National Park

Department of the Interior
National Park Service
Glacier National Park
Belton, Montana
August 11, 1934

For more than a month before the President was due to visit Glacier National Park, preparations were under way here to accommodate not only the Presidential party but also the hundreds of persons who were expected to visit the park—and the villages of Belton and Glacier Park—that day. In both instances foresight proved to be of extreme value and both the crowds and the special party were handled without the slightest hitch occurring.

On June 26 Colonel Ed Starling of the White House secret service detail visited the park for the first time to go over the President's route here and make preliminary arrangements. Colonel Starling was taken on the journey here by Superintendent E. T. Scoyen accompanied by Chief Ranger T. E. Whitcraft, A. A. Aszmann, Manager of the Glacier Park Hotel Company; Howard H. Hays, president of the Park Transport Company and Fred A. Noble, manager of the Transport Company. At Glacier Park station Secret Service Agent A. N. Becktel of the Seattle office was picked up and he returned to Belton with the party. Plans for the protection of the Presidential party were discussed and preliminary arrangements made. Again on July 29 Colonel Starling visited the park for a final checkup before the day of the President's arrival. He was accompanied on this trip by Mr. Scoyen, Mr. Hays, Mr. Noble, Mr. Whitcraft, Park Naturalist G. C. Ruhle, Park Engineer Ira S. Stinson and O. J. McGillis, general advertising agent of the Great Northern Railway. Colonel Starling held several conferences with the above officials and again went over the route to be taken by the President on August 5.

In preparation for the visit, various physical improvements had to be effected and those projects were handled by the National Park Service engineering forces, the Glacier Park Hotel Company and the Park Transport Company. Ramps were built at Belton, Going-to-the-Sun, Many Glacier and Two Medicine in order to facilitate walking for the President. At Going-to-the-Sun chalet a small road was built down to the lower chalets so it would not be necessary for the President to leave his car in order to enjoy the beauty of that spot. At Belton, Many Glacier and Two Medicine approximately nineteen miles of road were oiled and repairs made on portions of the previous oiling which had become rough from constant use. Along the east side of Logan Pass there is approximately fifteen miles of roadway which is graveled but not oiled, the roadbed was sprinkled with water in order to keep down the dust. Sprinkling operations started Friday evening and were kept up day and night until Sunday morning shortly before the Presidential party passed over that section. Throughout the length of Going-to-the-Sun highway crews of Civilian Conservation Corps workers from the various camps in the park were employed in clearing hazards from the sides of the highway for some time in advance of the Presidential visit. Dead trees, snags, fallen timber, rocks and other hazards were removed. The timber was placed in piles to be burned later in the year. At Belton the park engineering department erected a series of posts through which ropes were strung. These posts were set parallel to the siding where the Presidential special drew in and in this manner the crowds were kept back a short distance from the train. Also at the Belton parking area, several National Park Service pumps were employed all day Saturday and until early on Sunday morning in pumping water from the river to be sprinkled over the parking area. By this means the fire hazard was reduced as the field was covered with long, dry grass, and the dust was kept down as much as possible.

For protection of the Presidential party in the park and to facilitate its swift and uninterrupted passage, various measures were adopted. Registration stations at Belton and St. Mary remained open all of the night of August 4, tunnels on the highway were guarded for 24 hours preceding the tour, the chalet at Two Medicine was guarded for a like period as was his room at Many Glacier hotel. At Belton headquarters the fourteen automobiles used by the Glacier Park Transport Company to transport the Presidential party through the park were guarded for 12 hours preceding their use.

For communication purposes in order to expedite the party on its trip, short wave radiotelephones were installed temporarily at Logan Pass, Babb and the Browning wye. By use of these radios and the sets previously installed at other vantage points—such as Belton, St. Mary's and Many Glacier—progress of the party was reported in advance and traffic stoppages were effected far enough ahead of the party in order to effectively clear the road for it. A detailed traffic control program was worked out in advance by Chief Ranger T. E. Whitcraft so that there was no possibility of automobiles other than those belonging to the party breaking into the line of travel. Guards were posted at all points of intersection with branch roads and also at all points where crowds were expected to gather. The schedule was arranged so that no automobile was on any part of the highway at least thirty minutes before the pilot car of the Presidential party arrived there. In addition, the route was thoroughly patrolled in advance of the party.

At Belton the park forces were augmented by a detachment of Montana National Guardsmen from Kalispell, a group of United States Customs men and several deputy sheriffs from the Flathead County force. These men assisted in handling the crowds and in directing traffic. After the party had left Belton, the National Guardsmen were transported to Glacier Park where they again functioned as guards that evening, in addition to more park employees and deputy sheriffs of Glacier County.

In addition to all of these preparations, considerable work had been done to prepare a short program to be given in the President's honor at Two Medicine. Dr. George C. Ruhle, park naturalist, made several trips to Two Medicine and to Browning, agency for the Blackfeet Indian Reservation, arranging the portion of the program to be offered by the Indians. Mr. Charles Smith, educational advisor of the Olney Conservation Corps camp, visited the park several times during July and spent the week preceding the Presidential visit at the Two Medicine camp where he rehearsed and trained a picked chorus of forty Civilian Conservation Corps workers. Four boys were picked from each of eight camps in Glacier National Park and four from each of two camps in adjoining forests to make up this chorus.

During the week before the President's visit, a group of news reel photographers representing Fox, Paramount and Pathe spent two days in the park on their way to Portland to meet the Presidential party. At Two Medicine they photographed a brilliant Indian ceremony staged by about thirty members of the Blackfeet tribe in full regalia. Prayers were offered to the Great Spirit and all the evil spirits were purged from the valley so that the Great White Father from Washington might enjoy a safe and peaceful visit there.

President Roosevelt's special train arrived at Belton from the west early Sunday morning but it was not until 8:40 o'clock that it pulled into the track in front of the Belton depot. At that time a crowd of approximately 2,000 had gathered behind the ropes and a smaller group of Montana dignitaries, park service officials, representatives of the great Northern Railway, etc., had congregated around the rear coach to welcome the President when he left the train. The Kalispell band offered a concert for about an hour before the President left the train. Also Mayor J. P. Bruckhauser of Kalispell deposited a box of Flathead cherries in the baggage car of the train and later presented the President with a 10-gallon hat on behalf of the citizens of Kalispell.

At one time, Mrs. Roosevelt, escorted by Senator Wheeler, slipped off the front end of the rear car and mingled with the group inside the ropes, meeting many of them and chatting with them and several others she already knew.

Just before the party was ready to start on the park tour a group of persons including Senator B. K. Wheeler and Mrs. Wheeler, Senator John E. Erickson, Governor and Mrs. F. H. Cooney of Montana, Congressman and Mrs. Joseph P. Monaghan, and Frank Walker were called into the train to officially welcome the President to the state.

A little later the President appeared on the back platform and, amid cheers from the crowd, came down the ramp and seated himself in the right rear seat of one of the Glacier Park Transport Company's red Cadillac touring cars. Quickly the other members of the party found their places in the other cars of the fleet and the Presidential procession was under way. Thus, at 10:30 o'clock on the morning of August 5, 1934, Franklin D. Roosevelt became the first president of the United States to enter Glacier National Park.

Following the two patrol cars driven by Rangers Elmer Fladmark and Ben C. Miller which preceded the party by thirty and ten minutes respectively, the automobiles in the party and their occupants were, in order: Pilot car driven by Chief Ranger Thos. E. Whitcraft with Secret Service Agent Becktel as his passenger; Car No. 1, The President, James Roosevelt,

Governor F. H. Cooney, Superintendent Scoyen, two secret service men; Car No. 2, Secret Service men; Car No. 3, Mrs. Roosevelt, Mrs. Cooney, Senator B. K. Wheeler, Mrs. Wheeler; Car No. 4 Secretary to the President L. M. Howe, Secretary to the President Stephen T. Early, Captain W. Brown, Colonel E. M. Watson, Mr. H. M. Kannee; Car No. 5, Senator J. E. Erickson, Mr. James E. Murray, Representative J. P. Monaghan, Mrs. Monaghan, Arno B. Cammerer, director of the National Park Service; Car No. 6, Franklin Roosevelt, Jr., John Roosevelt, Mr. Jackson, Mr. Rudolph Forester, Dr. R. T. McIntire; Car No. 7, Secretary of Interior Harold L. Ickes, Secretary of War George H. Dern, Major Gruber, Mr. Lee, Mrs. E. T. Scoyen; Car No. 8, Mrs. Mary H. Rumsey and children, Mrs. Malvina Schneider, Mrs. Frank Walker.

The remaining six cars of the Transport Company's fleet were occupied by newspapermen, cameramen, news photographers, representatives of radio companies, telegraph and telephone services. Also various others were present, representing the National Park Service, the Great Northern Railway, Glacier National Park operators and several guests including Senator W. A. Buchannan of Alberta.

Following the procession was a government truck driven by Assistant Chief Ranger Charles L. Croghan at a distance of about three hundred yards behind the last car of the party. Several hundred yards behind Croghan's auto came the final two patrol cars driven by Assistant Chief Ranger Arthur R. Best and Ranger Francis X. Guardipee. They drove abreast throughout the trip, thus not permitting anyone to break into the line of the official party from the rear.

The Presidential car was driven throughout the entire trip by Mr. Fred A. Noble, manager of the Glacier Park Transport Company. President Roosevelt rode in the right rear seat with Governor Cooney in the center and Superintendent Scoyen in the left rear seat. James Roosevelt occupied the left jump seat and Richard Jorvis and Gus Gennerich rode in the front seat with Mr. Noble.

After proceeding up the McDonald Creek valley and along the Garden Wall, the procession stopped for the first time at Logan Pass, near the Stephen T. Mather plaque. The pause was short, however, and the cavalcade went on down into the St. Mary valley. A stop had been scheduled for Going-to-the-Sun chalets but, due to the late start, the party drove directly past that point. A five-minute pause, however, was made at Civilian Conservation

Corps Camp No. GNP-11 at Roes Creek. This camp, commanded by Captain Arthur E. McClarren, was the only one in the park to be visited by the President.

From Roes Creek the party proceeded on to Many Glacier Hotel, reaching that place about 2 o'clock in the afternoon. Their lunch was served to eighty-eight members of the official party. Leaving Many Glacier the party retraced its route to St. Mary and thence on down the Blackfeet Highway to Two Medicine Chalet, arriving there at 5:45 o'clock. There the President was greeted by a group of about forty Blackfeet Indians in full regalia and a like number of Civilian Conservation Corps workers. The CCC chorus entertained with several songs and the quartet of Negro boys offered a number. Favorites of the President were included.

Then the President, Mrs. Roosevelt and Secretary Ickes were inducted into the Blackfeet tribe and presented with suitable gifts. "Lone Chief" is the Chief Executive's Indian name. Mrs. Roosevelt was called "Medicine Pipe Woman" and Secretary Ickes, "Big Bear". Following this, the Indians presented a number of their tribal dances.

While all the program and other proceedings were going on, countless photographs and moving pictures were being snapped by both professional photographers and cameramen for the large news syndicates and moving picture companies and also by those attached to the special party. Glacier National Park's force of rangers, ranger-naturalists and others was well represented.

As an informal bit of recreation, Mrs. Roosevelt and her two sons, James and Franklin, Jr., enjoyed a dip in the cool waters of Two Medicine Lake before dinner and John Roosevelt was taken on a short fishing trip on the lake by Assistant Chief Ranger Arthur R. Best.

At 7:30 o'clock, Mountain Standard Time, President Roosevelt delivered a nation-wide broadcast from his room in the chalet fronting on the lake. This was the first time a Presidential broadcast ever had originated in any national park. Receiving sets were installed in the dining room of Two Medicine Chalet, at Glacier Park Hotel and other points throughout the park so that those interested could listen to the President's words. The text of his speech follows:

"I have been back on the soil of the continental United States for three days after most interesting visits to our fellow Americans in Puerto Rico, the Virgin

Islands, the Canal Zone and the Territory of Hawaii. I return with the conviction that their problems are essentially similar to those of us who live on the mainland and, furthermore, that they are enthusiastically doing their part to improve their conditions of life and thereby the conditions of life of all Americans.

"On Friday and Saturday I had the opportunity of seeing the actual construction work under way in the first two national projects for the development of the Columbia River Basin. At Bonneville, Oregon, a great dam, 140 miles inland, at the last place where the river leaps down over rapids to sea level, will provide not only a large development of cheap power but also will enable vessels to proceed another 70 or 80 miles into the interior of the country.

"At Grand Coulee in north central Washington, an even greater dam will regulate the flow of the Columbia River, developing power and, in the future will open up a large tract of parched land for the benefit of this and future generations. Many families in the days to come, I am confident, will thank us of this generation for providing small farms on which they will at least be able to make an honest and honorable livelihood.

"Today, for the first time in my life, I have seen Glacier Park. Perhaps I can best express to you my thrill and delight by saying that I wish every American, old and young, could have been with me today. The great mountains, the glaciers, the lakes and the trees make me long to stay here for all the rest of the summer.

"Comparisons are generally objectionable and yet it is not unkind to say, from the standpoint of scenery alone, that if many and indeed most of our American national parks were to be set down anywhere on the continent of Europe thousands of Americans would journey all the way across the ocean in order to see their beauties. There is nothing so American as our national parks. The scenery and wild life are native and the fundamental idea behind the parks is native.

"It is, in brief, that the country belongs to the people; that what it is and what it is in the process of making is for the enrichment of the lives of all of us. Thus the parks stand as the outward symbol of this great human principle.

"It was on a famous night, 64 years ago, that a group of men who had been exploring the Yellowstone country gathered about a campfire to discuss what could be done with that wonderland of beauty. It is said that one of the party, a lawyer from the State of Montana, Cornelius Hedges, advanced the idea that the region might be preserved for all time as a national park for the benefit of all the people of the Nation. As a result of that suggestion, Yellowstone national park was established in 1872 by act of congress as a 'pleasuring ground' for the people. I like that phrase because, in the years that have followed, our great series of parks in every part of the union have become indeed a 'pleasuring ground' for millions of Americans.

"My old friend, Franklin K. Lane, secretary of the interior in the Wilson administration, well described the policies governing the national park administration when he said:

"'The policy to which the service will adhere is based on three broad principles: First, that the national parks must be maintained in absolutely unimpaired form for the use of future generations as well as those of our own time; second, that they are set apart for the use, observation, health and pleasure of the people, and, third, that the national interest must dictate all decisions affecting public or private enterprise in the parks.'

"The present national park service stands as an example of efficient and farseeing governmental administration and to its former duties I added last year by transferring from other departments many other parks, battlefield sites, memorials and national monuments. This concentration of responsibility has thus made it possible to embark on a permanent park policy as a great recreational and educational project—one which no other country in the world has ever undertaken in such a broad way for protection of its natural and history treasures and for the enjoyment of them by vast numbers of people.

"Today I have seen some of the work of the Civilian Conservation Corps boys in this northwestern country. Of the 300,000 young men in these camps, 75,000 are at work in our national parks. Here, under trained leadership, we are helping these men to help themselves and their families and at the same time we are making the parks more available and more useful for the average citizen. Hundreds of miles of firebreaks have been built, fire hazards have been reduced on great tracts of timberland, thousands of miles of roadside have been cleared, 2,500 miles of trails have been constructed and 10,000 acres have been reforested. Other tens of thousands of acres have been treated for tree disease and soil erosion. This is but another example of our efforts to build, not for today alone, but for tomorrow as well.

"We should remember that the development of our national park system over a period of many years has not been a simple bed of roses. As is the case of the long fight for the preservation of national forests and water power and mineral deposits and other national possessions, it has been a long and fierce fight against many private interests which were entrenched in political and economic power. So, too, it has been a constant struggle to protect the public interest once cleared from private exploitation at the hands of the selfish few.

"It took a bitter struggle to teach the country at large that our national resources are not inexhaustible and that when public domain is stolen, a two-fold injury is done, for it is a theft of the treasure of the present and at the same time bars the road of opportunity to the future.

"We have won the greater part of the fight to obtain and to retain these great public park properties for the benefit of the public. We are at the threshold of even more important a battle to save our resources of agriculture and industry against the selfishness of individuals.

"The Secretary of the Interior in 1933 announced that this year of 1934 was to be emphasized as 'national parks year'. I am glad to say that there has been a magnificent response and that the number visiting our national parks has shown a splendid increase. But I decided today that every year ought to be 'national parks year'. That is why with all the earnestness at my command I express to you the hope that each and every one of you who can possibly find the means and opportunity for so doing will visit our national parks and use them as they are intended to be used. They are not for the rich alone. Camping is free; the sanitation is excellent. You will find them in every part of the union. You will find glorious scenery of every character; you will find every climate; you will perform the double function of enjoying much and learning much.

"We are definitely in an era of building, the best kind of building—the building of great public projects for the benefit of the public and with the definite objective of building human happiness.

"I believe, too, that we are building a better comprehension of our national needs. People understand, as never before, the splendid public purpose that underlies the development of great power sites, the improving of navigation, the prevention of floods and of the erosion of our agricultural fields, the prevention of forest fires, the diversification of farming and the distribution of industry. We know, more and more, that the east has a stake in the west and the west has a stake in the east, that the nation must and shall be considered as a whole and not as an aggregation of disjointed groups.

"May we come better to know every part of our great heritage in the days to come."

Later the President repeated certain parts of his talk for the benefit of sound and news photographers. This took place on the front porch of the chalet. Then the President and his immediate family retired to the front room of the chalet where dinner was served. Other members of the party ate in the main dining room. About 9:30 o'clock the party left Two Medicine and motored to Glacier Park station where the special train was waiting. A large crowd was in evidence for a glimpse of the Chief Executive when he arrived there. The party boarded the train and at 8 o'clock the next morning, August 6, the train left the park.

Thus President Roosevelt honored Glacier National Park by becoming the first Chief Executive in history to visit the playground from which the waters flow to three oceans. The President himself ate breakfast on the Pacific slope, lunched on the Arctic slope and dined on the Atlantic slope for Triple Divide Peak in Glacier National Park is the one spot in America which divides the three drainages each from the other.

The organization of Glacier National Park received many fine compliments for the manner in which the Presidential party was handled through the park. The following is quoted from a letter to the park superintendent from Secretary of the Interior Ickes:

"I appreciate the courtesies you showed me while I was at Glacier National Park. I was glad to renew, even if briefly, my acquaintance with the Park and I was particularly interested to realize that the Park is just as wonderful as it seemed to me to be when I first visited it in 1916.

"You had a heavy strain thrown upon yourself and your organization on account of the arrival of the President and Mrs. Roosevelt with such a large party. I congratulate you upon the manner in which you acquitted yourself. Everything went off beautifully. Every member of the party that I talked with was impressed not only with the Park physically, but the manner in which the National Park Service was doing its job."

Although some members of the park force had more responsibility in seeing that the party moved through the park efficiently and comfortably than others, it must be kept in mind that if any person had failed in his assigned task our plan of action would have collapsed entirely. Therefore, we prefer to take such praise as that above as an organization rather than individually. In the scope of the word organization it is meant to include park operators and their employees who cooperated beyond the limits expected of them.

The U.S. Bureau of Public Roads gave splendid cooperation in getting those sections of Going-to-the-Sun Highway under construction in condition so that the party would suffer no delays and inconvenience. Mr. A. V. Emery, Resident Engineer, worked as hard for the success of the trip as any of our park employees.

Others whose cooperation was needed and cheerfully given, includes members of the Blackfeet Reservation staff and Indians headed by Superintendent F. R. Stone; District Commander Maj. W. H. Hammond of the Army and CCC from Ft. Missoula; Gov. F. H. Cooney of Montana who ordered out the Kalispell National Guard Company to assist in handling traffic and crowds in Belton and we had fine assistance from Captain Carl Anderson, his officers and men of that organization; Sheriffs McMillan and Stewart of Flathead and Glacier counties were right on the job at all times; men from the U.S. Customs Service and many others.

On every hand were evidences that the people of Montana, and others in the park, were determined that the President was to receive only the best impression of the park. Not a single disagreeable or annoying incident occurred the entire trip so perhaps the crowds who were here to welcome him also deserve congratulations.

Source: Eivind T. Scoyen, *Superintendent's Annual Report: 857-09 Presidential Visit.* Report no. GLAC#: 01.09, File Unit: 026, Folder: 2. National Park Service, U.S. Department of the Interior. Glacier National Park Historical Records and Central Files, 1934.

Bibliography

Albright, Horace M., and Robert Cahn. *The Birth of the National Park Service: The Founding Years, 1913–33*. Salt Lake City, UT: Howe Brothers, 1985.

Albright, Horace M., and Marian Albright Schenck. *Creating the National Park Service: The Missing Years*. Norman, OK: University of Oklahoma Press, 1999.

American Academy for Park and Recreation Administration. "Stephen Tyng Mather." American Academy for Park and Recreation Administration. Accessed August 7, 2016. http://www.aapra.org/pugsley-bios/stephen-tyng-mather.

Ashby, Christopher S. *The Blackfeet Agreement of 1895 and Glacier National Park: A Case History*. Master's thesis, University of Montana, 1985. Ann Arbor, MI: ProQuest LLC, 2012. 1–42.

Brinkley, Douglas. *Rightful Heritage: Franklin D. Roosevelt and the Land of America*. New York, NY: HarperCollins Publishers, 2016.

Bristol, George. *On Politics and Parks*. College Station, TX: Texas A&M University Press, 2012.

Buchholtz, C. W. *Man in Glacier*. West Glacier, MT: Glacier Natural History Association, 1976.

Burns, Ken, and Dayton Duncan. "Episode Four: 1920–1933: Going Home." *The National Parks: America's Best Idea: A Film by Ken Burns*, 2009. Accessed September 2, 2016. http://www.pbs.org/nationalparks/history/ep4/2/.

Burns, Ken, and Dayton Duncan. "Theodore Roosevelt (1858–1919)." The National Parks: America's Best Idea: A Film by Ken Burns. 2009. Accessed September 2, 2015. http://www.pbs.org/nationalparks/people/historical/roosevelt/.

Carr, Ethan. *Mission 66: Modernism and the National Park Dilemma*. Amherst, MA: University of Massachusetts Press, 2007. PDF.

Catlin, George. "George Catlin: Letters and Notes on the Manners, Customs, and Conditions of the North American Indians, 2 Vols. (1860), 1: 260–64." Franklin & Marshall College. June 5, 1997. Accessed November 02, 2016. http://www.fandm.edu/david-schuyler/ams280/manners-customs-and-conditions-of-the-north-american-indians.

Chase, Candace. "Laura Bush Visits Glacier Park." *Daily Inter Lake*, July 16, 2011. Accessed September 01, 2016. http://www.dailyinterlake.com/members/laura-bush-visits-glacier-park/article_9e9a2d0a-af49-11e0-99f4-001cc4c03286.html.

Churchill, Ward. *Struggle for Land: Native North American Resistance to Genocide, Ecocide and Colonization*. San Francisco, CA: City Lights Books, 2002.

Davis, Ren, and Helen Davis. *Our Mark on This Land: A Guide to the Legacy of the Civilian Conservation Corps in America's Parks*. Granville, OH: McDonald & Woodward Publishing Company, 2011.

Devlin, Vince. "Glacier National Park Welcomes 100 Millionth Visitor: '#WINNER.'" *Missoulian*, June 11, 2015. Accessed August 30, 2016. http://missoulian.com/news/local/glacier

-national-park-welcomes-millionth-visitor-winner/article_9692204b-8804-544d-8d5d
-81893cb54d24.html.

Devlin, Vince. "Short Glacier Road Has Long Connection with Turning Points in Park History." *Missoulian*, June 2, 2015. Accessed August 8, 2016. http://missoulian.com/news/local
/short-glacier-road-has-long-connection-with-turning-points-in/article_2ceabe1c-49f9
-522c-89bc-4888b520a678.html.

Diettert, Gerald A. *Grinnell's Glacier: George Bird Grinnell and Glacier National Park*. Missoula,
MT: Mountain Press Publishing Company, 1992.

Djuff, Ray, and Chris Morrison. *View with a Room: Glacier's Historic Hotels & Chalets*. Helena,
MT: Farcountry Press, 2001.

Duncan, Dayton, and Ken Burns. *The National Parks: America's Best Idea: An Illustrated History*. New York, NY: Alfred A. Knopf, 2009.

Eisinger, Nikki. "Glacier National Park Conservancy Interview." Telephone interview by author, August 11, 2016.

Elias, Scott Armstrong. "First Americans Lived on Bering Land Bridge for Thousands of Years."
Scientific American, March 4, 2014. Accessed September 7, 2016. http://www.scientific
american.com/article/first-americans-lived-on-bering-land-bridge-for-thousands-of
-years/.

Ewers, John C. *The Blackfeet: Raiders on the Northwestern Plains*. Norman, OK: University of
Oklahoma Press, 1958.

Farr, William E. "How the Blackfeet Became the Guardians of Glacier." In *Center for the Rocky
Mountain West*. Proceedings of History and Memory: Glacier National Park's Centennial
Year Symposium, Flathead Valley Community College, Kalispell, MT. April 24, 2010. Accessed October 4, 2015. http://crmw.org/MP3Files/Kalispell Symposium 4-10.pdf.

Farr, William E. "'When We Were First Paid': The Blackfoot Treaty, the Western Tribes, and
the Creation of the Common Hunting Ground, 1855." *Great Plains Quarterly*, April 1, 2001,
131–154. Accessed September 5, 2016. http://digitalcommons.unl.edu/cgi/viewcontent.cgi
?article=3226&context=greatplainsquarterly.

Forest History Society. "U.S. Forest Service Fire Suppression." U.S. Forest Service History.
March 17, 2015. Accessed September 4, 2016. http://www.foresthistory.org/ASPNET/Policy
/Fire/Suppression/Suppression.aspx.

Fox, Stephen R. *The American Conservation Movement: John Muir and His Legacy*, 116. Madison, WI: University of Wisconsin Press, 1981.

Franz, Justin. "A Race Against Time." *Flathead Beacon*, September 2, 2015. Accessed September 8, 2015. http://flatheadbeacon.com/2015/09/02/a-race-against-time/.

Germann, Denise. "Glacier Creates $179 Million in Economic Benefit." National Park Service.
July 21, 2014. Accessed July 21, 2014. https://www.nps.gov/glac/learn/news/glacier-creates
-179-million-in-economic-benefit.htm.

Glacier Park Foundation. "The Fires of 2003: An Anthology." The Inside Trail. Winter 2004. Accessed September 01, 2016. http://www.glacierparkfoundation.org/InsideTrail/IT_2004
Win.pdf.

Great Northern Railway. "What Was the Great Northern Railway?" GN History. Accessed September 1, 2016. https://www.gnrhs.org/gn_history.htm.

Grinnell, George Bird. "Letter to Lawrence O. Vaught." George Bird Grinnell to Lawrence O.
Vaught, 1917. Lawrence O. Vaught Papers: File Unit 82: Correspondence, George Bird Grinnell: Glacier National Park Archives, Montana.

Guthrie, C. W. *All Aboard! for Glacier: The Great Northern Railway and Glacier National Park.* Helena, MT: Farcountry Press, 2004.

Guthrie, C. W. *Glacier National Park: The First 100 Years.* Helena, MT: Farcountry Press, 2008.

Guthrie, C. W. *Going-to-the-Sun Road: Glacier National Park's Highway to the Sky.* Helena, MT: Farcountry Press, 2006.

Haefele, Michelle, John Loomis, and Linda J. Bilmes. *Total Economic Valuation of the National Park Service Lands and Programs: Results of a Survey of the American Public.* Report. Colorado State University and Harvard University, 2016, 1–48.

Haeg, Larry. *Harriman vs. Hill: Wall Street's Great Railroad War.* Minneapolis, MN: University of Minnesota Press, 2013.

Hagovsky, Amy. "New Poll of Likely Voters Finds Unity in Public Support for National Parks." National Parks Conservation Association. August 7, 2012. Accessed November 26, 2015. https://www.npca.org/articles/693-new-poll-of-likely-voters-finds-unity-in-public -support-for-national-parks.

Hardner, Jared, and Bruce McKenney. "The U.S. National Park System: An Economic Asset at Risk." National Parks Conservation Association. May 30, 2006. Accessed February 20, 2016. https://www.npca.org/resources/1109-the-u-s-national-park-system-an-economic -asset-at-risk.

Harper, Andrew C. "Conceiving Nature: The Creation of Montana's Glacier National Park." *Montana: The Magazine of Western History,* Summer 2010, 3–24.

Hidy, Ralph W., and Muriel E. Hidy. "John Frank Stevens: Great Northern Engineer." *Minnesota History Magazine,* Winter 1969, 345–361. Accessed August 30, 2016. http://collections .mnhs.org/MNHistoryMagazine/articles/41/v41i08p345-361.pdf.

History Matters. "'Dam Hetch-Hetchy!': John Muir Contests the Hetch-Hetchy Dam." History Matters. Accessed September 5, 2016. http://historymatters.gmu.edu/d/5720/.

Hodges, Glenn. "First Americans." *National Geographic,* January 2015, 125–137.

Johnson-Humrickhouse Museum. "Civilian Public Service: An Experiment in Democracy." Johnson-Humrickhouse Museum. Accessed August 8, 2016. http://www.jhmuseum.org /ourstory/community-stories/256-civilian-public-service-an-experiment-in-democracy.

Jupiter, Frankie. "Gov. McAuliffe Accepts Deed to Natural Bridge." WDBJ7. May 12, 2014. Accessed August 31, 2016. http://m.wdbj7.com/news/local/gov-mcauliffe-to-accept-deed-to -natural-bridge-on-monday/25931884.

Kaufman, Polly Welts. *National Parks and the Woman's Voice: A History.* Albuquerque, NM: University of New Mexico Press, 1996.

King, Mari. "NITS-STI-TA-PII: The Real People: Imataa Manistsi: Blackfoot Dog Travois." Pitt Rivers Virtual Collections. 2010. Accessed September 7, 2016. http://web.prm.ox.ac.uk /blackfootshirts/attachments/028_Imataa Manistsi- Blackfoot Dog Travois.pdf.

Krech, Shepard, III. "Buffalo Tales: The Near-Extermination of the American Bison." Native Americans and the Land. Accessed September 7, 2016. http://nationalhumanitiescenter .org/tserve/nattrans/ntecoindian/essays/buffaloc.htm.

Kreider, Robert. "CPS Unit Number 055–01: The Civilian Public Service Story." The Civilian Public Service Story. Accessed August 26, 2015. http://civilianpublicservice.org/camps /55/1.

Kreider, Robert. "Selective Service: The Civilian Public Service Story." The Civilian Public Service Story. Accessed August 8, 2016. http://civilianpublicservice.org/storybegins/krehbiel /selective-service.

Landry, Alysa. "Native History: Dawes Act Signed into Law to 'Civilize' Indians." Indian Country Today Media Network. February 8, 2014. Accessed August 24, 2015. http://indiancoun trytodaymedianetwork.com/2014/02/08/native-history-dawes-act-signed-law-civilize -indians-153467.

Louie, Wayne. "Sturgeon-Nose Creations: History." Sturgeon-Nose Creations. Accessed August 30, 2016. http://www.sturgeon-nose-creations.com/history.

Mack, Dwayne. "May the Work I've Done Speak for Me: African American Civilian Corps Enrollees in Montana, 1933–1934." *The Western Journal of Black Studies* 27, no. 4 (2003): 236–45.

McCabe, Richard E. "George Bird Grinnell: 'The Noblest Roman of Them All,'" Outdoor Writers Association of America. Accessed August 7, 2016. http://owaa.org/owaa-legends/george -bird-grinnell-the-noblest-roman-of-them-all/.

McClintock, Walter. *The Old North Trail: Or, Life, Legends and Religion of the Blackfeet Indians.* London, UK: MacMillan and Company, Limited, 1910. Accessed September 7, 2016. https:// books.google.com/books/about/The_Old_North_Trail.html?id=ro_YAAAAMAAJ&print sec=frontcover&source=kp_read_button#v=onepage&q&f=false.

Meriam, Lewis. "Meriam Report: The Problem of Indian Administration." National Indian Law Library, 1936. Accessed September 7, 2016. http://www.narf.org/nill/resources/meriam .html.

Muir, John. *John Muir, in His Own Words: A Book of Quotations.* Edited by Peter Browning. Lafayette, CA: Great West Books, 1988.

Muir, John. *My First Summer in the Sierra.* San Francisco, CA: Sierra Club Books, 1990.

Muir, John. *Our National Parks.* San Francisco, CA: Sierra Club Books, 1991.

Muller, Christopher. "Railroad Engineering Records: Bridges & Tunnels." Railserv.com. Accessed August 30, 2016. http://www.railserve.com/stats_records/railroad_tunnels_bridges .html.

National Geographic. "Why Did the Woolly Mammoth Die Out?" March 26, 2011. Accessed August 29, 2016. http://www.nationalgeographic.com.au/history/why-did-the-woolly-ma mmoth-die-out.aspx.

National Park Service. "American Antiquities Act of 1906 (16 USC 431–433)." National Park Service. June 8, 1906. Accessed August 27, 2016. https://www.nps.gov/history/local-law /anti1906.htm.

National Park Service. "The CCC and the National Park Service, 1933–1942: An Administrative History." National Park Service. April 4, 2000. Accessed September 3, 2016. https://www .nps.gov/parkhistory/online_books/ccc/ccc2a.htm.

National Park Service. "Civilian Conservation Corps (CCC)." National Park Service. Accessed September 4, 2016. https://www.nps.gov/glac/learn/historyculture/ccc.htm.

National Park Service. "Frequently Asked Questions (U.S. National Park Service)." National Park Service. Accessed September 7, 2016. https://www.nps.gov/aboutus/faqs.htm.

National Park Service. "Glacier National Park: Fact Sheet." National Park Service. Accessed September 16, 2015. http://www.nps.gov/glac/learn/news/fact-sheet.htm.

National Park Service. "Glacier National Park: Through the Years in Glacier National Park: An Administrative History (Appendix A: Historic Place Names)." National Park Service. January 15, 2004. Accessed February 21, 2017. https://www.nps.gov/parkhistory/online_books /glac/appa.htm.

National Park Service. "Glacier National Park Press Kit: Glacier National Park and Other NPS Quotes." National Park Service. Accessed April 22, 2015. http://www.nps.gov/glac/learn /news/upload/press_quotes.pdf.

National Park Service. "Glaciers." National Park Service. Accessed August 30, 2016. https:// www.nps.gov/glac/learn/education/glaciers.htm.

National Park Service. "History (U.S. National Park Service)." National Park Service. Accessed September 2, 2016. https://www.nps.gov/aboutus/history.htm.

National Park Service. "Lyndon B. Johnson and the Environment." National Park Service. Accessed July 29, 2016. https://www.nps.gov/lyjo/planyourvisit/upload/EnvironmentCS2.pdf.

National Park Service. "Wilderness: Frequently Asked Questions." National Park Service. Accessed September 16, 2015. http://wilderness.nps.gov/faqnew.cfm.

Natural Resources Defense Council. "Wildfires in Western Forests." Natural Resources Defense Council. May 2003. Accessed July 27, 2007. www.nrdc.org/land/forests/pfires.asp.

Newcomb, Steven. "The 1887 Dawes Act: The U.S. Theft of 90 Million Acres of Indian Land." Indian Country. February 8, 2012. Accessed September 5, 2016. http://indiancountrytoday medianetwork.com/2012/02/08/1887-dawes-act-us-theft-90-million-acres-indian-land.

NOLO. "Servicemen's Readjustment Act (G.I. Bill)." NOLO. Accessed September 4, 2016. https://www.nolo.com/legal-encyclopedia/content/gi-bill-act.html.

Ober, Michael J. "The CCC Experience in Glacier National Park." *Montana: The Magazine of Western History*, Summer 1976, 30–39.

Olmsted, Frederick Law. *Yosemite and the Mariposa Grove: A Preliminary Report, 1865.* Yosemite National Park, CA: Yosemite Association, 1995.

Olsen, Jack. *Night of the Grizzlies.* Moose, WY: Homestead Publishing, 1996.

Parks Canada. "Waterton–Glacier International Peace Park." Parks Canada. February 19, 2015. Accessed September 4, 2016. http://www.pc.gc.ca/eng/pn-np/ab/waterton/natcul/inter .aspx.

Perrottet, Tony. "Chasing a Prairie Tale." *New York Times*, June 23, 2012. Accessed August 31, 2016. http://www.nytimes.com/2012/06/24/travel/buffalo-the-pawnee-and-an-old-story -on-a-trip-across-the-plains.html?_r=0.

Philanthropy Roundtable. "1916: Stephen Mather Builds the National Park Service." Philanthropy Roundtable: Nature and Parks. Accessed August 7, 2016. http://www.philanthropy roundtable.org/almanac/nature/1916_stephen_mather_builds_the_national_park _service.

Pommersheim, Frank. *Broken Landscape: Indians, Indian Tribes, and the Constitution.* Oxford, UK: Oxford University Press, 2009.

Potrero Group. *National Park Partners: Status and Trends.* Report. National Park Foundation, 2016, 1–56.

Punke, Michael. *Last Stand: George Bird Grinnell, the Battle to Save the Buffalo, and the Birth of the New West.* New York, NY: Smithsonian Books/Collins, 2007.

Ray, Arthur J. "Hudson's Bay Company." *The Canadian Encyclopedia*, April 2, 2009. Accessed August 24, 2016. http://www.thecanadianencyclopedia.ca/en/article/hudsons-bay-company/.

Reis, Patrick. "Obama Admin Strikes $3.4B Deal in Indian Trust Lawsuit." *New York Times*, December 8, 2009. Accessed September 7, 2016. http://www.nytimes.com/gwire/2009/12 /08/08greenwire-obama-admin-strikes-34b-deal-in-indian-trust-l-92369.html.

Richmond, Laura Lee. "Stephen Mather of the National Parks Believed That the Outdoors Ward off His Mental Illness." Lauraleerichmond. May 7, 2015. Accessed September 2, 2016. https://lauraleerichmond.wordpress.com/2015/05/07/stephen-mather-of-the-national -parks-believed-that-the-outdoors-ward-off-his-mental-illness/.

Rinehart, Mary Roberts. *Through Glacier Park*. Helena, MT: TWODOT, 2016.

Robinson, Donald H. "Glacier National Park: Through the Years in Glacier National Park: An Administrative History (Chapter 3)." National Park Service. May 1960. Accessed September 01, 2016. https://www.nps.gov/parkhistory/online_books/glac/chap3.htm.

Robinson, Donald H., Maynard C. Bowers, Richard W. Frost, and Glacier Natural History Association, Inc. *Through the Years in Glacier National Park*. Whitefish, MT: Sun Point Press, 1960.

Robinson, George. "Biographical Vignettes: Freeman Tilden, 1883–1980." National Park Service. December 1, 2000. Accessed August 7, 2016. https://www.nps.gov/parkhistory/online _books/sontag/tilden.htm.

Rockwell, David. *Glacier National Park: A Natural History Guide*. New York, NY: Houghton Mifflin, 1995.

Roosevelt, Franklin D. "Franklin D. Roosevelt: Radio Address from Two Medicine Chalet, Glacier National Park." The American Presidency Project. August 5, 1934. Accessed September 18, 2014. http://www.presidency.ucsb.edu/ws/?pid=14733.

Roosevelt, Theodore. *The Strenuous Life*. New York, NY: Century, 1902. Accessed August 31, 2016. http://www.theodore-roosevelt.com/images/research/thestrenuouslife.pdf.

Roosevelt, Theodore. *The Works of Theodore Roosevelt*. New York, NY: C. Scribner's Sons, 1923. Accessed October 1, 2014. http://www.theodore-roosevelt.com/images/research/txtspeeches /51.txt.

Roser-Renouf, Connie, Edward Maibach, Anthony Leiserowitz, Geoff Feinberg, Seth Rosenthal, and Jennifer Kreslake. "Global Warming's Six Americas' Perceptions of the Health Risks." Yale Program on Climate Change Communication. March 16, 2015. Accessed February 20, 2016. http://climatecommunication.yale.edu/publications/global-warmings-six -americas-perceptions-of-the-health-risks/.

Schlesinger, Arthur M. *The Coming of the New Deal*. Boston, MA: Houghton Mifflin, 2003. E-book.

Scott, Gary. "The Presidents and the National Parks." White House Historical Association. Accessed September 6, 2016. https://www.whitehousehistory.org/the-presidents-and-the -national-parks.

Scoyen, Eivind T. *Superintendent's Annual Report: 857-09 Presidential Visit*. Report no. GLAC#: 01.09, File Unit: 026, Folder: 2. National Park Service, U.S. Department of the Interior. Glacier National Park Historical Records and Central Files, 1934.

Shafroth, Will. "Jon Jarvis Quote." E-mail. August 7, 2016.

Shafroth, Will. "Your Book Chapter Review." E-mail. July 29, 2016.

Shea, Rachel Hartigan. "How Good Old American Marketing Saved the National Parks." *National Geographic*, March 24, 2015. Accessed September 01, 2016. http://news.national geographic.com/2015/03/150324-national-park-service-history-yellowstone-california -united-states/.

Shekell, Francis. "Walton Historical Interview." Interview by Janet Panebaker. *Glacier National Park Archives, Oral History Collection*. March 5, 1979.

Shribman, David M. "Getting Rid of Uncle Joe." *Pittsburgh Post-Gazette*, March 14, 2010. Accessed August 31, 2016. http://www.post-gazette.com/opinion/david-shribman/2010/03/14/Getting-rid-of-Uncle-Joe/stories/201003140237.

Sierra Club. "Quotations from John Muir." The John Muir Exhibit. Accessed September 1, 2016. http://vault.sierraclub.org/john_muir_exhibit/writings/favorite_quotations.aspx.

Smokey Bear. "About the Campaign." Smokey Bear. Accessed September 4, 2016. https://smokeybear.com/en/smokeys-history/about-the-campaign.

Speakman, Joseph M. "Into the Woods: The First Year of the Civilian Conservation Corps." National Archives, Fall 2006. Accessed September 3, 2016. http://www.archives.gov/publications/prologue/2006/fall/ccc.html.

St. Rosemary Educational Institution. "The Blackfoot Indians: History, Culture, Society." SchoolWorkHelper. 2016. Accessed September 5, 2016. http://schoolworkhelper.net/the-blackfoot-indians-history-culture-society/.

Thomas Jefferson Foundation, Inc. "Natural Bridge." Thomas Jefferson's Monticello. March 1997. Accessed August 27, 2016. https://www.monticello.org/site/research-and-collections/natural-bridge.

Thompson, Sally, Kootenai Culture Committee, and Pikunni Traditional Association. *People Before the Park: The Kootenai and Blackfeet Before Glacier National Park*. Helena, MT: Montana Historical Society Press, 2015.

Thoreau, Henry David. "The Henry D. Thoreau Quotation Page: Conservation." The Walden Woods Project. 1906. Accessed August 27, 2016. https://www.walden.org/Library/Quotations/Conservation.

Troy, Tia. "Reynolds Creek Fire Update: Montana's Glacier National Park." Glacier Country Montana. July 23, 2015. Accessed August 7, 2016. https://glaciermt.com/blog/reynolds-creek-fire-update-montanas-glacier-national-park/.

Uchytel, Roman. "Bison Antiquus (Ancient Bison)." Extinct Animals: Images: Prehistoric Fauna Reconstructions. 2012. Accessed November 29, 2014. http://prehistoric-fauna.com/Bison-antiquus.

U.S. Fish and Wildlife Service. "Timeline of the American Bison." U.S. Fish and Wildlife Service. Accessed August 25, 2016. https://www.fws.gov/bisonrange/timeline.htm.

Walter, Dave. "Past Times: The Ceded Strip: The Blackfeet, Glacier National Park, and the Badger-Two Medicine." *Montana Magazine*, September/October 1998, 55–61.

Warrick, Joby. "The Great Thaw: As Temperatures Rise, Many American Glaciers Could Vanish in a Few Decades." *Washington Post*, November 26, 2015. Accessed August 30, 2016. http://www.washingtonpost.com/sf/national/2015/11/26/ice-worlds/.

White, Christopher P. *The Melting World: A Journey Across America's Vanishing Glaciers*. New York, NY: St. Martin's Press, 2013.

Wilderness Society. "Wallace Stegner." The Wilderness Society. Accessed August 7, 2016. http://wilderness.org/bios/former-council-members/wallace-stegner.

Young, Biloine W., and Eileen R. McCormack. *The Dutiful Son, Louis W. Hill: Life in the Shadow of the Empire Builder, James J. Hill*. St. Paul, MN: Ramsey County Historical Society, 2010.

Further Reading

Albright, Horace M., and Robert Cahn. *The Birth of the National Park Service: The Founding Years, 1913–33*. Salt Lake City, UT: Howe Brothers, 1985.

Albright, Horace M., and Marian Albright Schenck. *Creating the National Park Service: The Missing Years*. Norman, OK: University of Oklahoma Press, 1999.

Alt, David D., and Donald W. Hyndman. *Roadside Geology of Montana*. Missoula, MT: Mountain Press Publishing, 1986.

Ashby, Christopher S. *The Blackfeet Agreement of 1895 and Glacier National Park: A Case History*. Master's thesis, University of Montana, 1985. Ann Arbor, MI: ProQuest LLC, 2012. 1–42.

Bottomly-O'looney, Jennifer, and Deirdre Shaw. "Glacier National Park: People, a Playground, and a Park." *Montana: The Magazine of Western History*, Summer 2010, 42–55.

Brinkley, Douglas. *Rightful Heritage: Franklin D. Roosevelt and the Land of America*. New York, NY: HarperCollins Publishers, 2016.

Brinkley, Douglas. *The Wilderness Warrior: Theodore Roosevelt and the Crusade for America*. New York, NY: Harper Collins, 2009.

Bristol, George. *On Politics and Parks*. College Station, TX: Texas A&M University Press, 2012.

Buchholtz, C. W. *Man in Glacier*. West Glacier, MT: Glacier Natural History Association, 1976.

Davis, Ren, and Helen Davis. *Our Mark on This Land: A Guide to the Legacy of the Civilian Conservation Corps in America's Parks*. Granville, OH: McDonald & Woodward Publishing Company, 2011.

Dempsey, Hugh A. "Blackfoot Confederacy." *The Canadian Encyclopedia*, December 6, 2010. http://www.thecanadianencyclopedia.ca/en/article/blackfoot-nation/.

Diettert, Gerald A. *Grinnell's Glacier: George Bird Grinnell and Glacier National Park*. Missoula, MT: Mountain Press Publishing Company, 1992.

Djuff, Ray. *High on a Windy Hill: The Story of the Prince of Wales Hotel*. Surrey, BC: Rocky Mountain Books, 1999.

Djuff, Ray, and Chris Morrison. *View with a Room: Glacier's Historic Hotels & Chalets*. Helena, MT: Farcountry Press, 2001.

Duncan, Dayton, and Ken Burns. *The National Parks: America's Best Idea: An Illustrated History*. New York, NY: Alfred A. Knopf, 2009.

Ewers, John C. *The Blackfeet: Raiders on the Northwestern Plains*. Norman, OK: University of Oklahoma Press, 1958.

Fagre, Daniel B. "Glacier National Park Biosphere Reserve: Its Suitability for the Mountain Research Initiative." In *Global Change Research in Mountain Biosphere Reserves*, 99–108. Proceedings of International Launching Workshop, Entlebuch Biosphere Reserve. 2003.

Fagre, Daniel B. "Glacier National Park: Glacier Repeat Photography Gallery." U. S. Geological Survey. https://www.usgs.gov/atom/13896.

Farr, William E. "How the Blackfeet Became the Guardians of Glacier." In *Center for the Rocky Mountain West.* Proceedings of History and Memory: Glacier National Park's Centennial Year Symposium, Flathead Valley Community College, Kalispell, MT, April 24, 2010. http://crmw.org/MP3Files/Kalispell Symposium 4-10.pdf.

Grinnell, George Bird. *Blackfeet Indian Stories.* Helena, MT: Riverbend Publishing, 2005.

Grubin, David, and Geoffrey C. Ward. "TR, The Story of Theodore Roosevelt: Theodore Roosevelt and the Environment." American Experience: PBS. 1996. http://www.pbs.org/wgbh/americanexperience/features/general-article/tr-environment/.

Guthrie, C. W. *All Aboard! for Glacier: The Great Northern Railway and Glacier National Park.* Helena, MT: Farcountry Press, 2004.

Guthrie, C. W. *Glacier National Park: The First 100 Years.* Helena, MT: Farcountry Press, 2008.

Guthrie, C. W. *Going-to-the-Sun Road: Glacier National Park's Highway to the Sky.* Helena, MT: Farcountry Press, 2006.

Haeg, Larry. *Harriman vs. Hill: Wall Street's Great Railroad War.* Minneapolis, MN: University of Minnesota Press, 2013.

Harmon, David, and National Park Foundation, eds. *Mirror of America: Literary Encounters with the National Parks.* Boulder, CO: Roberts Rinehart, 1989.

Harper, Andrew C. "Conceiving Nature: The Creation of Montana's Glacier National Park." *Montana: The Magazine of Western History,* Summer 2010, 3–24.

Hodges, Glenn. "First Americans." *National Geographic,* January 2015, 125–37.

Kaufman, Polly Welts. *National Parks and the Woman's Voice: A History.* Albuquerque, NM: University of New Mexico Press, 1996.

Kreider, Robert. "Work of National Importance: The Civilian Public Service Story." The Civilian Public Service Story. September 7, 2010. http://civilianpublicservice.org/national importance.

Mack, Dwayne. "May the Work I've Done Speak for Me: African American Civilian Corps Enrollees in Montana, 1933–1934." *The Western Journal of Black Studies* 27, no. 4 (2003): 236–45.

McClintock, Walter. *The Old North Trail: Or, Life, Legends and Religion of the Blackfeet Indians.* London, UK: MacMillan and Company, Limited, 1910.

Miller, Char. "The Fight for Conservation, by Gifford Pinchot: CHAPTER IX The Children." In *The Evolution of the Conservation Movement, 1850–1920,* ed. Jurretta Jordan Heckscher, 101–8. Milford, PA: Grey Towers Press, 1992.

Muir, John. *The Wilderness World of John Muir.* Edited by Edwin Way Teale. Boston, MA: Houghton Mifflin, 1954.

Ober, Michael J. "The CCC Experience in Glacier National Park." *Montana: The Magazine of Western History,* Summer 1976, 30–39.

Ojibwa. "Glacier National Park: What Came Before." Daily Kos. April 24, 2013. http://www.dailykos.com/story/2013/04/24/1204424/-Glacier-National-Park-What-Came-Before.

Olmsted, Frederick Law. *Yosemite and the Mariposa Grove: A Preliminary Report, 1865.* Yosemite National Park, CA: Yosemite Association, 1995.

Olsen, Jack. *Night of the Grizzlies.* Moose, WY: Homestead Publishing, 1996.

Reeves, Brian, and Sandy Peacock. *"Our Mountains Are Our Pillows": An Ethnographic Overview of Glacier National Park.* West Glacier, MT: Glacier National Park, 2001.

Rinehart, Mary Roberts. *Through Glacier Park.* Helena, MT: TWODOT, 2016.

Robinson, Donald H., Maynard C. Bowers, Richard W. Frost, and Glacier Natural History Association, Inc. *Through the Years in Glacier National Park*. Whitefish, MT: Sun Point Press, 1960.

Rockwell, David. *Glacier National Park: A Natural History Guide*. New York, NY: Houghton Mifflin, 1995.

Roosevelt, Franklin D. "Franklin D. Roosevelt: Radio Address from Two Medicine Chalet, Glacier National Park." The American Presidency Project. August 5, 1934. http://www.presidency.ucsb.edu/ws/?pid=14733.

Roser-Renouf, Connie, Edward Maibach, Anthony Leiserowitz, Geoff Feinberg, Seth Rosenthal, and Jennifer Kreslake. "Global Warming's Six Americas' Perceptions of the Health Risks." Yale Program on Climate Change Communication. March 16, 2015. http://climatecommunication.yale.edu/publications/global-warmings-six-americas-perceptions-of-the-health-risks/.

Salmond, John, and Duke University Press. "The Civilian Conservation Corps, 1933–1942: A New Deal Case Study (Chapter 1)." National Park Service. 1967. http://www.nps.gov/parkhistory/online_books/ccc/salmond/chap1.htm.

Shea, Rachel Hartigan. "How Good Old American Marketing Saved the National Parks." *National Geographic*, March 24, 2015. http://news.nationalgeographic.com/2015/03/150324-national-park-service-history-yellowstone-california-united-states/.

Sheire, James W. *Glacier National Park: Historic Resource Study*. Washington, DC: Office of History and Historic Architecture, Eastern Service Center, 1970.

Sontag, William H., ed. *National Park Service: The First 75 Years: Preserving Our Past for the Future*. Fort Washington, PA: Eastern National Park & Monument Association, 1990.

Thompson, Sally, Kootenai Culture Committee, and Pikunni Traditional Association. *People Before the Park: The Kootenai and Blackfeet Before Glacier National Park*. Helena, MT: Montana Historical Society Press, 2015.

United States History. "Theodore Roosevelt and Conservation." United States History. http://www.u-s-history.com/pages/h937.html.

University of Montana. "Blackfeet Relationship with US: The Shrinking Reservation." Trail tribes.org. http://trailtribes.org/greatfalls/shrinking-reservation.htm.

U.S. Geological Survey and National Park Service. "The Earth's Geologic Time Scale." Rocks in My Head Too. 2009. http://www.rocksinmyheadtoo.com/TimeLine.htm.

Walter, Dave. "Past Times: The Ceded Strip: The Blackfeet, Glacier National Park, and the Badger-Two Medicine." *Montana Magazine*, September/October 1998, 55–61.

White, Christopher P. *The Melting World: A Journey Across America's Vanishing Glaciers*. New York, NY: St. Martin's Press, 2013.

Young, Biloine W., and Eileen R. McCormack. *The Dutiful Son, Louis W. Hill: Life in the Shadow of the Empire Builder, James J. Hill*. St. Paul, MN: Ramsey County Historical Society, 2010.

About the Author

For more than forty years, George Bristol has been a successful entrepreneur, political organizer, fundraiser, and lobbyist. During those years, he formed a deep interest in national and state parks. In 1984, he was named chairman of the Texas Conservation Foundation by Governor Mark White and served until 1988. That experience heightened his awareness of the need for a stronger commitment to a conservation ethic. In 1994, he received a six-year appointment to the National Park Foundation Board of Directors by President Bill Clinton and Secretary of the Interior Bruce Babbitt.

Upon completing his term, Bristol formed the Texas Coalition for Conservation to advocate for better funding for Texas parks. As its president, he led a statewide effort that culminated in success in 2007 when the Texas Legislature nearly tripled appropriations to parks. In 2015, the legislature voted for permanent funding for state parks. He was honored in February 2016 by the staff of the State Parks Division of the Texas Parks and Wildlife Department. Among the awards of the day was a scholarship to be named in his honor for the leadership advancement of outstanding park employees.

From 1999 to 2009, Bristol cofounded and served on the board of Directors of the Glacier Fund (now the Glacier National Park Conservancy). He cofounded and served as chairman of the Texas State Parks Advisory Committee from 2009 to 2016. He has also served as chair of Audubon Texas. In 2006, he was deeply honored to be chosen to be an advisor to the PBS series *The National Parks: America's Best Idea* by Dayton Duncan and Ken Burns.

Included in the many awards and honors Bristol has received are the National Cornelius Pugsley Award from the American Academy for Park and Recreation Administration and the National Park Foundation in 2009 and selection as a Feature Author by the Texas Book Festival in 2012 and the San

Antonio Book Festival in 2013. In addition to *Glacier National Park: A Culmi-nation of Giants*, he has published his autobiography, *On Politics and Parks*, in 2012 with the Texas A&M University Press and a book of photography and poetry, *Visual Voices*, in 1991 with Leisure Time Publishing.

Bristol is also an award-winning photographer and poet.

Index

Note: Page numbers in *italics* refer to illustrations.
"GNP" refers to Glacier National Park. "NPS" refers to National Park Service.

water resources, 55, 154

waterskiing, 143

Waterton formation, 5

Waterton-Glacier International Peace Park, 128, *129*, 137, 144, 155

Waterton Lakes, 137

Waterton Lakes National Park, 144, 157

Waterton National Park in Canada, 79

western migration of Anglo population, 16–17

West Glacier (previously Belton)
  and Apgar Visitor Center, 137, 138
  and Civilian Conservation Corps, 119
  and flooding disaster (1964), 138
  lodging at, 79
  and road to East Glacier, 128
  and Roosevelt's trip to GNP, 179, 180, 181

West Glacier Bar, xv

Wetlands Preservation Bill (1967), 147

Wheeler, Burton, 135

Wheeler, William F., 18

White, Christopher, 10

White Calf, Chief, 18, 19, *20*

Wild and Scenic River System, 147

Wilderness Act (1964), 136, 140–41, 143, · 147

Wilderness Area status sought for Glacier National Park, 144, 155

Wilderness Letter (Stegner), 155

wildlife in Glacier National Park, 141–42, 144, 166–68, 170, 171. *See also* bison

Wilson, Woodrow, 39, 67, 104

Wirth, Conrad, 136

Wisconsin period, 8

"wisest and best use" policy, 85, 101

wolves, 144

women's support for national parks, 97–100

Wood, Maria, 37

woolly mammoth (*M. primigenius*), 8

World Heritage Site status of Glacier National Park, 155

World War II
  and Civilian Conservation Corps, 119
  and conscientious objectors, 123–24
  end of, 133
  and Great Northern Railway's investment in GNP, 120, 128

Wright, Orville, 134

Yard, Robert Sterling, 95, 100

Yellowstone National Park
  and concessionaires, 107
  and conservation ethic, 45
  early advocates for, 161
  establishment of, 176
  funding for, 160
  and Grinnell, 57
  and Hill, Louis, 56
  hunting and poaching in, 57
  military presence in, 106, 109
  and railroads, 74

Yellowstone Park Protection Act, 57

The Yosemite (Muir), 135

Yosemite National Park
  economic argument for, 55
  and Hetch-Hetchy dam, 135
  income generated by, 48
  and Mather, 106
  and Muir, xi, 49–53
  and Olmsted, 46, 47–49
  roads of, 97
  and Roosevelt (Theodore), 50–53